Edward Albert Wurtzburg

The Acts Relating to Building Societies

Comprising the Act of 1836, and the Building Societies Acts 1874, 1875, 1877,1884

Edward Albert Wurtzburg

The Acts Relating to Building Societies
Comprising the Act of 1836, and the Building Societies Acts 1874, 1875, 1877,1884

ISBN/EAN: 9783337159160

Printed in Europe, USA, Canada, Australia, Japan

Cover: Foto ©Suzi / pixelio.de

More available books at **www.hansebooks.com**

Edward Albert Wurtzburg

The Acts Relating to Building Societies
Comprising the Act of 1836, and the Building Societies Acts 1874, 1875, 1877,1884

ISBN/EAN: 9783337159160

Printed in Europe, USA, Canada, Australia, Japan

Cover: Foto ©Suzi / pixelio.de

More available books at **www.hansebooks.com**

THE ACTS

RELATING TO

BUILDING SOCIETIES:

COMPRISING

THE ACT OF 1836, AND THE BUILDING SOCIETIES ACTS 1874, 1875, 1877, 1884,

AND

THE TREASURY REGULATIONS, 1884;

WITH AN

INTRODUCTION, COPIOUS NOTES,

AND

PRECEDENTS OF RULES AND ASSURANCES.

BY

EDWARD ALBERT WURTZBURG,

OF LINCOLN'S INN, ESQ., BARRISTER-AT-LAW.

LONDON:

STEVENS AND SONS, 119, CHANCERY LANE,

Law Publishers and Booksellers.

1886.

PREFACE.

In the following pages the object has been to present in a concise and convenient form the whole law relating to Building Societies. All the Statutes on the subject are printed *in extenso*, with copious notes, together with the Regulations issued by the Treasury in December, 1884, and the Act of Sederunt, published in 1882, for regulating the proceedings in liquidations in the Sheriff Courts of Scotland. All cases have been cited which throw any light on the rights, duties and liabilities of these Societies, their Members, and those who act on their behalf; and references have invariably been given to all the Reports. A Precedent of Rules and some Precedents of Assurances have also been added.

The Author trusts that the book will be found of use to the large and increasing class of persons who are interested in Building Societies, and to those who have the responsibility of advising them.

E. A. W.

22, Old Buildings, Lincoln's Inn.
January, 1886.

TABLE OF CONTENTS.

TABLE OF CASES.

INTRODUCTION.

A BUILDING society may be defined as an association of persons subscribing to a common fund to be employed in making advances on house property or land, the sums advanced being generally, though not necessarily, repayable by instalments. These advances are almost invariably confined to members of the society, but it is a common practice for persons to become members for the sole purpose of borrowing, the taking out of shares and receiving an advance being, in fact, simultaneous transactions. Such members as do not desire to obtain an advance, but merely pay their subscriptions and other contributions to the funds of the society, are called unadvanced or investing members; and provision is generally made by the rules for enabling members to withdraw on certain specified terms. What is a building society.

In the preamble to the Building Societies Act of 1836, 6 & 7 Will. 4, c. 32, these societies are said to have been established in different parts of the kingdom, principally amongst the industrious classes, for the purpose of raising, by small periodical subscriptions, a fund to assist the members thereof in obtaining a small freehold or leasehold property. And in the Building Societies Act, 1874, 37 & 38 Vict. c. 42, s. 13, they are described as societies for the purpose of raising, by the subscriptions of the members, a stock or fund for making advances to members, out of the funds of the society, upon freehold, copyhold, or leasehold estate by way of mortgage.

Building societies are of two kinds, terminating and permanent.

Terminating societies.

Building societies are of two kinds; (1) Terminating; (2) Permanent. A terminating society is a society which by its rules is to terminate at a fixed date, or when a result specified in its rules is attained. The earlier societies were all of this class, the permanent society being an invention of a later date. The scheme of a terminating society is somewhat as follows. The society is constituted by several persons, each subscribing for a certain number of shares. Upon each of these shares a fixed subscription is made payable so long as the society lasts, the object being to continue the society until the subscriptions, with the interest that has arisen from their investment, shall have produced such an amount per share as may have been fixed by the rules. As soon as the society has sufficient funds in hand, advances are made to such members as may desire them, in anticipation of the shares which would be payable to them on the termination of the subscriptions; the sum advanced being the amount of the member's share or shares, less a discount, and the member who receives the advance executing a mortgage of real or leasehold estate to the society, for securing the due payment by him of his subscriptions and other contributions to the funds of the society. The Bowkett and Starr-Bowkett societies are both varieties of this class.

Permanent societies.

A permanent society, on the other hand, is a

society which has not by its rules any fixed date or specified result at which it shall terminate. Societies of this kind, which are undoubtedly the best and most equitable, may therefore continue their operations for an indefinite period. They are constituted by the agreement of several persons to take shares of a certain fixed value, on which payment has to be made, either in a lump sum or by instalments, until the full amount of the share has been paid up; and the sums so paid carry interest. Advances are made to members from time to time, as the funds will permit, on the security of land or house property, the money advanced being usually made repayable by equal instalments, composed of principal and interest and spread over a fixed period.

Nature and operations of a building society.

In his judgment in *Fleming* v. *Self* (1854), 3 De G. M. & G. 997; 24 L. J. Ch. 29; 1 Jur. N. S. 25; 3 W. R. 89; 24 L. T. (O. S.) 101; 3 Eq. Rep. 14; 18 J. P. 772, Lord Cranworth, L. C., thus describes the nature and operations of a building society. His lordship's remarks were addressed to the case of a terminating society, but they apply in great measure to permanent societies as well, and exhibit in a very clear light the different positions of advanced members, unadvanced or investing members, and withdrawing members. The question in the suit was as to the terms upon which an advanced member was entitled to redeem. His lordship said:—

"Building societies exist under the provisions of the Act 6 & 7 Will. 4, c. 32, sects. 1, 3, 4, 5; the principle is this, members subscribe monthly sums which are accumulated till the fund is sufficient to give a stipulated sum to each member, and then the whole is divided amongst them: in the society now in question the sum to be raised for each member is 100*l.* If this were all it would be a very simple transaction, mere accumulation, and the only question would be how to invest the sums subscribed to the greatest advantage. But this is not all; one main object is to enable members to obtain their 100*l.* by anticipation on their allowing a large discount. For this purpose, when a sufficient fund is in the hands of the treasurer, the members who desire to get their shares in advance bid, by a sort of auction, the sum which they are ready to allow as discount, and the highest bidder obtains the advance. Thus if at the end of a year a sum of 500*l.* is in the hands of the treasurer arising from the monthly subscriptions, and the holder of ten shares is willing to allow a discount of fifty per cent., (no one offering more,) the 500*l.* is or may be advanced to him, being 50*l.* in satisfaction of each of his ten shares. For this accommodation he is bound to pay monthly, till a fund is raised sufficient to give 100*l.* per share to all the other members, not only the original monthly subscription, but also a further monthly sum called redemption money. The statute provides that the shares shall not in any society exceed 150*l.* each: in this society the shares are fixed by the rules, as I have already stated, at 100*l.* each. The amount of the monthly subscriptions and redemption money is fixed by the rules of each society; here the monthly subscription on each share is 8*s.* 6*d.*, the monthly redemption money 3*s.* 6*d.*; so that the monthly payment by each member who has not received his share in advance is 8*s.* 6*d.*, by those who have been advanced it is 12*s*. If after such an advance as I have supposed no further advance were made, the natural course of the society would be that the members, other than the holder of the ten shares, would continue their monthly subscriptions, and the owner of the ten shares would continue his monthly subscriptions and redemption money, till the fund thus raised should be sufficient to pay 100*l*. per share to every member other than the holder of the ten satisfied shares. Thus if there were one hundred shares, and at the end of the first year there was 500*l*. in hand, the condition of each shareholder before any advance made would be, that he would be bound to pay 8*s*. 6*d*. per month, say 5*l*. per annum, till by means of these payments and the 500*l*. in hand the requisite amount, that is, 10,000*l*., being 100*l*. for each 100*l*. share, should have been raised by accumulation. After the advance, the condition of every shareholder, other than the holder of the ten advanced shares, is, that he is to contribute his monthly payments till they, together with the monthly payments and redemption money contributed by the holder of the advanced shares, are sufficient to realize, not 10,000*l*. but 9,000*l*., that is, 100*l*. for each share other than the ten shares of the advanced member, whose shares will have been already satisfied by the 500*l*. He loses his interest in the 500*l*. advanced to the holder of the ten shares, but, on the other hand, the sum to be raised is only 9,000*l*. instead of 10,000*l*., and the monthly contribution is increased by the amount of the redemption money paid by the member who has received his ten shares in advance. Further advances are made from time to time as funds are accumulated, and as members are inclined to give high discount in order to obtain payment of their shares by anticipation. The gain to the society arises mainly from the high rate of discount which members in want of money are ready to give; in truth, the whole scheme is but an elaborate contrivance for enabling persons having sums for which they have no immediate want to lend them to others at a very high rate of interest. In order to secure the due payment of the monthly subscriptions and redemption money by the members who have received their shares in advance, they are obliged to give satisfactory real security to the trustees of the society, and the statute protects such mortgages from the operation of the laws which, until last session, were in force against usury.

"Besides this advance to a member of his share, deducting discount, the rules provide also for the case of a member desiring to withdraw from the society altogether. By the sixteenth rule any member may withdraw on certain terms there laid down, the principle being that he is to pay a small sum by way of fine or penalty if he withdraws at an early date after the formation of the society; but if he withdraws after having been a member, and so having paid his subscriptions, for several years, then on withdrawing he is to receive back the full amount of his subscriptions, and also, if the directors think fit, a further sum to be from time to time fixed by them by way of bonus out of what are called the profits of the society. This is provided for by the sixteenth rule, which is thus. . . . . It is obvious that this is an arrangement which may, if the calculations be properly made, be carried into effect without injury to the society. When a member withdraws, the society thenceforth loses the benefit of his monthly subscriptions, but then they are relieved from the obligation of making up the 100*l.* to which he would eventually become entitled. If the member on withdrawing merely took back the amount of his subscriptions, the society would obviously benefit to the extent of the interest made by means of those subscriptions previously to the withdrawal. It is obvious that out of the interest so realized an allowance may be made to the withdrawing member, still leaving to the society some benefit from his past contributions. The sums subscribed by a member who withdraws have contributed to make up the fund out of which the shares of those members who have been advanced, that is, have taken a smaller sum at once, allowing a large discount in lieu of the full sum of 100*l.* at a distant day, have been made good. They have, therefore, enabled the society to obtain a larger monthly payment, that is, 12*s.* instead of 8*s.* 6*d.* on each share, and to reduce on favourable terms the number of shares to be eventually provided for; this is in truth substantially an investment at a high rate of interest, and the benefits thereby accruing may not inaptly be designated, together with the interest on ordinary investments, by the name of profit. What is the precise amount of benefit, which from these different causes may have resulted to the society from the subscriptions of each member, must be a problem very difficult to solve, not perhaps admitting of any absolutely accurate solution; but it may be possible to arrive at it in a rough way, so at least as to enable the directors to fix from time to time a sum which may, without detriment to the interests of the society, be paid to any member desirous of withdrawing beyond the amount of the principal sums subscribed by him; and the sixteenth rule enables the directors to fix on such a sum, it being not, I think, inaccurately described as a bonus out of the profits of the society. The interests of members, as well those taking their shares by anticipation as those quitting the society, are thus tolerably well provided for.

"But another case was contemplated, namely, that of members who, having received their shares by anticipation, might be desirous of relieving themselves from the burden of continuing the payment of their monthly subscriptions and redemption money. From the very nature of these societies it is impossible to know with certainty how long it may be necessary to continue the monthly payments: they must be made until the sum necessary to give to every unadvanced member the full amount of his share, that is, in this society, 100*l.*, has been accumulated: the time required for this purpose will be more or less, according to the amount of benefit which the society may derive from the discount given on advances of shares and from the interest made by investments, in other words, as the profits realized have been large or small. Reasoning *à priori*, the fair course would seem to be, that the society should ascertain as nearly as may be the period of time during which the monthly payments would have to be continued, and then should allow any advanced member to relieve himself from the obligation of continuing his monthly payments on paying down at once a sum equivalent to their present value. Thus, if the monthly payment is 12*s*., and it is ascertained that these payments must probably continue to be made for ten years, it would seem to be a reasonable arrangement that the advanced member, who is liable to pay 12*s*. per month for ten years, should be freed from his liability on paying down at once a sum which an actuary should say is equivalent in present money to such continued prospective payment. This, however, is not the principle on which the power of redemption is given in this society: the provision on this subject is to be found in the fourteenth rule, it is as follows . . . . It is impossible to read this rule without being strongly impressed with the belief that those who framed it had not duly considered how it would operate. When an unadvanced member withdraws from the society, it is reasonable, and not necessarily inconsistent with the interest of its remaining members, that he should receive back, not only the principal sums which he has contributed, but also by way of bonus a portion of the benefits which those sums have gained for the society. Up to the time of his withdrawing he has received nothing: when he withdraws he loses all right to the share, that is the 100*l*., to which, if he had not withdrawn, he would, like every continuing member, have been eventually entitled, and is content to take in lieu of it the amount of what for a series of years he has been paying, together with a portion of what has been, as it were, accumulating in respect of those payments towards the eventual realization of his 100*l*. share. This is the position in which a withdrawing member stands at the time of his withdrawal, but the condition of an advanced member redeeming, which is in truth withdrawing, is very different; he is not a member who has up to the time of his redeeming received nothing; in fact, he has received that which he was content to take, supposing redemption to be out of the question, as an equivalent for the whole of his share. The rule, therefore, which gives to him on redeeming his obligation the same sum under the name of profits as is given to the non-advanced member on withdrawing, appears to be hardly reasonable; still, the question to be decided is, not whether the provision is fair and just, but what is the meaning of the rule: if the meaning is clear, it is the duty of the Court, if possible, to give it effect." See also the observations of Sir George Jessel, M. R., in *Re Guardian Permanent Benefit Building Society*, cited *infra*, p. 15.

Status of building societies.

With respect to what may be called their legal *status* or position, building societies, so far as they are regulated by the Building Societies Acts, are divided into two classes—(1) Unincorporated; (2) Incorporated.

Unincorporated societies.

(1) The first class consists of societies which were formed under, and continue to be still governed by, the Act of 1836, 6 & 7 Will. 4, c. 32, and the Acts incorporated therewith. This Act was repealed by the Building Societies Act, 1874, 37 & 38 Vict. c. 42, which came into operation on November 2nd, 1874, and no new society can therefore be established under it; but this repeal does not affect any then existing society certified under the former Act until it has obtained a certificate of incorporation under the later Act, which many societies have not seen fit

to do, preferring rather to continue under the old law. The Act of 1874 provides, however, that with regard to such subsisting societies as may not obtain certificates of incorporation under it, all things required to be done by or sent to the barrister or advocate and the clerk of the peace, under the provisions of the repealed Act, shall be done by or sent to the Registrar of Friendly Societies.

Incorporated societies.

(2) The second class consists of societies regulated by the Building Societies Act, 1874, and the Acts amending the same. These are either (a) societies established since November 2nd, 1874, the date on which the Act came into operation, or (b) societies established previously thereto, under the Act of 1836, but which have obtained a certificate of incorporation under the Act of 1874.

Unregistered societies.

There is a third class of building societies, which should perhaps be mentioned, consisting of such as have not taken the precaution of registering under any of the Acts relating to building societies, and are therefore subject only to the general law. There appears to be no objection at common law to the formation of an ordinary building society; see *Murray* v. *Scott*, 9 App. Cas. p. 546, *per* Lord Blackburn. But such a society, if consisting of more than twenty members, would, it is conceived, be rendered illegal by sect. 4 of the Companies Act, 1862, unless registered under that Act, as being an association having for its object the acquisition of gain; see *Shaw* v. *Benson*, 11 Q. B. D. 563; 52 L. J. Q. B. 575; 49 L. T. 651; *Jennings* v. *Hammond*, 9 Q. B. D. 225; 51 L. J. Q. B. 493; 31 W. R. 40; *Shaw* v. *Simmons*, 12 Q. B. D. 117; 53

L. J. Q. B. 29; 32 W. R. 292; *Re Thomas, Ex parte Poppleton*, 14 Q. B. D. 379; 54 L. J. Q. B. 336; 33 W. R. 583; 51 L. T. 602. A freehold land society, however, is not within the mischief of this section; see *Re Siddall*, 29 Ch. D. 1; 54 L. J. Ch. 62; 33 W. R. 509; 52 L. T. 114; *Crowther* v. *Thorley*, 32 W. R. 330; 50 L. T. 43; reversing *S. C.* below, 31 W. R. 564; 48 L. T. 644; *Wigfield* v. *Potter*, 45 L. T. 612.

THE BUILDING SOCIETIES ACTS.

THE BUILDING SOCIETIES ACT, 1836.

6 & 7 Will. 4, c. 32.

An Act for the Regulation of Benefit Building Societies.

[14th July, 1836.]

Whereas certain societies commonly called building societies have been established in different parts of the kingdom, principally amongst the industrious* classes, for the purpose of raising by small periodical subscriptions a fund to assist the members thereof in obtaining a small freehold or leasehold property, and it is expedient to afford encouragement and protection to such societies and the property obtained therewith: Be it therefore enacted by the king's most excellent majesty, by and with the advice and consent of the lords spiritual and temporal, and commons, in this present parliament assembled, and by the authority of the same, That it shall and may be lawful for any number of persons in Great Britain and Ireland to form themselves into and establish societies for the purpose of raising, by the monthly or other subscriptions of the several members of such societies, shares not exceeding the value of one hundred and fifty pounds for each share, such subscriptions not to exceed in the whole twenty shillings per month for

* *Sic.*

Societies may be established for the purchase or erection of dwelling houses.

Sect. 1. each share, a stock or fund for the purpose of enabling each member thereof to receive out of the funds of such society the amount or value of his or her share or shares therein, to erect or purchase one or more dwelling house or dwelling houses, or other real or leasehold estate to be secured by way of mortgage to such society until the amount or value of his or her shares shall have been fully repaid to such society with the interest thereon, and all fines or other payments incurred in respect thereof, and to and for the several members of each society from time to time to assemble together, and to make, ordain, and constitute such proper and wholesome rules and regulations for the government and guidance of the same as to the major part of the members of such society so assembled together shall seem meet, so as such rules shall not be repugnant to the express provisions of this Act and to the general laws of the realm, and to impose and inflict such reasonable fines, penalties, and forfeitures upon the several members of any such society who shall offend against any such rules, as the members may think fit, to be respectively paid to such uses for the benefit of such society as such society by such rules shall direct, and also from time to time to alter and amend such rules as occasion shall require, or annul or repeal the same, and to make new rules in lieu thereof, under such restrictions as are in this Act contained; provided that no member shall receive or be entitled to receive from the funds of such society any interest or dividend, by way of annual or other periodical profit upon any shares in such society, until the amount or value of his or her share shall have been realized, except on the withdrawal of such member, according to the rules of such society then in force.

Sect. 1.

What societies are affected by the Act.

This Act, which is remarkably ill-drawn—indeed, this first section is not English, and is barely intelligible—was repealed by s. 7 of the Building Societies Act, 1874, *post*, p. 97; but the repeal does not affect any society in existence at the date of the repeal, and certified under the repealed Act until it has obtained a certificate of incorporation under the Act of 1874, except that the things required to be done by or sent to the barrister or advocate and clerk of the peace must be done by or sent to the registrar of friendly societies. Sections 10, 35, 36 and 39 of the later Act also affect societies established under the old law, although they have not been incorporated; and it must be remembered that owing to an error which crept into s. 8 of the Act of 1874 all societies whose rules had been certified under the Act of 1836 were from Nov. 2nd, 1874, to April 22nd, 1875, deemed to be societies under the Act of 1874, although they had not obtained a certificate of incorporation; see the Building Societies Act, 1874, s. 8, and note thereto, *post*, p. 98; and the Building Societies Act, 1875, s. 1, *post*, p. 155. No society, of course, can be established under the Act of 1836 since Nov. 2nd, 1874.

Scope and objects of the Act.

In his judgment in *Re Guardian Permanent Benefit Building Society*, 23 Ch. D. 440; 52 L. J. Ch. 857; 32 W. R. 73; 48 L. T. 134, Sir G. Jessel, M. R., made the following observations on the nature of building societies and the general scope and object of the Act of 1836. The decision in the case was ultimately reversed by the House of Lords in *Agnew v. Murray*, cited below, but the value of this part of the judgment is not thereby impaired. His lordship said:— "The first point to be observed is that, whatever the effect of the Act of Will. 4 may be, it applies to societies already in existence, and it professes to deal with those societies. It is familiar to all who are interested in the subject that at the time of the Act these societies consisted of two classes of members—investing members and borrowing members, sometimes called advanced and unadvanced. The scheme

Sect. 1. of those societies was this: there were certain persons who had saved or were saving money and were desirous of investing it at a higher rate of interest than the usury laws enabled them to obtain at the time; and other persons who were desirous of either building or buying houses for their own habitation. Those two classes of persons came together; the people who had saved money or were saving money paid it into the society, and it was lent to persons who were desirous of building or buying houses on the security of the houses, and on terms which compelled the borrowers to pay a larger sum by way of interest than five per cent. per annum. That this was the substance of those societies must have been known to the legislature. The societies were divided into two classes, those which were called terminable, and which came to an end at the expiration of a fixed period, sometimes of ten years and sometimes of fifteen, and the other class, called permanent societies, which came to an end when the shares were all paid up.* In both cases, at the termination of the society, the profits were realized and the surplus assets were divided amongst the members who had paid up their shares. They got back their money with an addition in the shape of interest, which, though always expected to be more than five per cent., was sometimes a good deal less. Therefore, the investing members got back their money and interest, and the advanced members got their houses on payment off of the mortgages which were given to secure the sums payable on their shares. Under those circumstances the 6 & 7 Will. 4, c. 32, for the regulation of building societies was passed, and it recited that certain societies, commonly called building societies, had been established in different parts of the kingdom, principally amongst the industrial classes, for the purpose of raising by small periodical subscriptions money to assist some of the members in obtaining small freehold or leasehold properties. That was only one of the objects of the societies. It must have been well known to the legislature that the other object

* Both these classes would now be considered terminating societies.

was that the investing members should get a high rate of interest for their money, and that it was known is obvious from another section. It was the object to assist, therefore, some of the members to obtain freehold or leasehold property and some a high rate of interest. Then the Act enacted that it might be lawful for those two classes to form themselves into societies for the purpose of raising by monthly or other subscriptions of the members of such societies shares not exceeding the value of 150*l.* each, and such subscriptions were not to exceed 20*s.* a month for each share. These words obviously refer to such subscriptions as were to be paid monthly, and do not prohibit other contributions. Such subscriptions were to form a stock or fund for the purpose of enabling each member of the society to receive out of the funds of the society the amount or value of their shares therein, and to erect dwelling-houses, or purchase real or leasehold estate to be secured by way of mortgage to the society until the amount of their shares should have been fully repaid to the society, together with interest thereon. There is no provision here as to investing members. It looks as if everybody was to get an advance, and that the framers of the Act were forgetting that the people who made the advance must be somewhere.

"Then the Act goes on, 'And to and for the several members of each society from time to time to assemble together, and to make, ordain, and constitute such proper and wholesome rules and regulations for the government and guidance of the same as to the major part of the members of such society so assembled together shall seem meet, so as such rules shall not be repugnant to the express provisions of this Act, and to the general laws of the realm.' Whether those rules were intended to be merely bye-laws to be made after the society was constituted or not does not appear to me to make any difference, because the legislature must have known that the society could not start without rules, and therefore, if you restrict those words to the subsequent rules or laws, there is no provision as to the original rules, and it appears to me that this is the true meaning of the clause—that the rules spoken of are not the original constitution of

Sect. 1.

the society, but subsequent 'as to the major part of the members of such society so assembled together shall seem meet;' but they must be members to make the rules. It seems to me to point to a period subsequent to the starting of the society, and that there is really in this very Act of Parliament no restriction, and no direction as to the original rules which govern the constitution of the society. But, however, whichever view you take, the only limitation as to the rules is this: that they shall not be repugnant to the law of the realm, or to the express provisions of this Act.

"Then the 2nd section of the Act clearly shows me this, that the legislature clearly had the investing member in view, for it provided that it might be lawful for any such society to receive from any member thereof any sums of money by way of bonus on any shares, for the privilege of receiving the same in advance prior to the same being realized, and also any interest for the shares so received, without being subject or liable on account thereof to any of the forfeitures or penalties imposed by any of the Usury Acts; or, in other words, the society was entitled to take from the borrowing members a larger rate of interest than the usury laws allowed. Those words can have no possible meaning unless they contemplated a body of lending members.

"By lending members, I do not mean lending in the actual sense of a loan proceeding from the members, but that class which I have described as investing members. Then the 7th section extended the benefit of the Act to all societies then existing which got their rules certified." See also as to the scope and objects of the Act, the judgment of Lord Blackburn in *Agnew* v. *Murray*, 9 App. Cas. 519; 53 L. J. Ch. 745; 33 W. R. 173; 51 L. T. 462.

Distinction between building societies and freehold land societies.

Building societies must not be confounded with freehold land societies. "A freehold land society buys land with the funds contributed by the members of the society, and then divides it amongst them; but a building society advances to its borrowing members money derived from the subscriptions, and which the borrowing members themselves lay out in the purchase of lands or buildings, and then mortgage them to the society" (*Grimes* v. *Harrison*, 26 Beav. 435; 28 L. J. Ch. 823; 5 Jur. N. S. 528; 33 L. T. (O. S.) 115; 23 J. P. 421, *per* Romilly, M. R.). **Sect. 1.**

Power of building society to buy land. A society whose rules are certified as those of a building society under this Act is not justified in acting as a freehold land society; but if the rules of such a society direct unemployed money to be invested "in such manner and upon such legal security" as the directors deem necessary, there is no objection to its being invested in a purchase of freeholds (*Grimes* v. *Harrison;* and see *Mullock* v. *Jenkins*, 14 Beav. 628; 21 L. J. Ch. 65; 18 L. T. (O. S.) 203). If, however, the directors or trustees invest more money in such a purchase than the rules allow, or endeavour to convert the society into a freehold land society, or, indeed, misapply the funds in any other way, they will be guilty of a breach of trust, and will be liable for any loss that may be sustained; and any such proceedings on their part may be restrained by injunction on the application of any member who thinks himself aggrieved. **Breach of rules.** But the society does not cease to exist because it or its directors do something which the rules do not warrant, and so long as the society exists the members are bound by the rules; see *Grimes* v. *Harrison; Re Kent Benefit Building Society*, 1 Dr. & Sm. 417; 30 L. J. Ch. 785; 7 Jur. N. S. 1045; 9 W. R. 686; 4 L. T. 610; 25 J. P. 805; *R.* v. *D'Eyncourt*, 4 B. & S. 820; 9 L. T. 712; 28 J. P. 116; *S. C. nom. Hughes* v. *Layton*, 33 L. J. M. C. 89; 10 Jur. N. S. 513; *nom. Hughes* v. *D'Eyncourt*, 3 N. R. 420; 12 W. R. 408, cited *post*, p. 75.

Incorporated societies. Incorporated societies have only a very limited power to hold land; see the Building Societies Act, 1874, ss. 13, 37, *post*, pp. 103, 140.

Land societies. As to land societies, see the Industrial and Provident Societies Act, 1876, 39 & 40 Vict. c. 45; sect. 19 of this Act was partly repealed by the Summary Jurisdiction Act, 1884, 47 & 48 Vict. c. 43.

"Shares not exceeding the value of 150*l*." The interest of a member in the society is not limited to 150*l*., though the shares must not exceed that amount (*Morrison* v. *Glover*, 4 Ex. 430; 19 L. J. Ex. 20; 14 L. T. (O. S.) 204; 14 J. P. 84, where Parke, B., said that his *dictum* to

Sect. 1.

the contrary in *Cutbill* v. *Kingdom*, 1 Ex. 494; 17 L. J. Ex. 177, was incorrect).

"Proper and wholesome rules and regulations."

As to the power to make rules conferred by the Act, see the judgment of the Earl of Selborne, L. C., in *Agnew* v. *Murray*, 9 App. Cas. p. 538; 53 L. J. Ch. 745; 33 W. R. 173; 51 L. T. 462; the remarks of Giffard, L. J., in *Laing* v. *Reed*, 5 Ch. 4; 39 L. J. Ch. 1; 18 W. R. 76; 21 L. T. 773; 34 J. P. 131; and the judgment of Jessel, M. R., cited above, p. 17. "The only real and true limit of the rule-making power, as to a matter not governed by the general law of the realm or by any express prohibition in the statute, must be that pointed out by Giffard, L. J.; the power cannot be so exercised as to make the society a thing different from a benefit building society, formed for the purposes and in the manner defined by the Act" (*Agnew* v. *Murray*, *loc. cit.*).

Alteration of rules.

As to the mode of altering the rules, see 10 Geo. 4, c. 56, s. 9, and note thereto, *post*, p. 49.

"Reasonable fines, penalties and forfeitures."

The fines must be "reasonable." A rule imposing fines for non-payment of their contributions by advanced members at the rate of a shilling per pound per month (sixty per cent.) was held reasonable in *Parker* v. *Butcher*, 3 Eq. 762; 36 L. J. Ch. 552. This case was followed by Hall, V.-C., in *Pilkington* v. *Baker* (2), W. N. (1877), 210, where the contract was for repayment of the advance by monthly instalments of principal and interest, and in default of payment on the day named, for payment of the sum of sixpence per pound per month.

Forfeiture.

In *Card* v. *Carr*, 1 C. B. N. S. 197; 26 L. J. C. P. 113, one of the rules provided that any unadvanced member who should have neglected to pay his monthly subscriptions for six consecutive monthly nights, should thereupon cease to be a member of the society and forfeit all his interest therein. The Court were clearly of opinion that there was nothing unreasonable or contrary to law in such a rule.

In a recent case one of the rules was as follows:—"The fines incurred by all present or future mortgagors by neglecting to make their monthly payments of principal, interest, fines and other payments, will be at the rate of five per cent. per month on the total amount in arrear." It was

Sect. 1.

held that the monthly fine was to be calculated at the rate of five per cent. per month on the amount of the previous fines and other payments, as well as of the principal and interest in arrear, and that the amount of the fine was not unreasonable (*Re The Middlesbrough Building Society*, 54 L. J. Ch. 592; 51 L. T. 743; 49 J. P. 278; W. N. (1884), 208). See also *Ex parte Voisey*, 21 Ch. D. 442; 52 L. J. Ch. 121; 31 W. R. 19; 47 L. T. 362; and for further cases on the construction of rules as to fines, see *Lovejoy* v. *Mulkern*, 46 L. J. Ch. 630; 37 L. T. 77; *Re Tierney's Estate*, Ir. R. 9 Eq. 1; 8 Ir. L. T. Rep. 29.

Power of societies to borrow money.

1. Where the rules contain a power to borrow.

With regard to the borrowing of money by societies under the Act, a point on which the Act itself is silent, an opinion at one time prevailed that, though a rule authorizing the directors to borrow money for the purposes of the society *to a limited extent* was good, a rule giving them an *unlimited* power to borrow for such purposes was illegal and void as being contrary to the scope and intent of the statute. See *Laing* v. *Reed*, 5 Ch. p. 8; 39 L. J. Ch. 1; 18 W. R. 76; 21 L. T. 773; 34 J. P. 134; *Hill's Case*, 9 Eq. 605; 39 L. J. Ch. 628; 18 W. R. 967; 22 L. T. 777; 34 J. P. 532; *Re Professional, Commercial, and Industrial Permanent Benefit Building Society*, 6 Ch. 856; 19 W. R. 1153; 25 L. T. 397; *Re Guardian Permanent Benefit Building Society, Calvert's Case*, 23 Ch. D. 440; 52 L. J. Ch. 857; 32 W. R. 73; 48 L. T. 134. The House of Lords, however, has recently held that this idea is erroneous, and that a rule authorizing the directors to borrow money for the purposes of the society, without any limit being expressed as to the amount, is perfectly good, and the loans contracted under it valid; see *Agnew* v. *Murray*, 9 App. Cas. 519; 53 L. J. Ch. 745; 33 W. R. 173; 51 L. T. 462, reversing the decision of the Court of Appeal in *Calvert's Case*, from which *Agnew* v. *Murray* was, in substance though not in name, an appeal. In that case the 32nd rule of the society was as follows:—

"The trustees or directors for the time being of this society may, from time to time as occasion may require, borrow and take up at interest any sum or sums of money from the society's banker, or from any banker, or from any other

Sect. 1.

person or persons; and any borrowed money shall be a first charge on the funds and property of the society. And in case the trustees or directors shall at any time give their joint and several promissory note or other security for money borrowed for and on behalf of the society, then and in such case the persons giving the security shall be indemnified by the society, and the funds and property of the society shall be held subject and liable to the repayment of the borrowed moneys, the borrowed moneys being always deemed a first charge on the society's funds and property." Under this rule the directors borrowed large sums for the proper purposes of the society, and deposited with the lenders as security title deeds of properties which had been mortgaged to the society by advanced members. The society was ordered to be wound up. The House of Lords held that the rule was valid, and that the lenders were entitled in the winding-up to payment out of the assets after satisfaction of the outside creditors and in priority to the claims of all shareholders or members.

Effect of provision that borrowed moneys shall be a first charge on the funds of the society.

It was held, however, in the case last cited, that the lenders must give up their securities to the official liquidator, the claim to special equitable charges upon specific properties being inconsistent with the true meaning of the rule, which was that all the moneys borrowed under it were to have the benefit, equally and *pari passu*, of a first charge upon the general funds and property of the society; and see also *Small* v. *Smith*, 10 App. Cas. p. 131.

In a recent case, the first rule of the society declared that it was established "for the purpose of raising by monthly subscriptions and deposits on loans a fund to make advances to members of the value of their shares, to enable them to erect or purchase one or more house or houses," &c. At a meeting of directors, it was resolved that the directors might receive deposits of money on debentures; and under that resolution they received loans from persons not otherwise members. On the society being wound up, it was held, by Mr. Justice Kay, that the rule sufficiently expressed the power to receive deposits on loan, and that the lenders were outside creditors, and entitled to be paid in priority to the

Sect. 1.

members of all classes, including those who had given notice of withdrawal before the commencement of the winding-up (*Re Mutual Aid Permanent Benefit Building Society*, 29 Ch. D. 182; 54 L. J. Ch. 493; 33 W. R. 575; 52 L. T. 406; affirmed on appeal, 30 Ch. D. 434).

2. Where the rules contain no power to borrow.

A building society, however, has no power to borrow money unless its rules authorize it so to do; see *Re National Permanent Benefit Building Society, Ex parte Williamson*, 5 Ch. 309; 18 W. R. 388; 22 L. T. 284; 34 J. P. 341; *Cunliffe Brooks & Co.* v. *Blackburn Benefit Building Society*, 9 App. Cas. 857; 54 L. J. Ch. 376; 33 W. R. 309; 52 L. T. 225; affirming *S. C.* below, 22 Ch. D. 61; 52 L. J. Ch. 92; 31 W. R. 98; 48 L. T. 33; though the power to borrow need not be express (*Blackburn Building Society* v. *Cunliffe Brooks & Co.*, 22 Ch. D. p. 70, *per* Lord Selborne, L. C.). "If it could be shown that the course of business authorized by the rules was such as to give, as incidental to it, a power to borrow, it would be authorized, though not expressly authorized;" *per* Lord Blackburn, in *Cunliffe Brooks & Co.* v. *Blackburn Benefit Building Society*, 9 App. Cas. p. 865. In that case the facts were as follows:—The society, whose rules contained no power to borrow, was allowed by its bankers to overdraw its account to a large amount. In 1876 a memorandum was signed by the officers of the society, and confirmed by the directors, stating that certain deeds of borrowing members which had been deposited with the bankers were deposited not only for safe custody, but as a security for the balance from time to time. In 1881 an order for winding-up the society was made, and the official liquidators brought an action to recover these deeds, which the bankers claimed to retain as security for the balance of their account. No evidence was given as to the application of the money which was drawn out by the society; but it was admitted that some part was applied in payment of members withdrawing from the society, and the remainder in payment of salaries, legal expenses, and expenses of mortgaged property.

The Court of Appeal held that the overdrafts were *ultra vires*, being a borrowing not authorized by the rules, and not properly incident to the course and conduct of the

Sect. 1. society's business for its proper purposes; and that the bankers were not creditors of the society in respect of the overdrafts; but that they were entitled, according to a well-settled principle of equity, to hold the deeds as a security for repayment of so much of the moneys advanced by them as was applied in payment of the debts and liabilities of the society properly payable and had not been repaid to the bankers, excluding payments to withdrawing members; that the burden of proving this lay on the bankers, and that in satisfying that burden the bankers could not have the benefit of the rule in *Clayton's Case* (1 Mer. 572). The Court of Appeal made an order accordingly, directing inquiries, with a declaration that in making the inquiries the bankers were to be charged with all sums received by them on account of the society, since it ceased to have any balance to its credit with the bankers, and that they were not to be allowed any sums advanced by them since that date, which were applied in making payments to withdrawing members or otherwise than in paying such debts and liabilities of the society as aforesaid. On an appeal by the bankers alone the House of Lords expressed no opinion upon the question of payments to withdrawing members or the bankers' right to hold the securities, but held that in other respects the decision and order of the Court of Appeal were right. The liquidators then brought an action against the bankers to recover all moneys which had been paid to them by the society and applied by the bankers in discharge of their loan. The Court of Appeal held that it was no answer to the action that the moneys had been so applied by the order of the directors of the society under a mistake of law as to their power to borrow, the borrowing and directing the application of the moneys being both unauthorized and not binding on the society; but the bankers were allowed to stand in the place of withdrawing members of the society, who had been paid out of moneys so advanced by the bankers, and to receive the amounts which would be payable to such members if they had not been paid off, and they were also allowed to have the benefit of securities obtained by the society by means of the overdrafts allowed by the bankers, and to have

Sect. 1.

the benefit of such securities according to their order of priority, without being postponed to other securities granted by the society (*Blackburn Benefit Building Society* v. *Cunliffe Brooks & Co.*, 29 Ch. D. 902). It was also held in the same case, that the fact that annual balance sheets, showing the amounts due to the bankers, had been sent to all members of the society and adopted at the annual meetings, did not amount to a ratification by the society of the acts of the directors, and that no ratification of such acts by the majority of the members would bind the minority.

3. Where the borrowing power has been exceeded.

If the rules of the society contain a limited power to borrow, it must be strictly pursued, and if the limits of the power are exceeded the loan will create no liability against the society. Thus, where the rules authorized the committee to obtain loans for the purpose of making advances to members, and the committee borrowed money for general purposes and in order to pay debts, the society were not liable (*Moye* v. *Sparrow*, 18 W. R. 400; W. N. (1870), 33; 22 L. T. 154). So, where the rules empowered the directors to borrow "for the purposes of the society," and the directors employed the money they borrowed in loan transactions with another society and in buying an estate (*Re Durham County Building Society*, *Davis' Case*, 12 Eq. 516; 41 L. J. Ch. 124; 25 L. T. 83). In another case, however, in the same winding-up, the Court refused to order the lender to give up deeds which had been deposited with him as security for the loan (*Wilson's Case*, 12 Eq. 521; 41 L. J. Ch. 125; 25 L. T. 84). It may, perhaps, be doubted whether this last decision can now be relied on; see *Cunliffe Brooks & Co.* v. *Blackburn Benefit Building Society*, cited above; though there is this difference between the two cases, that in *Wilson's Case* there was a power to borrow, though the money borrowed was misapplied, whereas in the Blackburn case there was no power to borrow at all. Again, where the rules authorized the directors to borrow up to a certain amount, and they contracted a loan after the prescribed limit had been already exceeded, the Court of Appeal held that the society, which had received no benefit from the loan, were not liable to

Sect. 1. repay it; though they also hold that, under the circumstances, the directors themselves were personally liable for the money which had been advanced (*Chapleo* v. *Brunswick Building Society*, 6 Q. B. D. 696; 50 L. J. Q. B. 372; 29 W. R. 529; 44 L. T. 449; reversing *S. C.* below, 5 C. P. D. 331; 49 L. J. C. P. 796; 29 W. R. 153). In his judgment in this case, Baggallay, L. J., said: "The acts of the directors would in no way give effect to that which was in itself unlawful, nor in my opinion would the assent of every shareholder to the transaction make it binding upon the society as a society, whatever might have been the liability of individual shareholders. . . . . If the society had received the benefit of the 100*l.*, if for instance that amount had found its way to the credit of their banking account, the plaintiffs might, upon the authority of some of the decisions which have been cited in their behalf, have been enabled to establish a claim against the society to the extent of the benefit derived by them from the transaction, but no such benefit was derived by the society from the transaction with which we are dealing. . . . . It has also been urged upon us that the plaintiffs had no means of knowing or ascertaining whether the society had exhausted its powers of borrowing; or whether indeed there was any limit to such power. To this argument I can only reply, that persons who deal with corporations and societies that owe their constitution to or have their powers defined or limited by Acts of Parliament, or are regulated by deeds of settlement or rules, deriving their effect more or less from Acts of Parliament, are bound to know or to ascertain for themselves the nature of the constitution and the extent of the powers of the corporation or society with which they deal. The plaintiffs and every one else who have dealings with a building society are bound to know that such a society has no power of borrowing, except such as is conferred upon it by its rules, and f in dealing with such a society they neglect or fail to ascertain whether it has the power of borrowing, or whether any imited power it may have has been exceeded, they must take the consequences of their carelessness. It may be that the plaintiffs in the present case have been misled, by the misrepresentations or conduct of others, into the belief that

Sect. 1.

the company had full authority to accept the loan from them; that is a question which I shall have to consider when dealing with the other appeal; such representations or conduct may doubtless give rise to a claim against the parties making such misrepresentations or so conducting themselves, but in my opinion they can in no way give rise to or support a claim against the society."

Overdrawing banking account is borrowing.

There is no distinction between borrowing by overdrawing the society's banking account and borrowing by obtaining a loan in the ordinary way (*Cunliffe Brooks & Co.* v. *Blackburn Benefit Building Society; Looker* v. *Wrigley, Leigh* v. *Wrigley*, 9 Q. B. D. 397; 46 J. P. 758); the cases to the contrary (*post*, p. 108) cannot now be relied on.

Incorporated societies.

As to the power of incorporated societies to borrow money, see the Building Societies Act, 1874, s. 15, and note thereto, *post*, p. 106; and as to loans made to unincorporated societies in the interval between Nov. 2, 1874, and April 22, 1875, see *post*, p. 99.

Preference shares.

A rule giving the directors power to issue deposit or paid-up shares at a fixed rate of interest, with a right to withdraw the money in preference to the ordinary unadvanced members, is valid, and the holders will be entitled in the event of the society being wound up to be paid in priority to the unadvanced members. Such shares are, in fact, true preference shares; and there is nothing either in the statute itself or in the general law to render their issue, when authorized by the rules of the society, illegal (*Re Guardian Permanent Benefit Building Society, Scott's Case*, 23 Ch. D. 440, 453; 52 L. J. Ch. 857; 32 W. R. 73; 48 L.T. 134; affirmed on appeal, *nom. Murray* v. *Scott*, 9 App. Cas. 519; 53 L. J. Ch. 745; 33 W. R. 173; 51 L. T. 462).

Shares are not within Mortmain Act.

Shares in a building society are not within the Mortmain Act, 9 Geo. 2, c. 36, and may therefore be bequeathed to a charity (*Entwistle* v. *Davis*, 4 Eq. 272; 36 L. J. Ch. 825; 31 J. P. 708).

County vote.

As to the mode of ascertaining the value to an advanced member of the property mortgaged by him to the society, in order to determine whether he is entitled in respect of such property to a vote for the county, see *Rolleston* v. *Cope*,

Sect. 1. L. R. 6 C. P. 292; 1 Hop. & Colt. 488; 40 L. J. C. P. 160; 19 W. R. 927; 24 L. T. 390, and cases there cited; Rogers on Elections, p. 42, 14th ed.

Winding-up. An unincorporated building society may be wound up under the Companies Act, 1862 (*Re No. 3 Midland Counties Benefit Building Society*, 4 De G. J. & S. 468; 33 L. J. Ch. 739; 11 Jur. N. S. 229; 13 W. R. 399; 4 N. R. 536; 29 J. P. 613, reversing *S. C.* below, 33 L. J. Ch. 520; 10 Jur. N. S. 505; 10 L. T. 258; 28 J. P. 295; *Re Doncaster Permanent Building Society*, 3 Eq. 158; 15 W. R. 102; 15 L. T. 270; 31 J. P. 310; *Re Queen's Benefit Building Society*, 6 Ch. 815; 40 L. J. Ch. 381; 19 W. R. 597; 24 L. T. 346); and the winding-up proceeds in the same way as in the case of an ordinary unregistered company.

On whose petition. An order to wind up may be made at the instance of an outside creditor (*Re No. 3 Midland Counties Benefit Building Society*), of an unadvanced member who has given notice of withdrawal (*Re Queen's Benefit Building Society*), or of an advanced member (*Re Professional Commercial and Industrial Benefit Building Society*, 6 Ch. 856; 19 W. R. 1153; 25 L. T. 397). But though an outside creditor is, except under special circumstances, entitled to a winding-up order *ex debito justitiæ*, there is no such absolute right in the case of a member; and if the Court sees that an order to wind up will be prejudicial to the best interests of the society, and in fact will do more harm than good, or is sought for the purpose of obtaining an undue advantage over other members, the petition will be dismissed: see *Re Professional Commercial and Industrial Benefit Building Society; Re Planet Benefit Building and Investment Society*, 14 Eq. 441; 41 L. J. Ch. 738; 20 W. R. 935; 27 L. T. 638; *Re London Permanent Benefit Building Society*, 17 W. R. 513, 717; 20 L. T. 388; 21 L. T. 8; *Martin v. Scottish Savings Investment and Building Society*, 17 Sc. L. R. 221.

Loan *ultra vires*. Where the petitioner had lent money to a society which had *no power to borrow*, it was held that the loan created no debt, and the petition was accordingly dismissed (*Re National Permanent Benefit Building Society, Ex parte Williamson*, 5 Ch. 309; 18 W. R. 388; 22 L. T. 284; 34 J. P. 341).

Sect. 1.

Advanced members.

Both advanced and unadvanced members are liable in a winding-up to contribute towards payment of debts due to outside creditors (*Re Doncaster Permanent Building Society*, 3 Eq. 158; 15 W. R. 102; 15 L. T. 270; 31 J. P. 310); but when all these debts had been paid, and the advanced members had redeemed their shares, it was held, the rules providing that the funds of the society should belong to the members in proportion to the time they had been subscribers, that no further call could be made, and that the surplus assets must be distributed among the unadvanced members according to their respective periods of subscription (*Re Doncaster Permanent Building Society*, 4 Eq. 579; 36 L. J. Ch. 871).

Sharing losses.

Where the rules provided that advanced members, as well as the unadvanced, should be entitled to a share in the profits, in proportion to the amounts respectively standing to the credit of their shares, it was held, there being no outside creditors, that the advanced members must bear a share of the losses in proportion to the sums standing to their credit at the time when the society resolved to wind up (*Trustees of The North British Building Society*, 12 R. 1271; 22 Sc. L. R. 833).

Incorporated societies.

In the case of incorporated societies the liability of members is strictly limited: see the Building Societies Act, 1874, s. 14, and note thereto, *post*, p. 104. In *Scottish Property Investment Company Building Society* v. *Boyd*, 12 R. 127; 22 Sc. L. R. 43, it was held, there being no outside creditors unpaid, that an advanced member could not be compelled, on the society going into liquidation, to repay his loan otherwise than by instalments as stipulated in his bond. The liquidator contended that the effect of the winding-up was to compel the advanced member to pay the whole balance remaining due from him at once, and cited *Brownlie* v. *Russell* (see *post*, p. 31) in support of this view. The Lord Justice Clerk in the course of his judgment (12 R., p. 137) said:—"I am of opinion that there is neither principle nor authority which can maintain such a demand; that the company, although in liquidation, continues to subsist for the purpose of winding-up, for the realizing of

Sect. 1.

its funds, and fulfilment of its obligations, and that as it was effectually bound to accept payment of the alleged debt by the stipulated instalments, the liquidator is not entitled to evade these stipulations but is bound to fulfil them. It does not seem to me of much moment to inquire whether this building society comes strictly under the category of a trading partnership or not. It is certainly primarily regulated by the Acts of Parliament which have been passed in regard to such associations, and by the rules of the special association. Subject, however, to these, I should have thought that it belonged to the category of society or partnership as understood in our law. But such a society must, at all events, continue to exist for the purpose of winding-up, and it must fulfil its obligations in the terms and on the conditions to which its contract binds it, whatever may be the legal character of its constitution. There is no provision in any Act of Parliament, or in the rules of this society, which justifies the violation of deliberate contract, or which empowers the company or the shareholders to terminate them by going into liquidation. This may, and no doubt does, put an end to future transactions, but it cannot affect the rights of creditors constituted by prior obligations. Neither do I think it of moment to consider minutely the precise position of an advanced shareholder under this contract. My own opinion is that under such a contract he is more of a debtor than of a shareholder, and that there is nothing in the fact of his being on the roll of shareholders which in any way limits his right to receive fulfilment of the obligations of the company in terms of their undertaking; neither does it seem necessarily to imply any future or contingent obligation after the contract of repayment has been fulfilled. Much, of course, will depend on the particular rules of any given society, but I know of no authority for holding it to be a general rule that the liquidation of a building society of this kind alters the terms of contracts made with advanced shareholders, or renders it illegal to continue to receive payments on such debts by instalments in terms of the obligation."

Security for costs.

In a recent case the official liquidator took out a summons

in the winding-up against the manager to make him liable for certain moneys of the society. The manager applied for security for costs under sect. 69 of the Companies Act, 1862, and Bacon, V.-C., held that the Court had general jurisdiction to make the order asked for (*Re Seventh East Central Building Society*, 51 L. T. 109). **Sect. 1.**

The rights and liabilities of members who have given notice of withdrawal depend upon the rules of the society, subject, however, to this—that if the society is wound up, and there are outside creditors whose claims have to be met, they must be paid first. Members who have given notice to withdraw cannot compete with outside creditors, though they may be entitled under the rules to priority over members who have not given such notice. The following cases have been decided as to the effect of a winding-up order on the right to withdraw. Withdrawal. **Effect of winding-up order.**

In *Brownlie* v. *Russell*, 8 App. Cas. 235; 48 L. T. 881; 47 J. P. 757, the society was registered under the Act of 1874. The rules provided that an unadvanced member on withdrawal should receive the whole instalments paid on his shares with interest, and that an advanced member should pay up the whole of his debt interest and penalties, after deducting the amount of the monthly instalments paid upon his shares with interest thereon. A member obtained an advance, executing a bond in common form as security, and the society granted him a back letter to the effect that they agreed not to enforce the bond so long as the regular payments of the instalments interest and other sums due upon his shares were paid. He regularly paid his instalments with interest on the whole sum lent. In February 1880, the society went into liquidation, there being no outside creditors. In the following July the member gave notice of withdrawal, claiming a discharge of his bond on payment of the difference between his loan and the total amount of the instalments paid by him, with interest. The liquidators denied his right to withdraw unless he paid up the whole loan, and left the instalments to be refunded according to the result of the liquidation. The House of Lords held that *Brownlie v. Russell.*

Sect. 1.

the advance had *pro tanto* been extinguished by the total amount of the instalments paid; and that after the winding-up order the member had a right to redeem by paying to the liquidators the difference between his advance and his instalments, with interest added thereon as against excess of interest which he had been charged; and that on payment of such difference, with interest thereon, he would be relieved from all further liability whatever.

The Lord Chancellor (Earl of Selborne) in his judgment said:—"I cannot but think that the true effect of the winding-up order is that which was put to your lordships by Mr. Davey in his able argument. I think that it prevents the exercise of the option of retiring or withdrawing which was given to all the members, to the unadvanced members under the 9th rule and to the advanced members under the 12th, as to which I hold that the rules contemplate a going concern. That is consistent with the opinion expressed by Vice-Chancellor Wood in the case before him, who spoke of the winding-up order as substantially putting a stop to the whole thing. It takes away the option which otherwise, if the concern had been a going one, would have belonged to each member—it, by a *vis major*, as the Vice-Chancellor said, puts a close to the whole concern—it terminates, at that date, the account of each shareholder—it cuts off all chance of profit which, if the thing had gone on, both classes of members might have had under the 5th rule. It is equivalent, not to an optional withdrawal or retirement by individual members, but to a compulsory withdrawal by the operation of the winding-up order as against them all. That cannot take away from the advanced member the right to redeem his mortgage by paying up all that is due upon it; and it appears to me that although the terms, in my view, of the 12th rule do not specifically apply, yet it comes to exactly the same thing in the practical result. The respondent has a right to redeem his security—he in that way gets rid of future interest. I agree that he is not entitled to discount, but he has a right to redeem his security by paying up all that is justly due from him; and in reckoning what is justly due from him he should, as against excess of interest with which he has been charged, be allowed interest on his actual payments." Sect. 1

In another case the rules allowed any investing member to withdraw, "provided the funds permit," upon giving notice, and declared that "no further liabilities shall be incurred by the society till such member has been repaid." The society was ordered to be wound up, and the assets were insufficient to pay everybody. It was held that those investing members who had given notice of withdrawal, and whose notices had expired before the winding-up began, were entitled to be paid out of the assets (after payment of the outside creditors), in priority to those members who had not given notice of withdrawal, notwithstanding the fact that between the giving of the notices and the winding-up there never were any funds available for their payment, and that some of the notices accepted by the directors were not in the form prescribed by the rules (*Walton* v. *Edge*, 10 App. Cas. 33; 54 L. J. Ch. 362; 33 W. R. 417; 52 L. T. 666; 49 J. P. 468; affirming *S. C.* below, *nom. Re Blackburn and District Benefit Building Society*, 24 Ch. D. 421; 52 L. J. Ch. 894; 32 W. R. 159; 49 L. T. 730). "Then what is there in this contract to say that, if the funds do permit the payment to be made, though it was not possible before the winding-up, yet if it becomes possible after that time, it shall not be done? Certainly there is nothing on the face of the contract to that effect; there is nothing to say that in any case when there are funds with or without winding-up, the non-withdrawing members are to come into competition with the right thus given to the withdrawing members. Is there anything to that effect in the Act under which building societies are liable to be wound up? Nothing whatever. The particular terms of that Act have not been referred to, but they are familiar to your lordships. It provides that when there is a winding-up the transactions of the society are to stop; there can be no new contracts entered into; there can be no change of the position in which the parties stand at that time; no new notice of withdrawal can be given or anything of that character; and an official liquidator is appointed, who is to

Walton v. *Edge.*

Sect. 1.

collect the assets of the society and to administer them in a due course of administration, paying creditors first and the costs of the winding-up, and then if there is a surplus that surplus is to be applied according to the rights of the members *inter se.* If the members had contracted with each other before the winding-up that in an event which had happened before the winding-up a particular member should have a right to be paid off his share or a sum which he desired to withdraw, as soon as the funds should permit, then the moment the funds of the society are cleared from claims prior to his right that right must take effect in a due course of administration under the winding-up, just as it would have done before. In adjusting the rights of the members *inter se*, without going into any technical questions as to the use of the word "creditor," those members are to be preferred who under the contract have a right to a preferable payment out of the free assets, the free funds, when they exist:" *per* the Earl of Selborne, L. C., 10 App. Cas. 37. This decision was followed by the Court of Appeal in *Re Alliance Society*, 28 Ch. D. 559; 54 L. J. Ch. 540; 52 L. T. 695; and by the Court of Session in Scotland, in *Trustees of the North British Building Society*, 12 R. 1271; 22 Sc. L. R. 833.

Re Norwich &c. Building Society.

In *Re Norwich and Norfolk Provident Permanent Benefit Building Society, Ex parte Rackham*, W. N. (1876), 186, 230; 45 L. J. Ch. 785, there were three classes of members, viz., 1st, "realized members," who had paid up in full what was due from them; 2nd, "withdrawal members," who had not paid up in full, but had given notice to withdraw; 3rd, "investing members," who had neither paid up in full nor given notice to withdraw. It was held that the realized and withdrawal members must be paid in priority to the investing members.

Scotch cases.

In a case that recently came before the Court of Session in Scotland, the 71st rule provided that the books of the society should be balanced and the profits ascertained as on February 1st in each year, in such way as the directors should think proper. The 75th rule provided that "any member holding unadvanced shares shall be entitled to withdraw from the society on application to the directors in writing, and shall be entitled to receive the amount standing at his credit in the books of the society in respect of his shares as at the immediately preceding annual balance, together with the amount of subscriptions paid by him thereafter." The 76th rule provided that "applications for withdrawal shall be considered and granted by the directors in the order of priority and the dates on which these applications shall have been received by the manager, and payment shall be made to such applicants so soon as the directors shall have sufficient funds at their disposal, and not otherwise." The annual balance sheet of the society for the year ending January 31st, 1881, was embodied in the directors' report, dated March 30th. It was disapproved by the society, and, after an investigation by the shareholders, an amended balance sheet was submitted by the directors, and approved by the society on July 28th. The amended balance sheet, instead of showing an apparent profit as in the original balance sheet, showed a loss, attributable to over-valuation of the assets, estimated at 40 per cent. of the value of the shares of all unadvanced members who had not given notice of withdrawal previous to February 1st, and stated that the deficiency must be written off these shares. In November the society went into liquidation. Certain unadvanced members, who had given notice of withdrawal on March 3rd, objected to the writing off of 40 per cent. from the value of their shares as they stood in the books of the society on February 1st. The Court held that the balance sheet approved on July 28th showed the balance for the year ending January 31st, and that 40 per cent. had been rightly written off the value of the objectors' shares (*Liquidators of The Scottish Property Investment Company Building Society* v. *Stewart*, 12 R. 925; 22 Sc. L. R. 619).

In *Glasgow Working Men's Provident Investment Building Society* v. *Galbraith*, 21 Sc. L. R. 782, a member gave notice to withdraw, but before he had been paid out the society resolved that a certain proportion per £ be deducted from all shareholders' accounts, and placed to a suspense account, and this resolution was intimated to him. He was subsequently paid out, subject to this deduction, and gave a receipt for the sum paid him as "placed to the debit of my share account." It was held that he was not precluded either by the receipt

Sect. 1.

or by what passed on the giving of it, from afterwards insisting on payment of the balance on the society becoming in funds to pay him in full. See, however, *Auld v. Glasgow Working Men's Provident Investment Building Society*, 12 R. 1320; 22 Sc. L. R. 883.

Cancellation of notice of withdrawal.

As to cancellation of a notice to withdraw, see *Liquidators of The Scottish Property Investment Company Building Society v. Stewart*, where it was held that, under the circumstances, the cancellation was conditional only, and the condition not having been performed the notice remained good.

In *Trustees of The North British Building Society*, 12 R. 1271; 22 Sc. L. R. 833, the directors issued a circular to the members intimating that, looking to the state of the finances and to the fact that a number of members had given notice to withdraw, they had resolved to take steps "to put all the members on an equal footing." With this view they suggested that all members should give notice of withdrawal. After the issue of this circular, no business was done and no new members admitted. On the society afterwards going into liquidation, it was held that the liability of members to share losses must be calculated as at the date of the circular, and that notices of withdrawal subsequent thereto could not receive effect.

Re Middlesbrough Building Society.

In *Re The Middlesbrough &c. Benefit Building Society*, 53 L. T. 203, the rules provided that a withdrawing member should receive back his subscription money; that withdrawing members, whose shares were fully paid up should receive 5 per cent. interest from the time such shares were so paid up, or from the time the previous dividend was paid; and that if more than one should give notice to withdraw they should be paid according to priority of notice. Mr. Justice Kay held, following *Walton v. Edge*, that those members who gave notice of withdrawal prior to the commencement of the winding-up, must be repaid the amount of their shares in priority to the other members in rotation, according to the respective dates of their notices. And his lordship held further, that such of the members whose shares were fully paid up at the dates of their respective notices were entitled to interest on the amounts due to them, in the same order of

Interest.

Sect. 1.

priority, from the times when such shares were fully paid up, or from the times of the payment of the last dividend, until payment of the amounts due to them.

Compound interest. Compound interest will be allowed to withdrawing members if the rules so provide (*Re Doncaster Permanent Benefit Building and Investment Society*, 14 L. T. 13).

Arbitration after notice of withdrawal. The acceptance by the trustees of a notice of withdrawal does not prevent the application of a rule providing for the settlement of disputes by arbitration; see *post*, p. 73.

New rules. A member is not bound by new rules made after he has given notice to withdraw (*Armitage* v. *Walker*, *post*, p. 73).

Payment to a registered owner of shares, without notice that he is only a trustee, discharges the society from liability to the real owner (*Nolloth* v. *Simplified Building Society*, 34 W. R. 73).

Bonus, &c. not to be usurious. **2.** And be it enacted, that it shall and may be lawful to and for any such society to have and receive from any member or members thereof any sum or sums of money, by way of bonus on any share or shares, for the privilege of receiving the same in advance prior to the same being realized, and also any interest for the share or shares so received or any part thereof, without being subject or liable on account thereof to any of the forfeitures or penalties imposed by any Act or Acts of Parliament relating to usury.

The repeal of the usury laws rendered this provision unnecessary.

Rules may be made to provide forms of conveyance, &c. **3.** And be it further enacted, that it shall and may be lawful to and for any such society, in and by the rules thereof, to describe the form or forms of conveyance, mortgage, transfer, agreement, bond, or other instrument which may be necessary for carrying the purposes of the said society into execution; and which shall be specified and set forth in a

Sect. 3. schedule to be annexed to the rules of such society, and duly certified and deposited as hereinafter provided.

Nature of mortgages to building societies.

Mortgages to building societies are of two kinds, depending on the constitution and rules of the society. In the case of a terminating society a mortgage by an advanced member is intended to secure, not the repayment of the sum advanced with interest, but the due payment by him of his subscriptions and other contributions to the funds of the society until the full amount of the shares of the unadvanced or investing members is realized according to the rules. In permanent societies, on the other hand, a mortgage for an advance to a member is usually in the nature of an ordinary security for repayment of the advance by equal instalments, composed of principal and interest combined, and spread over a fixed period. See Davidson's Precedents, Vol. II. Pt. II. p. 704, 4th ed.

The general law of mortgages applies in the case of mortgages to a building society, subject to such variations as arise from the special nature of these securities: see *Provident Permanent Building Society* v. *Greenhill*, 9 Ch. D. 122; 27 W. R. 110; 38 L. T. 140; *Bell* v. *London & South Western Bank*, W. N. (1874), 10.

Redemption.

The terms of redemption depend on the rules of the society and the provisions of the mortgage deed, and questions of considerable difficulty have arisen occasionally in consequence of the want of care and knowledge displayed in framing the rules, which in some instances have been little better than obscure nonsense. In the case of a permanent society it is comparatively easy to ascertain how much must be paid by an advanced member who wishes to redeem his security; but in the case of a terminating society, owing to the impossibility of saying exactly how long the society will last, the calculation is one of some difficulty, and in fact can scarcely be made with perfect theoretical accuracy.

In terminating societies. *Seagrave* v. *Pope*.

In *Seagrave* v. *Pope*, 1 De G. M. & G. 783; 22 L. J. Ch. 258; 16 Jur. 1099; 19 L. T. (O. S.) 173; 20 L. T. (O. S.) 158, the mortgagor claimed to be entitled to redeem on payment of the sums advanced to him by the society less the amount of the subscriptions which he had paid and the proportion of profits in the society to which he was entitled; it was held, however, by the Lord Chancellor, reversing the decision below, that he could only redeem on payment of all sums which, according to the rules, were then due or might thereafter become due during the *probable duration* of the society; and see *Mosley* v. *Baker*, 1 H. & T. 301; 3 De G. M. & G. 1032, n.; 18 L. J. Ch. 457; 13 L. T. (O. S.) 317; affirming *S. C.* below, 6 Ha. 87; 17 L. J. Ch. 257; 12 Jur. 551; 10 L. T. (O. S.) 461; Seton, Vol. II., p. 1174, where the form of decree is given. Sect. 3.

Fleming v. *Self.* In *Fleming* v. *Self*, 3 De G. M. & G. 997; 24 L. J. Ch. 29; 1 Jur. N. S. 25; 3 W. R. 89; 24 L. T. (O. S.) 101; 18 J. P. 772; 3 Eq. Rep. 14, the decree directed calculation of the *longest possible* duration of the society at the date of the notice to redeem, having regard to the net assets of the society and to the monthly subscriptions and redemption money * still continuing payable, and to the number of shares to be provided for, and charged the plaintiff as a present debt with all subscriptions and redemption money which would become payable by him, assuming the society to last for the whole of the calculated period, and crediting him with the amount of bonus payable at the date of the notice to withdrawing members. This decision was followed in *Smith* v. *Pilkington*, 1 De G. F. & J. 120; 29 L. J. Ch. 227; 24 J. P. 227; *S. C.* below, 4 Jur. N. S. 58; where it was further held that the mortgagor was also entitled to deduct redemption money paid by him, the Court being of opinion that this point had in fact been determined by the Lord Chancellor in *Fleming* v. *Self*, though not expressly referred to in his Lordship's judgment in that case. See also *Archer* v. *Harrison*, 7 De G. M. & G. 404; 3 Jur. N. S. 194; 29 L. T. (O. S.) 71; 21 J. P. 515, where the trustees, forgetting that advanced members on redeeming would be

* "Redemption money" is the increased monthly subscription payable by a member who obtains an advance.

Sect. 3.

entitled to participate, allowed a bonus on too liberal a scale, and the Court declined to relieve the society from the consequences of the mistake.

Sparrow v. Farmer.

In *Sparrow* v. *Farmer*, 26 Beav. 511; 28 L. J. Ch. 537; 5 Jur. N. S. 530; 33 L. T. (O. S.) 216; 23 J. P. 500, the estimated duration of the society, as shown by a table annexed to the rules, was thirteen years. The manager embezzled the moneys of the society and absconded, whereupon it became evident that the requisite amount (120*l.*) per share would certainly not be realized at the end of thirteen years. One of the rules empowered advanced members to redeem on payment of their subscriptions "up to the end of the thirteenth year of this company;" and the Court held that on payment of this amount an advanced member must be allowed to redeem, although he would remain liable under the rules to pay subscriptions until 120*l.* a share had been realized for the investing members; and see *Farmer* v. *Smith*, 4 H. & N. 196; 28 L. J. Ex. 226; 5 Jur. N. S. 533, n.; 7 W. R. 362; 32 L. T. (O. S.) 371; 23 J. P. 230; *Handley* v. *Farmer*, 29 Beav. 362.

In permanent societies.

The following cases have been decided as to redemption in permanent societies:—

In *Harvey* v. *Municipal Permanent Investment Building Society*, 26 Ch. D. 273; 52 L. J. Ch. 349; 53 L. J. Ch. 1126, it was held by Pollock, B., on the construction of the mortgage deed, and the rules, that a premium of 2*s.* a share per annum, payable by advanced members, must be added to the capital sum advanced, and interest charged on the combined amount, and that the borrower was not entitled on redeeming to a rebate in respect of the premiums contracted to be paid. The case was taken to the Court of Appeal, but went off there on another point.

Where property sold under the power of sale.

In *Matterson* v. *Elderfield*, 4 Ch. 207; 17 W. R. 422; 20 L. T. 503; 33 J. P. 326, the mortgage, which was in the ordinary form of a mortgage to a permanent society, contained a power of sale in the event of the subscriptions falling into arrear, and the purchase-money was to be applied in satisfaction of all moneys due, or to become due from the mortgagor in respect of subscriptions, fines, insurance, or otherwise under the mortgage deed, and the surplus was to be paid to the mortgagor. The subscriptions fell into arrear, and the directors sold the property. Lord Hatherley, C., held, reversing the decision of Giffard, V.-C., that the mortgagor was not entitled to any rebate or discount upon the amount of subscriptions not due at the time of the sale, although the rules directed that such an allowance should be made in the case of a mortgagor *redeeming* his mortgage before the expiration of the full period of payment. The society in this case was a permanent one, but the Lord Chancellor was of opinion that there was no substantial difference in a question of that kind between a permanent and a terminating society. Sect. 3.

Costs of suit to redeem.

The society will, of course, be entitled to its costs of a suit to redeem, unless its conduct has been vexatious and oppressive; see *Cotterell* v. *Stratton*, 8 Ch. 295; 42 L. J. Ch. 417; 21 W. R. 234; 28 L. T. 218; 37 J. P. 4; Morgan and Wurtzburg on Costs, p. 221 *et seq.*; R. S. C. 1883, Ord. LXV. r. 1.

Foreclosure.

A building society may obtain a foreclosure decree against an advanced member, and the form of decree does not differ materially from that in the case of an ordinary mortgage; see *Provident Permanent Building Society* v. *Greenhill*, 9 Ch. D. 122; 27 W. R. 110; 38 L. T. 140; *Ingoldby* v. *Riley*, 28 L. T. 55; W. N. (1873), 38; *Bell* v. *London and South Western Bank*, W. N. (1874), 10; sect. 13, *post*, p. 103.

Decree for sale.

Where, however, the mortgage is in the form of a *trust for sale* to secure the moneys due to the society, a decree for sale, and not foreclosure, is the proper remedy (*Schweitzer* v. *Mayhew*, 31 Beav. 37; and see *Jenkin* v. *Row*, 5 De G. & S. 107; 16 Jur. 1131).

Fines.

Fines for default in payment of the instalments of principal and interest due under a mortgage to a permanent society must be treated as principal in taking the account between the parties, and will carry interest accordingly (*Provident Permanent Building Society* v. *Greenhill*, Bacon, V.-C., 9 Ch. D. 122; 27 W. R. 110; 38 L. T. 140). This decision is difficult to reconcile with *Ingoldby* v. *Riley*, 28 L. T. 55, and *Parker* v. *Butcher*, 3 Eq. 762; 36 L. J. Ch. 552, where Lord Romilly held that though fines at the rate

Sect. 3.

of a shilling per £ per month were not unreasonable, they did not carry interest; see *Clarkson* v. *Henderson*, 14 Ch. D. 350; *Re The Middlesbrough Building Society*, cited *ante*, p. 21.

Claim for interest on bankruptcy of mortgagor.

It is a well-established rule in bankruptcy that there can be no proof for interest accruing due after the receiving order, unless the estate is more than sufficient to pay the creditors in full, and a mortgage to a permanent building society being generally in the form of a security for the payment of money by instalments, consisting partly of principal and partly of interest, questions have arisen as to the proper application of this rule in these cases.

Ex parte Osborne.

In *Ex parte Osborne, Re Goldsmith*, 10 Ch. 41; 31 L. T. 366, the mortgage was similar in its terms to that in *Matterson* v. *Elderfield*. The mortgagor, after paying a few subscriptions, became bankrupt, and the trustees of the society sold the property under the power of sale. The Court held that they were entitled to retain out of the proceeds of sale all subscriptions and fines payable up to the time of the completion of the sale, and such further sum as represented the balance of the principal sum remaining at that time unpaid, but that they were not entitled to any payment in respect of interest accruing after the principal had been all repaid. See, however, *Re O'Donohoe's Estate*, Ir. R. 10 Eq. 221.

Ex parte Bath.

In a recent case, a member of a building society borrowed 1,200*l.*, for which he was to pay 144*l.* premium and interest at 5 per cent. per annum. The principal, premium, and interest were made payable in a fixed number of monthly instalments, each of which consisted of principal, premium, and interest. The mortgagor filed a liquidation petition, and the society claimed to prove in the liquidation for the total amount of the monthly instalments which remained due under the deed, less the amount at which they valued their security. The Court of Appeal held—(1) That no proof could be made in respect of so much of the sum claimed as represented interest payable subsequently to the filing of the petition (*Ex parte Bath, Re Phillips*, 22 Ch. D. 450; 31 W. R. 281; 48 L. T. 293); but (2) That the premium was not in the nature of interest, and that the society were entitled to prove for it in the liquidation (*Ex parte Bath, Re Phillips*,

27 Ch. D. 509; 32 W. R. 808). In the course of his judgment, Lindley, L. J., said:—"On looking at the mortgage deed and considering the mode of working these societies, I am quite satisfied that this premium has nothing whatever to do with interest. It is a sum which is not altogether arbitrary, because it is calculated with reference to the duration of the loan. The object is to fix a sum which it will be worth the borrower's while to pay for the accommodation granted him by the society, that accommodation being the payment of the principal and interest by instalments. It is not a cloak for getting compound interest, or anything of that kind; it is a charge made for the convenience granted to the borrower. There is nothing illegal in it, nothing uncommon, nothing oppressive, and it appears to me that it would be an entire mistake to call it interest in any sense or shape. If you look at the deed it is quite plain it is not treated as interest, because the deed draws a distinction between the actual sum advanced, the 1,200*l.*, the premium, and the interest. The advance and the premium are first capitalized, and interest is charged on the aggregate sum; and then there is the clause which provides for the application of the instalments. But we must look at the substance of the thing, and I am satisfied that the premium is not in the nature of interest." **Sect. 3.**

Alteration in rules. An advanced member is not bound by an alteration in the rules introduced subsequently to the date of his mortgage, and making advanced members liable for further contributions as a condition of redeeming their securities, although such mortgage contains a covenant by the member to observe the rules of the society "for the time being" (*Smith's Case*, 1 Ch. D. 481; 45 L. J. Ch. 143; 24 W. R. 103).

Winding-up. As to the position of advanced members in the event of a winding-up, see *ante*, p. 29 *et seq.*

If the mortgaged property is sold by the society under a power of sale, no solicitor or other agent who acts for them in the matter of the sale can buy it; see *Martinson* v. *Clowes*, 21 Ch. D. 857; 51 L. J. Ch. 594; 30 W. R. 795; 46 L. T. 882; W. N. (1885), 41, where a purchase by the secretary of the society was set aside, though he had bought at an auction and there was no proof of undervalue.

Executor. An executor may execute a mortgage to a building society;

Sect. 3. see *Cruikshank* v. *Duffin*, 13 Eq. 555; 41 L. J. Ch. 317; 20 W. R. 354; 26 L. T. 121; 36 J. P. 708, cited *post*, p. 77.

Settlement of disputes. A dispute between the society and a member who has executed a mortgage to secure an advance is not a matter to be settled by arbitration; it must be decided by the Courts in the ordinary way, whether the society is incorporated or unincorporated: see *post*, pp. 71, 136.

Statutory receipt. As to the discharge of a mortgage to a building society by the indorsement of a statutory receipt, and the effect of such a receipt, see *post*, pp. 90, 143.

Conversion of mortgaged premises. As to conversion in incorporated societies in the case of an advanced member dying intestate, leaving an infant heir, see the Building Societies Act, 1874, s. 30, *post*, p. 124.

Deduction for income tax. A member of a permanent building society, who has executed a mortgage to the society in the usual form to secure an advance, is entitled to deduct income tax on so much of each periodical instalment as is in fact payment of interest (*Ex parte Wythes*, 53 L. T. 492; *Mosse* v. *Salt*, 32 Beav. 269; 32 L. J. Ch. 756; *Crane* v. *Kilpin*, 6 Eq. 334; 37 L. J. Ch. 913; 18 L. T. 350); but not on such portion as is repayment of principal, this not being income at all but capital (*Foley* v. *Fletcher*, 3 H. & N. 769; 28 L. J. Ex. 100; 22 J. P. 819). The case seems to be within both sect. 102 of the 5 & 6 Vict. c. 35, and sect. 40 of the 16 & 17 Vict. c. 34, as the words "yearly interest of money" in those sections include every payment of interest at a fixed rate per cent. per annum, although made at weekly or monthly intervals (*Bebb* v. *Bunny*, 1 K. & J. 216; 1 Jur. N. S. 203). If the society should refuse to allow the deduction, it will become liable to a penalty of £50 (16 & 17 Vict. c. 34, s. 40).

Premium. The premium commonly charged for an advance is not in the nature of interest, although made payable by instalments; see *Ex parte Bath, Re Phillips*, cited *ante*, p. 42.

Register of mortgages. The secretary should keep a register of all mortgages made to the society, and particularly of all notices received from subsequent incumbrancers; see *West London Bank* v. *Reliance Building Society*, 29 Ch. D. 954; 53 L. T. 442.

Provisions of Friendly Society **4.** And be it further enacted, that all the provisions of a certain Act made and passed in the tenth year of the reign of his late Majesty King George the Fourth, intituled "An Act to consolidate and amend the Laws relating to Friendly Societies," and also the provisions of a certain other Act made and passed in the fourth and fifth years of the reign of his present Majesty King William the Fourth, intituled "An Act to amend an Act of the Tenth Year of His late Majesty King George the Fourth, to consolidate and amend the Laws relating to Friendly Societies," so far as the same, or any part thereof, may be applicable to the purpose of any benefit building society, and to the framing, certifying, enrolling, and altering the rules thereof, shall extend and apply to such benefit building society and the rules thereof in such and the same manner as if the provisions of the said Acts had been herein expressly re-enacted.

Sect. 4.

Acts of 10 Geo. 4, c. 56, and 4 & 5 Will. 4, c. 40, extended to this Act.

The provisions of these two Acts, it will be observed, extend to building societies only so far as they are applicable to the purposes of such societies; see *Mulkern* v. *Lord*, 4 App. Cas. 182; 48 L. J. Ch. 745; 27 W. R. 510; 40 L. T. 594; 43 J. P. 492.

The Act 10 Geo. 4, c. 56 (19th June, 1829), is as follows:—

10 Geo. 4, c. 56.

Sect. 1 repeals several old Acts relating to friendly societies.

Sect. 1.

Sect. 2 provides that any number of persons may form themselves into a society, and raise a fund for their mutual benefit, and make rules, &c.

Sect. 2.

3. "And be it further enacted, that every such society so to be established as aforesaid, *before any of the rules thereof shall be confirmed by the justices in the manner hereinafter directed*, shall, in or by one or more of the rules *to be confirmed*

Societies, in their rules, to declare the pur-

Sect. 4.

poso of their establishment, &c.

by such justices, declare all and every the intents and purposes for which such society is intended to be established, and shall also in and by such rules direct all and every the uses and purposes to which the money which shall from time to time be subscribed, paid, or given to or for the use or benefit of such society, or which shall arise therefrom, or in anywise shall belong to such society, shall be appropriated and applied, and in what shares and proportions and under what circumstances any member of such society, or other person, shall or may become entitled to the same or any part thereof; provided that the application thereof shall not in anywise be repugnant to the uses, intents, and purposes of such society, or any of them, so to be declared as aforesaid; and all such rules, during the continuance of the same, shall be complied with and enforced; and the moneys so subscribed, paid, or given, or so arising, to or for the use or benefit of such society, or belonging thereto, shall not be diverted or misapplied either by the treasurer, trustee, or any other officer or member of such society entrusted therewith, under such penalty or forfeiture as such society shall by any rule impose and inflict for such offence."

So much of this Act as required that rules should be confirmed by justices was repealed by 4 & 5 Will. 4, c. 40, s. 3, *post*, p. 83.

Sect. 4.

Sect. 4 provided that a transcript of all rules should be sent to the barrister acting as Registrar of Savings Banks to be certified. The transcript, when certified, was to be deposited with the clerk of the peace, and laid by him before the justices for confirmation. The clerk then enrolled the transcript, and certified the enrolment on a duplicate copy of the rules, which he returned to the society. This section was repealed, though in a very clumsy manner, by sect. 3 of the Act 4 & 5 Will. 4, c. 40, the fourth section of which substitutes the following procedure:—Two transcripts of the rules are to be sent to the registrar and certified by him. One of these transcripts is then returned to the society and the other is sent to the clerk of the peace and enrolled by him after confirmation by the justices; the rules become binding, however, as soon as they are certified by the registrar. See this section and note thereto, *post*, p. 83. **Sect. 4.**

The 12th section of the Friendly Societies Act of 1846, 9 & 10 Vict. c. 27, which (sect. 22) is to be construed with and as part of these two Acts of Geo. 4 and Will. 4, repeals so much of the Act of Geo. 4 as requires that a transcript of the rules of any society established under that Act, or to which the provisions of that Act have been extended and made applicable, shall be deposited with or filed by the clerk of the peace and a certificate returned to the society, and that the same shall be confirmed by the justices, and provides that all rules then on the file shall be taken off and sent to the registrar, and that the registrar shall in future keep these rules and one of the transcripts of all rules certified by him. 9 & 10 Vict. c. 27.

It seems doubtful if this section ever applied to building societies. See *Walker* v. *Giles*, 6 C. B. 662; 18 L. J. C. P. 323; 13 Jur. 588; 13 L. T. (O. S.) 209, where the question was raised, but not decided. In a case in Ireland, however, it was held that it did apply, and that the registrar was the proper depositary of the rules of the society (*Stamers* v. *Preston*, 9 Ir. C. L. R. 351).

5. "Provided always, and be it further enacted, that in case any such *barrister or advocate* shall refuse to certify all or any of the rules so to be submitted for his perusal and examination, it shall then be lawful for any such society to submit the same to the Court of Quarter Sessions, together with the reasons assigned by the said *barrister or advocate*, in writing, for any such rejection or disapproval of any one or more such rules; and that the justices at their said Quarter Sessions shall and may, if they think fit, confirm and allow the same, notwithstanding any such rejection or disapproval by any such *barrister or advocate*." Manner of proceeding in case barrister shall refuse to certify.

Sect. 7 of the Building Societies Act, 1874, *post*, p. 97, provides that with regard to such subsisting societies as may not obtain certificates of incorporation under that Act, all things required to be done by or sent to the barrister or advocate, and the clerk of the peace, under the provisions of

Sect. 4. 6 & 7 Will. 4, c. 32, shall be done by or sent to the Registrar of Friendly Societies.

Sect. 6. Sect. 6, providing that rules are not to be allowed unless the justices are satisfied with the tables, was repealed by 4 & 5 Will. 4, c. 40, s. 1.

No society entitled to the benefit of this Act, unless their rules have been confirmed.

7. "And be it further enacted, that no such society as aforesaid shall have the benefit of this Act, unless all the rules for the management thereof shall be entered in a book to be kept by an officer of such society appointed for that purpose, and which book shall be open at all seasonable times for the inspection of the members of such society, *and unless all such rules shall be fairly transcribed, and such transcript deposited with the clerk of the peace for the county wherein such society shall be established as aforesaid;* but nevertheless nothing contained herein shall extend to prevent any alteration in or amendment of any such rules so entered *and deposited and filed* as aforesaid, or repealing or annulling the same, or any of them, in the whole or in part, or making any new rules for the management of such society, in such manner as by the rules of such society shall from time to time be provided; but such new rules, or such alterations in or amendments of former rules, or any order annulling or repealing any former rules in the whole or in part, shall not be in force until the same respectively shall be entered in such book as aforesaid, and certified, when necessary, by such barrister or advocate as aforesaid, *and until a transcript thereof shall be deposited with such clerk of the peace as aforesaid, who shall file and certify the same as aforesaid; and that no such rule, or alteration in or amendment of any former rule, shall be binding or have any force or effect until the same shall have been confirmed by such justices, and filed as aforesaid.*"

The words in italics are repealed by sect. 3 of 4 & 5 Will. 4, c. 40, *post*, p. 83.

Where a building society took a mortgage from a member *before* its rules had been certified and deposited, but these formalities were afterwards complied with, it was held that the deed was nevertheless exempt from stamp duty under the Act (*Williams* v. *Hayward*, 22 Beav. 220; 25 L. J. Ch. 289; 1 Jur. N. S. 1128; 26 L. T. (O. S.) 134; 19 J. P. 788). As to exemption from stamp duty, see sect. 37 and note thereto, *post*, p. 78. Sect. 4.

8. "And be it further enacted, that all rules from time to time made and in force for the management of such society as aforesaid, and duly entered in such book as aforesaid, *and confirmed by the justices as aforesaid*, shall be binding on the several members and officers of such society, and the several contributors thereto, and their representatives, all of whom shall be deemed and taken to have full notice thereof by such entry and contribution as aforesaid; and the entry of such rules in such book as aforesaid, or the transcript thereof *deposited with such clerk of the peace as aforesaid*, or a true copy of such transcript, examined with the original and proved to be a true copy, shall be received as evidence of such rules respectively in all cases; and no certiorari, suspension, advocation, reduction, or other legal process shall be brought or allowed to remove any such rules into any of his Majesty's Courts of Record; and every copy of any such transcript *deposited with any clerk of the peace as aforesaid* shall be made without fee or reward, except the actual expense of making such copy."

Rules, when entered and deposited, to be binding on members and depositors.

Copy of transcript to be received in evidence.

The words in italics are repealed by 4 & 5 Will. 4, c. 40, s. 3, *post*, p. 83.

In *R.* v. *Boynes*, 1 Car. & K. 65, it was held that to give evidence of the transcript of the rules of a benefit society enrolled at the office of the clerk of the peace, by proof of an examined copy of it, the witness who examined the copy with the transcript must prove that he examined the copy of *all* the rules with the transcript.

9. "And be it further enacted, that no rule *confirmed by the justices of the peace in manner aforesaid* shall be altered, rescinded, or repealed, unless at a general meeting of the members of such society as aforesaid, convened by public

No confirmed rule to be altered but at a general meeting of

Sect. 4.

the society, &c.

notice, written or printed, signed by the secretary or president or other principal officer or clerk of such society, in pursuance of a requisition for that purpose by seven or more of the members of such society, which said requisition and notice shall be publicly read at the two usual meetings of such society to be held next before such general meeting for the purpose of such alteration or repeal, unless a committee of such members shall have been nominated for that purpose at a general meeting of the members of such society convened in manner aforesaid, in which case such committee shall have the like power to make such alterations or repeal, and unless such alterations or repeal shall be made with the concurrence and approbation of three-fourths of the members of such society then and there present, or by the like proportion of such committee as aforesaid, if any shall have been nominated for that purpose."

The words in italics are repealed by 4 & 5 Will. 4, c. 40, s. 3, *post*, p. 83.

Special meeting.

Where the rules required that no action should be brought or defended without the sanction of a majority of members present at "*a special meeting*," it was held that the sanction of a majority present at *a special general meeting* was sufficient (*Cutbill* v. *Kingdom*, 1 Ex. 494; 17 L. J. Ex. 177). "The meaning of a special meeting is that the meeting shall not be convened unless the parties have notice of the purpose of meeting. A meeting may be both general and special—general for the purpose of doing general business, and special for a particular purpose, then it becomes a special general meeting:" *per* Alderson, B., 1 Ex. p. 504.

Under this section the officers of the society are *bound* to summon a meeting of the members upon a requisition to that effect being duly made to them, they have no discretion in the matter (*R.* v. *Oldham and United Parishes Insurance Society*, 21 L. J. Q. B. 1; 16 J. P. 149; *S. C. nom. R.* v. *Bannatyne*, 18 L. T. (O. S.) 74; overruling *R.* v. *Bannatyne*, 2 L. M. & P. 213; 20 L. J. Q. B. 210).

Rules shall specify place of

10. "And be it further enacted, that the rules of every society formed under the authority of this Act shall specify the place or places at which it is intended such society shall hold its meetings, and shall contain provisions with respect to the powers and duties of the members at large, and of such committees or officers as may be appointed for the management of the affairs of such society: provided always, that it shall and may be lawful for any such society to alter their place or places of meeting whenever they may consider it necessary, upon giving notice thereof in writing to the *clerk of the peace for the county within which such society shall be held*, the said notice to be given within seven days before or after such removal, and signed by the secretary or other principal officer, and also by three or more of the members of the said society; and provided that the place or places at which such society intend to hold their meetings shall be situate within the county in which the rules of the said society are enrolled."

Sect. 4. — meeting and duties of officers. Societies may alter place of meeting.

Where the officers of a friendly society took upon themselves to convene a general meeting of the society at Manchester, when according to the rules the place of business was at Liverpool, the Court of Queen's Bench held that new rules adopted at the meeting were entirely null and void (*R.* v. *Tidd Pratt*, 6 B. & S. 672; 29 J. P. 388, a case decided under the Friendly Societies Act, 1855, now repealed, sect. 28 of which contained a similar provision to that in the above section).

Place of meeting.

The notice is now sent to the Registrar of Friendly Societies; see the Building Societies Act, 1874, s. 7, *post*, p. 97.

A building society cannot remove its place of meeting out of the county in which for the purposes of its business it was originally established; see *R.* v. *Registrar of Friendly Societies*, 16 J. P. 613; 19 L. T. (O. S.) 182.

11. "And be it further enacted, that every such society shall and may from time to time, at any of their usual meetings, or by their committee, if any such shall be appointed for that society, elect and appoint such person into the office of steward, president, warden, treasurer, or trustee of such society, as they shall think proper, and also shall and may from time to time elect and appoint such clerks and other

Society may appoint officers.

Sect. 4.

officers as shall be deemed necessary to carry into execution the purposes of such society, for such space of time and for such purposes as shall be fixed and established by the rules of such society, and from time to time to elect and appoint others in the room of those who shall vacate or die; and such treasurer, trustee, and all and every other officer or other person whatever who shall be appointed to any office in anywise touching or concerning the receipt, management, or expenditure of any sum of money collected for the purpose of any such society, before he, she, or they shall be admitted to take upon him, her, or them the execution of any such office or trust, (if required so to do by the rules of such society to which such officer shall belong,) shall become bound in a bond, according to the form prescribed in the schedule to this Act annexed, with two sufficient sureties, for the just and faithful execution of such office or trust, and for rendering a just and true account according to the rules of such society, and in all matters lawful to pay obedience to the same, in such penal sum of money as by the major part of such society at any such meeting as aforesaid shall be thought expedient, and to the satisfaction of such society; and that every such bond to be given by or on the behalf of such treasurer or trustee, or of any other person appointed to any other office or trust, shall be given to the clerk of the peace of the county where such society shall be established, for the time being, without fee or reward; and in case of forfeiture it shall be lawful to sue upon such bond in the name of the clerk of the peace for the time being, for the use of the said society, fully indemnifying and saving harmless such clerk of the peace from all costs and charges in respect of such suit; provided that such bond shall have in Scotland the same force and effect as a bond in the form in use in Scotland containing a clause of registration."

Securities to be given for offices of trust if required.

Treasurer or trustees to give bond to the clerk of the peace.

Officers.

As to the terms on which officials of a building society are held to give their services, see *Alexander* v. *Worman*, 6 H. & N. 100; 30 L. J. Ex. 198; 3 L. T. 477; 25 J. P. 312. In that case the surveyor of a building society did certain work on behalf of the society. The society collapsed for want of funds, whereupon the surveyor brought an action for his

Sect. 4.

commission against one of the managing directors. The Court held that there was no proof that the defendant had ever contracted that he, or he and his fellow-directors would pay the plaintiff for his services; and Martin, B., in delivering judgment, said:—"We think it a mistake to suppose that, in societies of the kind, the surveyor or secretary or the officers do work and labour upon the same terms as professional men of their class ordinarily do. They generally have a much greater interest in them than the directors, and in the great majority of cases are the individuals who get them up, and at whose request the directors consent to accept the office and take upon themselves the liabilities and duties of their situation; and it is to us very clear that such officers discharge duties and perform services with the understanding on all hands that they are to be remunerated out of the funds, and that if the funds fail the officers must remain unpaid."

Directors. As to the general powers of the directors of a building society, see *Small* v. *Smith*, 10 App. Cas. 119, where it was held that they had no power to bind the society by giving a guarantee, such a transaction not being authorized by the rules nor incidental to the conduct of the society's business.

Mandamus. An officer of a building society who has been dismissed by a resolution of the society has no remedy by mandamus, which lies only to reinstate a person in an office where the office and its tenure are of a permanent character; see *Evans* v. *Hearts of Oak Benefit Society*, 12 Jur. N. S. 163.

Bond. Assuming that the provision as to the giving of a bond applied to building societies, then it would seem from sect. 7 of the Building Societies Act, 1874, that the bond ought now to be given to the Registrar of Friendly Societies, though the words "done by or sent to" do not quite meet the case of a bond; see the section, *post*, p. 97.

Appointment of committees. **12.** "And be it further enacted, that every such society shall and may from time to time elect and appoint any number of the members of such society to be a committee, the number thereof to be declared in the rules of every such society, and shall and may delegate to such committee all or

Sect. 4.

Powers of standing committees to be declared in the rules of the society, and of particular ones entered in a book.

any of the powers given by this Act to be executed, who, being so delegated, shall continue to act as such committee, for and during such time as they shall be appointed, for such society, for general purposes, the powers of such committee being first declared in and by the rules of such society, *confirmed by the justices of the peace at their sessions, and filed in the manner hereinbefore directed;* and in all cases where a committee shall be appointed for any particular purpose, the powers delegated to such committee shall be reduced into writing and entered into a book by the secretary or clerk of such society, and a majority of the members of such committee shall at all times be necessary to concur in any act of such committee; and such committee shall, in all things delegated to them, act for and in the name of such society; and all acts and orders of such committee, under the powers delegated to them, shall have the like force and effect as the acts and orders of such society at any general meeting thereof could or might have had in pursuance of this Act:

Committee controllable by society.

Provided always, that the transactions of such committee shall be entered in a book belonging to such society, and shall be from time to time and at all times subject and liable to the review, allowance or disallowance and control of such society, in such manner and form as such society shall by their general rules, *confirmed by the justices and filed as aforesaid,* have directed and appointed, or shall in like manner direct and appoint."

The words in italics are repealed by 4 & 5 Will. 4, c. 40, s. 3, *post*, p. 83.

Treasurer or trustees to lay out surplus of contributions;

13. "And be it further enacted, that it shall and may be lawful to and for the treasurer or trustee for the time being of any such society, and he, she, and they is and are hereby authorized and required, from time to time, by and with the consent of such society, to be had and testified in such manner as shall be directed by the general rules of such society, to lay out or dispose of such part of all such sums of money as shall at any time be collected, given, or paid to and for the beneficial ends, intents, and purposes of such society, as the exigencies of such society shall not call for the immediate application or expenditure of, either on real or heritable securities or heritable property, to be approved of as aforesaid, (such securities to be taken in the name of such treasurer or trustee for the time being,) or to invest the same in the public stocks or funds, *savings banks*, or government securities, or in any of the chartered banks in Scotland, or in the bank of the Commercial Banking Company of Scotland, and not otherwise, in the proper name of such treasurer or trustee; and from time to time, with such consent as aforesaid, to alter and transfer such securities and funds, and to make sale thereof respectively; and that all the dividends, interests, and proceeds which shall from time to time arise from the monies so laid out or invested as aforesaid shall from time to time be brought to account by such treasurer or trustee, and shall be applied to and for the use of such society, according to the rules thereof."

Sect. 4.

and to bring the proceeds to account.

Savings banks.

Sect. 6 of 6 & 7 Will. 4, c. 32, *post*, p. 91, forbids any building society to invest in any savings bank, or with the Commissioners for the Reduction of the National Debt.

Investment of surplus funds.

There is nothing, it seems, to prevent a building society under the old law from investing its surplus funds in the purchase of real estate; though such a society will not be allowed to convert itself into a freehold land society by speculating in land beyond this limit; see *Grimes* v. *Harrison*, 26 Beav. 435; 28 L. J. Ch. 823; 5 Jur. N. S. 528; 33 L. T. (O. S.) 115; 23 J. P. 421; *Mullock* v. *Jenkins*, 14 Beav. 628; 21 L. J. Ch. 65; 18 L. T. (O. S.) 203; *Re Kent Benefit Building Society*, 1 Dr. & Sm. 417; 30 L. J. Ch. 785; 7 Jur. N. S. 1045; 9 W. R. 686; 4 L. T. 610; 25 J. P. 805, cited *ante*, p. 19.

A society may lend its surplus funds on real security to persons not members of the society (*Cutbill* v. *Kingdom*, 1 Ex. 494; 17 L. J. Ex. 177); and of course may advance money on mortgage to one of its own members (*Morrison* v. *Glover*, 4 Ex. 430; 19 L. J. Ex. 20; 14 L. T. (O. S.) 204; 14 J. P. 84).

Where the directors of a building society had deposited money of the society with a finance company in a manner not authorized by the rules, the Court held that it was trust

Sect. 4.

money in the hands of the company and might be recovered accordingly (*Hardy* v. *Metropolitan Land & Finance Co.*, 7 Ch. 427; 41 L. J. Ch. 257; 20 W. R. 425; 26 L. T. 407); see also *Re Coltman*, 19 Ch. D. 64; 51 L. J. Ch. 3; 30 W. R. 342; 45 L. T. 392, cited *infra*, p. 120.

Treasurers, &c. to render accounts, and pay over balances, &c.;

14. "And be it further enacted, that every person who shall have, or receive any part of the monies, effects, or funds of or belonging to any such society, or shall in any manner have been or shall be entrusted with the disposal, management, or custody thereof, or of any securities, books, papers or property relating to the same, his or her executors, administrators and assigns respectively, shall, upon demand made, or notice in writing given or left at the last or usual place of residence of such persons, in pursuance of any order of such society, or committee to be appointed as aforesaid for that purpose, give in his or her account at the usual meeting of such society, or to such committee thereof as aforesaid, to be examined and allowed or disallowed by such society or committee thereof, and shall, on the like demand or notice, pay over all the monies remaining in his or her hands, and assign and transfer or deliver all securities and effects, books, papers, and property, taken or standing in his or her name as aforesaid, or being in his or her hands or custody, to the treasurer or trustee for the time being, or to such other person as such society or committee thereof shall appoint; and in case of any neglect or refusal to deliver such account, or to pay over such monies, or to assign, transfer or deliver such securities and effects, books, papers and property, in manner aforesaid, it shall and may be lawful to and for every such society, in the name of the treasurer or trustee or other principal officer thereof, as the case may be, to exhibit a petition in the *Court of Exchequer in England or Ireland, or in the Court of Session in Scotland, or the Courts of Great Sessions in Wales respectively*, who shall and may proceed thereupon in a summary way, and make such order therein, upon hearing all parties concerned, as to such Court in their discretion shall seem just, which order shall be final

and in case of neglect, application may be made to the Court of Exchequer, &c.

Sect. 4.

and conclusive; and all assignments, sales, and transfers made in pursuance of such order shall be good and effectual in law to all intents and purposes whatsoever."

See *Re Heanor Friendly Society*, 1 Beav. 508; *Re Lord Hill Friendly Society*, 2 J. P. 84.

The jurisdiction of the Court of Exchequer is now transferred to the High Court of Justice (Jud. Act, 1873, s. 16).

Where trustees, &c. are out of jurisdiction of Court, or it be uncertain whether they are alive, or they refuse to convey, &c., Court of Exchequer may appoint a person to convey.

15. "And be it further enacted, that when and so often as any person seised or possessed of any lands, tenements, or hereditaments, or other property, or any estate or interest therein, as a trustee of any such society, shall be out of the jurisdiction of or not amenable to the process of the *Court of Exchequer in England or Ireland, or the Court of Session in Scotland, or of the Court of Great Sessions in Wales*, or shall be idiot, lunatic, or of unsound mind, or it shall be unknown or uncertain whether he or she be living or dead, or such person shall refuse to convey or otherwise assure such lands, tenements, hereditaments, or property, or estate or interest, to the person duly nominated as trustee of such society in their stead, either alone or together with any continuing trustee, as occasion shall require, then and in every or any such case it shall be lawful for the judges of the said Courts respectively to appoint such person, as to such Court shall seem meet, on behalf and in the name of the person seised or possessed as aforesaid, to convey, surrender, release, assign, or otherwise assure the said lands, tenements, hereditaments, or property, or estate or interest, to such trustee so duly nominated as aforesaid; and every such conveyance, release, surrender, assignment, or assurance shall be as valid and effectual to all intents and purposes as if the person being out of the jurisdiction or not amenable to the process of the said Courts, or not known to be alive, or having refused, or as if the person being idiot, lunatic, or of unsound mind, had been at the time of the execution thereof of sane mind, memory, and understanding, and had by himself or herself executed the same."

See *Ex parte Armstrong and Shallcross*, 16 Sim. 296; *Re Eclipse Mutual Benefit Association*, 23 L. J. Ch. 280; Kay.

Sect. 4. App. xxx.; 2 Eq. Rep. 318. As to the Court of Exchequer, see Jud. Act, 1873, s. 16.

When trustees shall be absent, &c. Courts may order stock to be transferred and dividends paid.

16. "And be it further enacted, that when and as often as it shall happen that all and every person in whose name any part of the several stocks, annuities and funds transferable, or which hereafter shall be made transferable at the Bank of England, or in the books of the Governor and Company of the Bank of England, is, are, or shall be standing as a trustee of any such society, shall be absent, out of the jurisdiction or not amenable to the process of the said *Court of Exchequer in England or Ireland, or the Court of Session in Scotland, or the Courts of Great Session in Wales*, or shall be a bankrupt, insolvent or lunatic, or it shall be uncertain or unknown whether such trustee is living or dead, that then and in such case it shall and may be lawful to and for the judges of the said Courts respectively to order and direct that the accountant general, or the secretary or deputy secretary, or other proper officer for the time being of the Governor and Company of the Bank of England, do transfer in the book of the said company such stock, annuities or funds standing as aforesaid, to and into the name of such person as such society may appoint, and also pay over to such person as aforesaid the dividends of such stock, annuities or funds; and when and as often as it shall happen that one or more only, and not all or both of such trustees as aforesaid, shall be so absent, or not amenable to such process as aforesaid, or a bankrupt, insolvent or lunatic, or it be uncertain or unknown whether any one or more of such trustees is or are living or dead, that then, and in all and every such last-mentioned case and cases, it shall and may be lawful to and for the judges of the said courts respectively to order and direct that the other and others of such trustees who shall be forthcoming and ready and qualified to act do transfer such stock, annuities or funds to and into the name of such person as aforesaid, and also that such forthcoming trustee do also receive and pay over the dividends of such stock, annuities or funds as such society shall direct; and that all such transfers and payments so

made shall be and are hereby declared to be valid and effectual to all intents and purposes whatsoever, any former statute, law, usage or custom to the contrary thereof in anywise notwithstanding." Sect. 4.

See note to sect. 14.

17. "And be* further enacted, that no fee, reward, emolument or gratuity whatsoever shall be demanded, taken or received by any officer or minister of such Courts for any matter or thing done in such Courts in pursuance of this Act; and that upon the presenting of any such petition it shall be lawful for the judges of the said Courts respectively to assign counsel learned in the law, and to appoint a clerk or practitioner of such Court, to advise and carry on such petition on the behalf of such society, who are hereby respectively required to do their duties therein without fee or reward."

* *Sic.*

No fee to be taken for any proceeding in such Courts, &c.

18. "Provided always, and be it further enacted, that in all cases in which orders shall be made by any of the Courts aforesaid for the transfer of stocks or funds transferable at the Bank of England the persons to be named in such orders respectively for making such transfers shall be the secretary, deputy secretary or accountant general of the Governor and Company of the Bank of England for the time being, or one of them, except in cases where one or more of the trustees in whose name such stocks or funds shall stand shall be ordered to transfer the same without the concurrence of any other or others of such trustees, anything herein contained to the contrary thereof in anywise notwithstanding."

Who shall be named in the orders of the Court for making transfers.

19. "And be it further enacted, that this Act shall be and is hereby declared to be a full and complete indemnity and discharge to the Governor and Company of the Bank of England, and their officers and servants, for all acts and things done or permitted to be done pursuant thereto, and that such acts and things shall not be questioned or impeached in any court of law or equity to their prejudice or detriment."

Act to be an indemnity to the Bank.

Sect. 20 was repealed by sect. 1 of the Act 4 & 5 Will. 4, Sect. 20.

Sect. 4. c. 40, the twelfth section of which contains a more comprehensive provision to the same effect; see this section, *post*, p. 88.

Effects of societies to be vested in the trustees or treasurers for the time being, who may bring and defend actions, &c.

21. "And be it further enacted, that all real and heritable property, monies, goods, chattels, and effects whatever, and all titles, securities for money, or other obligatory instruments and evidences or muniments, and all other effects whatever, and all rights or claims belonging to or had by such society, shall be vested in the treasurer or trustee of such society for the time being, for the use and benefit of such society and the respective members thereof, their respective executors or administrators, according to their respective claims and interests, and after the death or removal of any treasurer or trustee shall vest in the succeeding treasurer or trustee, for the same estate and interest as the former treasurer or trustee had therein, and subject to the same trusts, without any assignment or conveyance whatever, except the transfer of stocks and securities in the public funds of Great Britain and Ireland, and also shall, for all purposes of action or suit, as well criminal as civil, in law or in equity, in anywise touching or concerning the same, be deemed and taken to be, and shall in every such proceeding (where necessary) be stated to be, the property of the person appointed to the office of treasurer or trustee of such society for the time being, in his or her proper name, without further description; and such person shall and he or she is hereby respectively authorized to bring or defend, or cause to be brought or defended, any action, suit, or prosecution, criminal as well as civil, in law or in equity, touching or concerning the property, right, or claim aforesaid of or belonging to or had by such society; provided such person shall have been thereunto duly authorized by the consent of the majority of members present at any meeting of the society or committee thereof, and such person so appointed shall and may, in all cases concerning the property, right, or claim aforesaid of such society, sue and be sued, plead and be impleaded, in his or her proper name, as treasurer or trustee of such society, without other description; and no such suit,

Sect. 4.

action, or prosecution shall be discontinued or abate by the death of such person, or his or her removal from the office of treasurer or trustee, but the same shall and may be proceeded in by the succeeding treasurer or trustee in the proper name of the person commencing the same, any law, usage, or custom to the contrary notwithstanding; and such succeeding treasurer or trustee shall pay or receive like costs as if the action or suit had been commenced in his or her name, for the benefit of or to be reimbursed from the funds of such society."

"Treasurer or trustee."

The words "treasurer or trustee" include treasurers or trustees; see sect. 38 of the Act, *post*, p. 82.

Probably the true construction of this section is that securities taken in the name of the treasurer vest in his successors, and if taken in the name of the trustee or trustees vest in the succeeding trustee or trustees (*Morrison* v. *Glover*, 4 Ex. p. 443, *per* Alderson, B.).

The trustees for the time being can sue on securities given to their predecessors even in a case where the rules of the society provide that on the removal of a trustee he shall assign all securities to the succeeding trustees, and no such assignment has been made (*Morrison* v. *Glover*, 4 Ex. 430; 19 L. J. Ex. 20; 14 L. T. (O. S.) 204; 14 J. P. 84; and see *Cartridge* v. *Griffiths*, 1 B. & Ald. 57).

In *Walker* v. *Giles*, 6 C. B. 662; 18 L. J. C. P. 323; 13 Jur. 588; 13 L. T. (O. S.) 209, one of two trustees resigned and another was appointed in his stead. A question having arisen as to the effect of this appointment, Maule, J., said:—"The effect of the 21st section of the 10 Geo. 4, c. 56, as it seems to me, is, to make the continuing and the new trustees joint tenants. It operates as a new appointment of *all*" (6 C. B. p. 692).

Where, however, the amended rules of a society directed that three trustees should be appointed, of whom one should be treasurer, in whose names the funds of the society should be invested, and three trustees were appointed but a fourth person was appointed treasurer, the Court held that these three trustees could not sue the former treasurer for a balance in his hands on account of the society (*Dewhurst* v.

Sect. 4.

Clarkson, 3 E. & B. 194; 23 L. J. Q. B. 247; 2 C. L. R. 1143; 18 Jur. 693; 23 L. T. (O. S.) 109; 18 J. P. 535).

Personal liability of trustees.

As to the personal liability of a trustee or treasurer against whom an action is brought, see *Wormwell* v. *Hailstone*, 4 M. & P. 512; 6 Bing. 668; *Harrison* v. *Timmins*, 4 M. & W. 510; and see further as to the liability of trustees, sect. 22 and note thereto. The provision in sect. 21 that the trustee may sue and be sued relates only to the form of suing or being sued (*Price* v. *Taylor*, 5 H. & N. p. 544, *per* Wilde, B.).

Limitation of responsibility of treasurers or trustees.

22. "And be it further enacted, that the treasurer or trustee, or any other officer of any society established under the authority of this Act, shall not be liable to make good any deficiency which may arise in the funds of such society, unless such persons shall have respectively declared by writing under their hands, deposited and registered in like manner with the rules of such society, that they are willing so to be answerable; and it shall be lawful for each of such persons, or for such persons collectively, to limit his, her, or their responsibility to such sum as shall be specified in any such instrument or writing: provided always, that the said treasurer, trustee, and every other the officer of any such society, shall be and they are hereby declared to be personally responsible and liable for all monies actually received by him, her, or them on account of or to and for the use of the said society."

Treasurer, &c. liable for money actually received.

Liability of officers of society.

This section does not increase the liability of the treasurer of a building society beyond that of a bailee, in respect of the loss of money immediately after its receipt. Thus, where an action was brought against a guarantee association to make good a sum of 170*l.* which a treasurer, for whom they were sureties, had received, and of which he had been immediately robbed, the Court held that they were not liable. Lord Campbell, C. J., in delivering judgment, said: "This plea (found to be true) alleges a loss of the monies by *irresistible violence;* and the general doctrine is not denied, that if the subject-matter bailed be lost by *vis major*, which we translate *irresistible violence*, the bailee is discharged. If J. Jones, the principal, was guilty of no default, the defendants, as his sureties, cannot be liable. Reliance, however, is placed on the 6 & 7 Will. 4, c. 32, s. 4, and the 10 Geo. 4, c. 56, s. 20,* by which it is said that as soon as the treasurer of such a society receives any money on account of the society, he, *eo instanti*, becomes a debtor to the society: so that payment alone can discharge him from his liability. But we think this must be confined to such monies received by him as he might use as his own, he being at liberty to pay the debt with other monies. He cannot, in respect of one receipt by him as treasurer, be considered at the same time as bailee of specific, ear-marked monies, and a debtor to the same amount, with the power of discharging his engagement by payment of an equivalent sum from any source, or in any denomination of coin, or in any paper securities which pass as cash. According to the averment in this declaration, J. Jones was undoubtedly bailee of the 170*l.*, and, therefore, he was not a debtor to that amount. As bailee, the true relation in which he stood to the society, he was discharged by the robbery. If this were not so, his liability would be greater than that of a common carrier; for he would not even be discharged by the act of God or of the Queen's enemies; and indeed Mr. Knowles was driven to contend that if while carrying to the bankers a bag of gold representing the 170*l.* within a few minutes after receiving it an earthquake had swallowed it up, he still would have been debtor to the society for the amount. But we are of opinion that the statutes relied upon were not intended to cast such an extraordinary liability upon an officer of such a society or upon his sureties" (*Walker* v. *The British Guarantee Association*, 21 L. J. Q. B. 257; 16 Jur. 885; 19 L. T. (O. S.) 87; 16 J. P. 582).

Sect. 4.

Qy. 22.

In *Grimes* v. *Harrison*, 26 Beav. 435; 28 L. J. Ch. 823; 5 Jur. N. S. 528; 33 L. T. (O. S.) 115; 23 J. P. 421, the directors of a building society misapplied 800*l.*, part of the funds of the society. The cheques for this sum were signed by the trustees, but as they had acted only ministerially and by the order of the directors the Court held that they were not liable, notwithstanding there was some informality in the authority given to them by the directors. As the trustees, however, instead of simply relying upon their position as

Trustees acting ministerially only not liable.

Sect. 4.

mere servants of the directors, took upon themselves to defend and support the transactions in question, they got no costs.

But where two members of a building society, acting as trustees *pro hâc vice* and not being the general trustees of the society, concurred in a transaction which was *ultra vires* and not acquiesced in by all the members, and in the course of it entered into personal covenants for the payment of money under which they were subsequently made liable, it was held that they could not compel contribution among the shareholders to recoup their loss (*Re Kent Benefit Building Society*, 1 Dr. & S. 417; 30 L. J. Ch. 785; 7 Jur. N. S. 1045; 9 W. R. 686; 25 J. P. 805; 4 L. T. 610). The decision would no doubt have been the same had they been the general trustees of the society.

Liability on bills or notes.

Where a bill or note is drawn by a trustee or other official of a building society he must be careful, if he mean to exempt himself from personal responsibility, to use clear and explicit words to show that intention; the mere addition to his name of the word "trustee" or "secretary" will not suffice.

Price v. Taylor.

In *Price v. Taylor*, 5 H. & N. 540; 29 L. J. Ex. 331; 6 Jur. N. S. 402; 8 W. R. 419; 2 L. T. 221; 24 J. P. 470, a promissory note was made in the following form:—

"Midland Counties Building Society, No. 3.

"Birmingham, March 12th, 1858.

"Two months after demand in writing we promise to pay to Mr. Thomas Price the sum of 100*l.*, with interest after the rate of six pounds per centum per annum, for value received.

"£100.

"W. R. HEATH, } *Trustees.*
"JOHN TAYLOR, }
"W. D. FISHER, *Secretary.*"

On an action being brought on the note against Taylor and Fisher the Court held that the parties who had signed the note were personally liable upon it, and that the right of the holder to sue them was not affected by the 6 & 7 Will. 4, c. 32, and the 10 Geo. 4, c. 56, s. 21.

Sect. 4.

In *Allan* v. *Miller*, 22 L. T. 825, a promissory note was made in the following form:—

Allan v. *Miller*.

"£200. "Gateshead, Oct. 18, 1864.

"On demand we promise to pay Mr. James Allan 200*l*., value received for the Second Gateshead Provident Benefit Building Society, and interest thereon at 5 per cent. per annum, payable half-yearly.

"GEORGE MILLER,
"C. D. GARBUTT,
"JOHN NEDDLE, } *Trustees*.
"THOMAS NEILSON, *Secretary*."

The Court held that the case was not substantially different from *Price* v. *Taylor*, and that the defendants were personally liable.

Bottomley v. *Fisher*.

In *Bottomley* v. *Fisher*, 1 H. & C. 211; 31 L. J. Ex. 417; 10 W. R. 669; 6 L. T. 688; 27 J. P. 23, a promissory note was made in the following form:—

"Midland Counties Building Society, No. 3.

"Birmingham, 1st Sept., 1856.

"One month after demand, we jointly and severally promise to pay to Mr. John Bottomley the sum of one hundred and twenty pounds, with interest thereon after the rate of six pounds per cent. per annum (payable half-yearly), for value received.

"W. R. HEATH,
"S. B. SMITH, } *Directors*.
"W. D. FISHER, *Secretary*."

An action was brought on this note against Fisher alone. *Held*, that he was personally liable.

See further as to the liability of trustees and directors on bills and notes, Lindley on Partnership, Vol. I., p. 340 *et seq.* 4th ed.

Work done for society on the order of the secretary.

The directors of a building society are liable to pay for work done by order of the secretary if there is evidence to satisfy the jury that the secretary was the general agent of the directors, even though the work was not ordered at a board meeting (*Allard* v. *Bourne*, 15 C. B. N. S. 468; 3 N. R. 42).

Liability of secretary

In a recent case the secretary of a building society employed a private clerk who assisted him in transacting the business

Sect. 4.

for the acts of his clerk.

of the society. The directors from time to time with the knowledge and assent of the secretary handed cheques to this clerk for the purpose of being paid to withdrawing members, though according to the rules the directors ought themselves to have paid the cheques to the withdrawing members direct. The clerk misappropriated the cheques; *held*, upon the society being wound up, that the secretary was liable to make good the sums so misappropriated (*Ex parte James*, 48 J. P. 54).

Purchase by officer of society.

An officer of the society, employed about a sale of property mortgaged to the society and sold under the power of sale, is disabled from purchasing; see *Martinson* v. *Clowes*, cited *ante*, p. 43.

Allowing commission.

It is not uncommon for the directors of a building society to allow a commission to any of their number who introduce business to the society. It is conceived that this is illegal, as being a breach of the rule that a trustee may not make a profit out of his trust.

Payment to persons appearing to be next of kin declared valid.

23. "And be it further enacted, that whenever the trustees of any society established under this Act, at any time after the decease of any member, have paid and divided any sum of money to or amongst any person or persons who shall at the time of such payment appear to such trustees to be entitled to the effects of any deceased intestate member, the payment of any such sum or sums of money shall be valid and effectual with respect to any demand of any other person or persons as next of kin of such deceased intestate member, or as the lawful representative or representatives of such member, against the funds of such society or against the trustees thereof; but nevertheless such next of kin or representatives shall have remedy for such money so paid as aforesaid against the person or persons who shall have received the same."

For payment of sums not exceeding 20*l*. where members die intestate.

24. "And be it further enacted, that in case any member of any society shall die, who shall be entitled to any sum not exceeding twenty pounds, it shall be lawful for the trustees or treasurer of such society, and they are hereby authorized and permitted, if such trustees or treasurer shall be satisfied that no will was made and left by such deceased member, and that no letters of administration

Sect. 4.

or confirmation will be taken out, of the funds, goods, and chattels of such depositor, to pay the same at any time after the decease of such member according to the rules and regulations of the said institution, and in the event of there being no rules and regulations made in that behalf, then the said trustees or treasurer are hereby authorized and permitted to pay and divide the same to and amongst the person or persons entitled to the effects of the deceased intestate, and that without administration in England or Ireland, and without confirmation in Scotland."

Justices may hear cases of fraud, and punish by fine or imprisonment.

25. "And be it further enacted, that for the more effectually preventing fraud and imposition on the funds of such societies, if any officer, member, or any other person being or representing himself or herself to be a member of such society, or the nominee, executor, administrator, or assignee of any member of such society, or any other person whatever, shall in or by any false representation or imposition fraudulently obtain possession of the monies of such society or any part thereof, or, having in his or her possession any sum of money belonging to such society, shall fraudulently withhold the same, and for which offence no especial provision is made in the rules of such society, it shall be lawful for any one justice of the peace residing within the county within which such society shall be held, upon complaint made on oath or affirmation by an officer of such society appointed for that purpose, to summon such person against whom such complaint shall be made to appear at a time and place to be named in such summons; and upon his or her appearance, or, in default thereof, upon due proof, upon oath or affirmation of the service of such summons, it shall and may be lawful for any two justices residing within the county aforesaid to hear and determine the said complaint according to the rules of the said society, *confirmed as directed by this Act;* and upon due proof of such fraud the said justices shall convict the said party, and award double the amount of the money so fraudulently obtained or withheld to be paid to the treasurer, to be applied by him to the purposes of the society so proved to have been imposed upon and defrauded, together with such costs as shall be awarded by the said

Sect. 4. justices, not exceeding the sum of ten shillings; and in case such person against whom such complaint shall be made shall not pay the sum of money so awarded to the person and at the time specified in the said order, such justices are hereby required, by warrant under their hands and seals, to cause the same to be levied by distress and sale of the goods of such person on whom such order shall have been made, or by other legal proceeding, together with such costs as shall be awarded by the said justices, not exceeding the sum of ten shillings, and also the costs and charges attending such distress and sale or other legal proceeding, returning the overplus (if any) to the owner; and, in default of such distress being found, the said justices of the peace shall commit such person so proved to have offended to the common gaol or house of correction, there to be kept to hard labour for such a period, not exceeding three calendar months, as to them shall seem fit: provided nevertheless, that nothing herein contained shall prevent the said society from proceeding by indictment or complaint against the party complained of; and provided also, that no party shall be proceeded against by indictment or complaint, if a previous conviction has been obtained for the same offence under the provisions of this Act."

The words in italics are repealed by 4 & 5 Will. 4, c. 40, s. 3.

Sect. 26. Sect. 26 related to the proceedings necessary for the dissolution of a society. It does not seem to be applicable to building societies.

Rules to be made directing how disputes shall be settled.

27. "Provided always, and be it further enacted, that provision shall be made by one or more of the rules of every such society, *to be confirmed as required by this Act*, specifying whether a reference of every matter in dispute between any such society, or any person acting under them, and any individual member thereof, or person claiming on account of any member, shall be made to such of his Majesty's justices of the peace as may act in and for the county in which such society may be formed, or to arbitrators to be appointed in manner hereinafter directed; and if the matter so in dispute shall be referred to arbitration, certain arbitrators shall be

Appointment of arbitrators.

named and elected at the first meeting of such society, or general committee thereof, that shall be held after the enrolment of its rules, none of the said arbitrators being beneficially interested, directly or indirectly, in the funds of the said society, of whom a certain number, not less than three, shall be chosen by ballot in each such case of dispute, the number of the said arbitrators and mode of ballot being determined by the rules of each society respectively; the names of such arbitrators shall be duly entered in the book of the said society in which the rules are entered as aforesaid;* and in case of the death, or refusal or neglect of any or all of the said arbitrators to act, it shall and may be lawful to and for the said society, or general committee thereof, and they are hereby required, at their next meeting, to name and elect one or more arbitrator or arbitrators as aforesaid to act in the place of the said arbitrator or arbitrators so dying or refusing or neglecting to act as aforesaid; and whatever award shall be made by the said arbitrators, or the major part of them, according to the true purport and meaning of the rules of such society, *confirmed by the justices according to the directions of this Act*, shall be in the form to this Act annexed, and shall be binding and conclusive on all parties, and shall be final, to all intents and purposes, without appeal, or being subject to the control of one or more justices of the peace, and shall not be removed or removable into any Court of law, or restrained or restrainable by the injunction of any Court of equity; and should either of the said parties in dispute refuse or neglect to comply with or conform to the decision of the said arbitrators, or the major part of them, it shall and may be lawful for any one justice of the peace residing within the county within which such society shall be held, upon good and sufficient proof being adduced before him of such award having been made, and of the refusal of the party to comply therewith, upon complaint made by or on behalf of the party aggrieved, to summon the person against whom such complaint shall be made to appear at a time and place to be named in such summons; and upon his or her appearance, or in default thereof, upon due proof, upon oath, of the service of such summons, any two justices of the peace may

Sect. 4.

* See s. 7, *ante*, p. 48.

Justices shall enforce compliance with the decision of arbitrators.

Sect. 4.

proceed to make such order thereupon as to them may seem just; and if the sum of money so awarded, together with a sum for costs not exceeding the sum of ten shillings, as to such justices shall seem meet, shall not be immediately paid, then such justices shall, by warrant under their hands and seals, cause such sum and costs as aforesaid to be levied by distress or by distress and sale of the monies, goods, chattels, securities, and effects belonging to the said party or to the said society, or other legal proceeding, together with all further costs and charges attending such distress and sale or other legal proceeding, returning the overplus (if any) to the said party, or to the said society, or to one of the treasurers or trustees thereof; and in default of such distress being found or such other legal proceeding being ineffectual, then to be levied by distress and sale of the proper goods of the said party or of the officer of the said society so neglecting or refusing as aforesaid, by other legal proceedings, together with such further costs and charges as aforesaid, returning the overplus (if any) to the owner: provided always, that whatever sums shall be paid by any such officer, so levied on his or her property or goods in pursuance of the award of arbitrators or order of any justices, shall be repaid, with all damages accruing to him or her, by and out of the monies belonging to such society, or out of the first monies which shall be thereafter received by such society."

The words in italics were repealed by sect. 3 of the Act 4 & 5 Will. 4, c. 40.

Disputes must be referred to arbitrators or justices:

The statutory provisions now in force relating to the settlement of disputes between an unincorporated society and its members may be shortly stated as follows:—

1. The rules of every society must direct whether disputes are to be referred to arbitrators or to justices (sect. 27).

1. To arbitrators.

2. If they direct a reference to arbitration the arbitrators must be chosen in the manner pointed out in the above section; and their award, which must be in a prescribed form, is final (sect. 27).

3. The award may be enforced by two justices in the manner above mentioned (sect. 27); and their order is final (sect. 29).

4. If either party declines to arbitrate, or the arbitrators

fail to make an award, the county court judge may decide the dispute (Building Societies Act, 1874, s. 35), and his decision is final (*ibid.* s. 36). Sect. 4.

5. If the rules direct a reference to justices the county court judge may determine the dispute (Building Societies Act, 1874, s. 35 (2)), and his determination will be final (*ibid.* s. 36); but he may state a case for the opinion of the High Court and may grant discovery (*ibid.*). 2. To justices.

There has been some difference of opinion as to what is a "dispute" within the meaning of these statutory provisions; but it may, it is conceived, be taken to be now settled that the parties will not be compelled to arbitrate, and so deprived of their ordinary right to have recourse to a Court of law, except in a case where the dispute is—(1) between the society and one of its members *simply quâ member;* and (2) of such a character that the *machinery provided by the Acts is adequate to its complete settlement.* To this it may be added, that where arbitration is the proper course either party can *insist* on its being adopted, and that when the relation of *mortgagor and mortgagee* has once been created between a member and the society the provisions as to arbitration no longer apply. What is a "dispute" within the Acts.

"When you come to look into the authorities which were cited, they amount to this, that where the case went beyond the internal arrangements of the society, and introduced something which might be within their functions in the ordinary course of their business but yet still outside the whole scheme and scope of the society itself, then a person who had a much larger interest than any of those contemplated among the ordinary members could not be deprived of recourse to the ordinary tribunals of the land. And more especially he could not be so deprived in regard to mortgages, where, as in this case, possession was taken, where there was a question as to account against mortgagees for wilful default, and where there was an account also for outlay and expenditure on the mortgaged premises by the mortgagees, and where certain other questions had arisen which could not be properly sifted unless you go to the proper Court, which has all the means and the powers of sifting and dealing with them. I think therefore, my Lords, *Mulkern v. Lord.*

Sect. 4.

when you see what the real nature of the case is, there cannot be a doubt that this tribunal fell short of the requirements of the case, and that the party who sought to have a decree for account and redemption was entitled to it" (*Mulkern* v. *Lord*, 4 App. Cas. p. 192, *per* Lord Hatherley).

And in the same case Lord O'Hagan in the course of his speech said:—"This being the nature of the transaction, what is the machinery which the appellants seek to apply to it? That which manifestly was intended to deal with small affairs amongst humble people, and with simple controversies easily brought to a short and final issue. It aimed to secure mutual assistance to the working classes, in circumstances of difficulty, and to settle their ordinary disputes and enforce their limited demands, at the least expense and in the promptest way. It contemplated the daily dealing of the members one with another, and was in no way adopted to the arrangement of considerable claims and the solution of doubtful questions."

Where an action, and not a reference to arbitration, is the proper remedy.

In the following cases it was held that an action or suit was the proper method of deciding the matter in dispute, and that the parties could not be compelled to arbitrate:—*Mulkern* v. *Lord*, 4 App. Cas. 182; 48 L. J. Ch. 745; 27 W. R. 510; 40 L. T. 594; 43 J. P. 492, which was an action by an advanced member against the trustees, who were mortgagees in possession under mortgages amounting to upwards of 16,000*l.*, for an account and general relief, the rules simply directing that disputes between a member and the society should be referred to arbitration pursuant to the 10 Geo. 4, c. 56: *Morrison* v. *Glover*, 4 Ex. 430; 19 L. J. Ex. 20; 14 L. T. (O. S.) 204; 14 J. P. 84, which is indistinguishable from *Mulkern* v. *Lord*; and see *Doe dem. Morrison* v. *Glover*, 15 Q. B. 103; 15 L. T. (O. S.) 111, between the same parties: *Farmer* v. *Giles*, 5 H. & N. 753; 30 L. J. Ex. 65; 8 W. R. 649; 2 L. T. 387; 24 J. P. 663, an action against a member on a covenant in a mortgage deed for payment of the subscriptions and interest payable on his shares: *Cutbill* v. *Kingdom*, 1 Ex. 494; 17 L. J. Ex. 177, also an action on a covenant in a mortgage, but the question in this case was decided on the construction of a particular rule of the society: *Fleming* v. *Self*, 3 De G. M. &

Sect. 4.

G. 997; 24 L. J. Ch. 29; 1 Jur. N. S. 25; 3 Eq. Rep. 14; 3 W. R. 89; 24 L. T. (O. S.) 101; 18 J. P. 772, a redemption suit: *Prentice* v. *London*, L. R. 10 C. P. 679; 44 L. J. C. P. 353; 33 L. T. 251; 39 J. P. 711, where the real question was whether the plaintiff, who claimed as transferee of certain shares which the trustees had cancelled, was a member of the society at all: *Smith* v. *Lloyd*, 26 Beav. 507, a suit by an unadvanced withdrawing member for an account and payment of what should be found due: *Doubleday* v. *Hosking*, 15 Eq. 344, *n.*, a similar case to *Smith* v. *Lloyd:* and see *Harmer* v. *Gooding*, 3 De G. & Sm. 407; 13 Jur. 400; 13 L. T. (O. S.) 134, where the suit was stopped by a demurrer for want of parties and not afterwards proceeded with.

In *R.* v. *Trafford*, 4 El. & Bl. 122; 24 L. J. M. C. 20; 1 Jur. N. S. 252; 24 L. T. (O. S.) 308; 19 J. P. 6, a dispute arose between the society and a withdrawing member as to the terms on which he was entitled to redeem a mortgage. The society refused to refer the dispute to arbitration, and two justices therefore made an order under 4 & 5 Will. 4, c. 40, s. 7. *Held*, that they had no jurisdiction, the dispute having arisen not solely from the relation of member and society but from that of mortgagor and mortgagee.

Where reference to arbitration is the proper remedy.

On the other hand where a member withdrew from the society; and on the trustees refusing to pay him the value of his shares brought an action against them for the amount, it was held that the Court had no jurisdiction (*Ex parte Payne*, 5 D. & L. 679; 18 L. J. Q. B. 197; 13 Jur. 634); and see *Crisp* v. *Bunbury*, 8 Bing. 394; 1 M. & Sc. 646; *Timms* v. *Williams*, 3 Q. B. 413; 11 L. J. Q. B. 210. To the same effect are *Huckle* v. *Wilson*, 2 C. P. D. 410; 26 W. R. 98, and *Johnson* v. *Altrincham Permanent Benefit Building Society*, 49 L. T. 568; 48 J. P. 24; and the fact that a notice of withdrawal has been given and assented to by the trustees does not prevent the application of a rule providing for arbitration (*Wright* v. *Deeley*, 4 H. & C. 209; 30 J. P. 631; W. N. (1866), 74; *Huckle* v. *Wilson*); the person who withdraws being treated as a member, for the purpose of arbitration, until his rights are determined (*Armitage* v. *Walker*, 2 K. & J.

Sect. 4. p. 222; 2 Jur. N. S. 13; 26 L. T. (O. S.) 182; 20 J. P. 53, *per* Wood, V.-C.).

Thompson v. Planet Benefit Building Society.

In *Thompson* v. *Planet Benefit Building Society*, 15 Eq. 333; 42 L. J. Ch. 364; 21 W. R. 474; 28 L. T. 549; 37 J. P. 468, a bill was filed by a shareholder against the society and its directors, alleging misconduct against the latter. The plaintiff prayed a declaration that he was not bound by certain new rules that had been passed, and he also prayed the benefit of certain of the original rules and for relief against the directors personally. The bill was demurred to both by the society and the directors, and after full argument it was held by Bacon, V.-C., that the dispute was one for the decision of which arbitrators were the proper authority, and the demurrers were allowed, but, in consideration of the state of the authorities, without costs. His lordship declined to follow *Doubleday* v. *Hosking*, considering the weight of authority was against it; and he did not feel himself much bound by *Smith* v. *Lloyd*, being of opinion that that case had been decided by Lord Romilly under the erroneous idea that the 10 Geo. 4, c. 56 had been repealed.

In *Trott* v. *Hughes*, 16 L. T. (O. S.) 260, a member who had given notice of withdrawal moved to restrain the directors from parting with the funds of the society, on the ground that he had a primary lien on them for the return of the subscriptions he had paid and that he apprehended a misapplication of the funds by the directors. Lord Cranworth, V.-C., held that the Court of Chancery was not the proper forum for the decision of such questions in face of a rule referring disputes to the directors, and if their decision was not satisfactory then to arbitration, and refused the motion with costs.

Reeves v. White.

In *Reeves* v. *White*, 17 Q. B. 995; 21 L. J. Q. B. 169; 16 Jur. 637; 18 L. T. (O. S.) 271; 16 J. P. 118, it was held that the trustees could not sue on covenants in a mortgage made by an advanced member to the society; but this is clearly not the law now, see *Mulkern* v. *Lord* and the other cases cited above.

A claim by the trustees of a society against the treasurer for money which he has received and has failed to pay over

Sect. 4.

to them is not a "dispute" which must be referred to arbitration, and an action will lie for its recovery (*Sinden* v. *Banks*, 3 El. & El. 623; 30 L. J. Q. B. 102; 7 Jur. N. S. 910; 9 W. R. 415; 3 L. T. 775; *S. C. nom. Lindon* v. *Banks*, 25 J. P. 390).

For the form of an award see *post*, p. 82.

Notice must be given by arbitrators.

The arbitrators must give notice of their intention to proceed with the reference. Where one of the rules of the society provided that all notices should be deemed duly served by posting the same to the members at their last registered address, the Court held that this only related to the ordinary business of the society and did not apply to notices by arbitrators (*Hilton* v. *Hill*, 9 L. T. 383; 27 J. P. 760).

The arbitrators may decline to hear counsel (*Re Macqueen*, 9 C. B. N. S. 793).

Award cannot be altered by the Court.

When the arbitrator has made his award the Court has no power to alter it unless there is error on the face of it or it is shown to have been corruptly obtained (*Armitage* v. *Walker*, 2 K. & J. 211; 2 Jur. N. S. 13; 26 L. T. (O. S.) 182; 20 J. P. 53).

A justice is bound to issue his warrant to enforce the performance of the award when once made; he cannot decline to do so on the ground that there has been a misapplication of the funds of the society (*Hughes* v. *Layton*, 33 L. J. M. C. 89; 10 Jur. N. S. 513; *S. C. nom. R.* v. *D'Eyncourt*, 4 B. & S. 820; 9 L. T. 712; 28 J. P. 116; *S. C. nom. Hughes* v. *D'Eyncourt*, 3 N. R. 420; 12 W. R. 408).

Incorporated societies.

As to arbitration in incorporated societies, see *post*, p. 134.

Reference of disputes to justices, if so directed by the rules of the society.

28. "And be it further enacted, that if by the rules of any such society it is directed that any matter in dispute as aforesaid shall be decided by justices of the peace, it shall and may be lawful for any such justice, on complaint being made to him of any refusal or neglect to comply with the rules of such society by any member or officer thereof, to summon the person against whom such complaint shall be made to appear at a time and place to be named in such summons; and upon his or her appearance, or in default thereof, upon due proof, on oath or affirmation, of the service of such sum-

Sect. 4. mons, it shall and may be lawful for any two justices to proceed to hear and determine the said complaint according to the rules of the said society; and in case the said justices shall adjudge any sum of money to be paid by such person against whom such complaint shall be made, and such person shall not pay such sum of money to the person and at the time specified by such justices, they shall proceed to enforce their award in the manner hereinbefore directed to be used in case of any neglect to comply with the decision of the arbitrators appointed under the authority of this Act."

Where the rules direct disputes to be referred to justices the County Court may determine the matter; see Building Societies Act, 1874, s. 35 (2), *post*, p. 139; and see note to sect. 27, *ante*, p. 70.

Orders of justices to be final.

29. "And be it further enacted, that every sentence, order, and adjudication of any justices under this Act shall be final and conclusive to all intents and purposes, and shall not be subject to appeal, and shall not be removed or removable into any court of law, or restrained or restrainable by the injunction of any court of equity, and that no suspension, advocation, or reduction shall be competent."

Sect. 30.

Sect. **30**, providing that funds might be subscribed into savings banks, was repealed; see 6 & 7 Will. 4, c. 32, s. 6, *post*, p. 91.

Sect. 31.

Sect. **31** does not apply to building societies.

Minors may be members, and have legal authority to act.

32. "And be it further enacted, that a minor may become a member of any such society, and shall be empowered to execute all instruments, give all necessary acquittances, and enjoy all the privileges and be liable to all the responsibilities appertaining to members of matured age, notwithstanding his or her incapacity or disability in law to act for himself or herself: provided always, that such minor be admitted into such society by and with the consent of his or her parents, masters, or guardians."

Married women.

As to married women see the Married Women's Property Act, 1882, 45 & 46 Vict. c. 75, particularly sects. 6—10.

Sect. 4.

Executors.

An executor became a member of a building society and mortgaged leaseholds of his testator to secure an advance, the mortgage deed showing on the face of it that the money was borrowed for executorship purposes. Malins, V.-C., held that there was no objection to the mortgage except in so far as it purported to be a security not only for repayment of what might become due from the borrower *quâ* executor, but also for any sums which might be due from him individually, if he subscribed for other shares in the society; this latter clause his lordship considered to be at variance with the rest of the deed *and therefore inoperative* (*Cruikshank* v. *Duffin*, 13 Eq. 555; 41 L. J. Ch. 317; 20 W. R. 354; 26 L. T. 121; 36 J. P. 708). It is not unusual for societies to advance money to executors, but they should exercise some caution in doing so.

Societies shall make annual audits and statements of the funds to the members.

33. "And be it further enacted, that the rules of every such society shall provide that the treasurers, trustees, stewards, or other principal officer thereof shall, once in every year at least, prepare or cause to be prepared a general statement of the funds and effects of or belonging to such society, specifying in whose custody or possession the said funds or effects shall be then remaining, together with an account of all and every the various sums of money received and expended by or on account of the said society since the publication of the preceding periodical statement; and every such periodical statement shall be attested by two or more members of such society appointed auditors for that purpose, and shall be countersigned by the secretary or clerk of such society; and every member shall be entitled to receive from the said society a copy of such periodical statement, on payment of such sum as the rules of such society may require, not exceeding the sum of sixpence."

Audited account may be impeached on the ground of fraud.

In *Holgate* v. *Shutt*, 27 Ch. D. 111; 53 L. J. Ch. 774; 32 W. R. 773; 51 L. T. 433, one of the rules of the society provided that the accounts should be audited every year "by auditors appointed by the society," and that after the accounts had been audited and signed the treasurer should not be answerable for mistakes, omissions or errors afterwards proved in the accounts. In an action by members

Sect. 4. against the treasurer the Court held that though the audited accounts must be received as *primâ facie* evidence the rule did not prevent the members from impeaching the accounts on the ground of fraud. The plaintiffs then raised a further point, viz. that the accounts having been audited by one person only who was not a member of the society the accounts were not even *primâ facie* evidence for the defendant. The Court was of opinion that the accounts had not been audited in accordance with the rules, but held that the defendant was not precluded from showing that the audited account ought to be treated as a settled account upon other grounds (*Holgate* v. *Shutt*, 28 Ch. D. 111; 54 L. J. Ch. 436; 51 L. T. 673; 49 J. P. 228). In the course of his judgment Fry, L. J., said:—"The 7th rule provides that 'The books of the secretary, vice-president, and treasurer shall be audited every twelve calendar months by auditors appointed by the society, and signed by such auditors to denote their accuracy in the secretary's book.' It appears to me to be plain that the auditors referred to in that passage must be the auditors pointed out by the statute of 10 Geo. 4, that is to say, there must be two auditors for every yearly audit, and those auditors must be members of the society. Now in the present case the audit was for years made by a single person and that person was not a member of the society. It follows, in my judgment, that the audit has not been an audit in accordance with rule 7, or with any other rules of the society. It has been suggested that the general power given to the society of regulating their affairs by a majority covers this case. In my view it cannot override the express provisions of rule 7 and the provisions of the Act of Parliament."

Sects. 34—36. Sects. **34—36** do not apply to building societies.

Exemption from stamp duties. **37.** "And be it further enacted, that no copy of rules, power, warrant or letter of attorney granted or to be granted by any persons as trustee of any society established under this Act for the transfer of any share in the public funds standing in the name of such trustee, nor any receipts given for any dividend in any public stock or fund or interest of exchequer bills, nor any receipt, nor any entry in any book

Sect. 4.

of receipt, for money deposited in the funds of any such society, nor for any money received by any member, his or her executors or administrators, assigns or attorneys, from the funds of such society, nor any bond nor other security to be given to or on account of any such society, or by the treasurer or trustee or any officer thereof, nor any draft or order, nor any form of assurance, nor any appointment of any agent, nor any certificate or other instrument for the revocation of any such appointment, nor any other instrument or document whatever required or authorized to be given, issued, signed, made or produced in pursuance of this Act, shall be subject or liable to or charged with any stamp duty or duties whatsoever."

Stamps on mortgages.

It was decided in *Walker* v. *Giles*, 6 C. B. 662; 18 L. J. C. P. 323; 13 Jur. 588; 13 L. T. (O. S.) 209, and *Barnard* v. *Pilsworth*, 6 C. B. 698, *n.*; 18 L. J. C. P. 330, *n.*; 14 L. T. (O. S.) 132, that mortgages to a building society came within this section and were exempt from duty; and the same was held in *Thorn* v. *Croft*, 3 Eq. 193; 36 L. J. Ch. 68; 15 W. R. 54; 15 L. T. 205; 31 J. P. 356, by Wood, V.-C., who extended the decision to the case of mortgages to the society by persons not members of it.

Stamp Act, 1870, s. 112.

The Stamp Act, 1870, 33 & 34 Vict. c. 97, s. 112 (Aug. 10, 1870), now provides as follows, in substitution for 31 & 32 Vict. c. 124, s. 11 (July 31, 1868), to the same effect:—"The exemption from stamp duty conferred by the Act of the sixth and seventh years of King William the Fourth, chapter thirty-two, for the regulation of benefit building societies, shall not extend to any mortgage to be made after the passing of this Act, except a mortgage by a *member* of a benefit building society for securing the repayment to the society of money *not exceeding five hundred pounds.*"

In *Williams* v. *Hayward*, 22 Beav. 220; 25 L. J. Ch. 289; 1 Jur. N. S. 1128; 26 L. T. (O. S.) 134; 19 J. P. 788, a mortgage to a building society executed before the rules had been certified and deposited, though this was done subsequently, was held to be exempt from stamp duty.

Receipt.

In *Attorney-General* v. *Phillips*, 24 L. T. 832; 19 W. R. 1146, a member mortgaged a cottage to the society to secure

Sect. 4.

an advance. The society entered into possession, and received rent from the tenant of the mortgaged premises, for which they gave him a receipt in the following form:—

"Temperance Permanent Land and Building Society (enrolled as The Temperance Permanent Benefit Building Society.)

"4, Ludgate Hill,

"No. 2667. "London, 15th Oct., 1870.

"Received of Mr. G. C. Knight twelve pounds, rent of premises, Barnhove Cottage, East Moulsey, due at Michaelmas 1870.

"For the Trustees of the Society,

"£12. "HENRY J. PHILLIPS, *Secretary.*"

The Court of Exchequer held that this was simply a receipt between landlord and tenant, and was liable to stamp duty.

"Bond nor other security."

In *Re Royal Liver Friendly Society*, L. R. 5 Ex. 78; *S. C. nom. Trustees of The Royal Liver Friendly Society* v. *Commissioners of Inland Revenue*, 39 L. J. Ex. 37; 18 W. R. 349; 21 L. T. 721, a case on the construction of the Friendly Societies Act, 1855, s. 37, which is almost identical with the section in the text, except that the words "nor other security" are omitted after the word "bond,"—Martin, B., said:—"My impression is that the word 'bond,' which occurs in both the earlier and the present section, refers, not to a loan or investment of the society's funds in or upon bonds, such as the Harbour Bonds of the Mersey Docks, but to bonds given, whether with or without sureties, by clerks, agents to receive money, and others, as security for their duly accounting, or otherwise discharging, the functions of their office. That, I think, also, was the nature of the 'security' mentioned in the earlier Act [10 Geo. 4, c. 56]; but a more extensive meaning having been attributed to it, the word was afterwards omitted."

"Draft or order."

Where a building society paid withdrawing members the amounts due to them by drafts to bearer, and made half-yearly payments of interest to members of the society in respect of their shares by similar drafts, both were held liable to stamp duty (*Att.-Gen.* v. *Gilpin*, L. R. 6 Ex. 193;

Sect. 4.

40 L. J. Ex. 134; 19 W. R. 1027). Kelly, C. B., in delivering judgment, said:—"The section of the Act which is relied on is sect. 37, which contains among the list of exempted instruments, 'draft or order;' it is necessary, therefore, to inquire what sort of drafts and orders are contemplated by the section. They must be drafts or orders 'required or authorized to be given, issued, signed, made, or produced, in pursuance of' the Act; and I think the words limit the drafts and orders mentioned to such as are drawn by an officer of the society for its purposes, or by a member upon the society, payable to himself only. The rules of the society evidently contemplate a payment to the member personally, on the production of his pass-book, and after its examination, and not a payment made on the draft of a member at a distance, and perhaps abroad, payable to the bearer, and passing from hand to hand with or without indorsement. Indeed, looking at the facts stated in the case, it may be doubted whether this is really a benefit building society at all; at all events this is not a transaction falling within the ordinary transactions of a building society, but is a transaction between banker and customer. The society has possessed itself of deposits amounting to more than one million pounds, which remain in its hands in the ordinary mode of banking business. A notice is required of a member's intention to withdraw his deposit, but on the expiration of the limited time, the member is entitled to withdraw either his completed share or shares of 30*l*., or the whole or any part of his uncompleted shares. This is clearly a banking transaction, and not a transaction within the operations either of a benefit building society or a friendly society, or within the spirit and meaning of 10 Geo. 4, c. 56, or 6 & 7 Will. 4, c. 32."

Rules and transfers of shares.

By sect. 8 of 6 & 7 Will. 4, c. 32, no rules of any building society, nor any transfer of any share in any such society, shall be liable to any stamp duty; see the section *post*, p. 92.

Incorporated societies.

As to the exemption from stamp duty in the case of incorporated societies, see the Building Societies Act, 1874, s. 41, *post*, p. 142.

Sect. 4.

Construction of Act.

38. "And be it further enacted, that the word 'society' in this Act shall be understood to include friendly society or societies, institution or institutions; the word 'rules' to include rules, orders, and regulations; the word 'county' to include county, riding, division, or place; and the words 'treasurer or trustee' to include treasurers or trustees; and the word 'person' to include persons; and the word 'book' to include books; and the word 'bond' to include bonds; 'name' to include names; 'account' to include accounts; 'member' to include members and honorary members; 'clerk of the peace' to include town clerk; unless it be otherwise specially provided."

Sects. 39—41.

The three remaining sections contain only temporary and formal provisions.

Form of award.

The form of award and form of bond given in the Act are as follows:—

"FORM OF AWARD.

"We, the major part of the arbitrators duly appointed by the Society established at , in the county of , do hereby award and order, that A. B. [*specifying by name the party or the officer of the society*] do, on the day of , pay to C. D. the sum of [*or* we do hereby reinstate in *or* expel A. B. from the said society, *as the case may be*]. Dated this day of , One thousand eight hundred and .

"E. F.
"G. H."

"FORM OF BOND.

Form of bond.

"Know all men by these presents, that we, A. B. of , treasurer [*or* trustee, &c.] of the Society established at , in the county of , and C. D. of , and G. H. of (as sureties on behalf of the said A. B.), are jointly and severally held and firmly bound to E. F., the present clerk of the peace [*or* town clerk] for the county [*or* county of a city, *or* county of a town, riding, division, *or* place, *as the case may be*] of , in the sum of , to be paid to the said E. F. as such clerk of the peace [*or* town clerk], or his successor, clerk of the peace [*or* town clerk] of the said county [*or* county of a city, &c.] for the time being, or his certain attorney; for which payment well and truly to be made we jointly and severally bind ourselves, and each of us by himself, our and each of our heirs, executors, and administrators, firmly by these presents, sealed with our seals. Dated the day of , in the year of our Lord . **Sect. 4.**

"Whereas the above-bounden A. B. hath been duly appointed treasurer [*or* trustee, &c.] of the Society established as aforesaid, and he, together with the above-bounden C. D. and G. H. as his sureties, have entered into the above-written bond, subject to the condition hereinafter contained; now, therefore, the condition of the above-written bond is such, that if the said A. B. shall and do justly and faithfully execute his office of treasurer [*or* trustee] of the said society established as aforesaid, and shall and do render a just and true account of all monies received and paid by him, and shall and do pay over all the monies remaining in his hands, and assign and transfer or deliver all securities and effects, books, papers, and property of or belonging to the said society in his hands or custody to such person or persons as the said society shall appoint, according to the rules of the said society, together with the proper or legal receipts or vouchers for such payments, and likewise shall and do in all respects well and truly and faithfully perform and fulfil his office of treasurer [*or* trustee, &c.] to the said society, according to the rules thereof, then the above-written bond shall be void and of no effect, otherwise shall be and remain in full force and virtue."

The Act 4 & 5 Will. 4, c. 40 (30th July, 1834) is as follows:— 4&5 Will. 4, c. 40.

Sect. 1 repeals sects. 6, 20 and 30, parts of sects. 34 and 35, and sect. 36 of 10 Geo. 4, c. 56. Sect. 1.

Sect. 2 does not relate to building societies. Sect. 2.

3. "And be it further enacted, that so much of the said Repeal of 10 Geo. 4,

Sect. 4.

c. 56, s. 4, and part of s. 7.

recited Act as relates to the rules of friendly societies being transmitted to the barrister or advocate, and deposited with the clerk of the peace and certified by him, as well as so much as relates to alterations of rules being certified by the clerk of the peace, and that no rule or alteration or amendment should be binding until confirmed by the justices, and filed under the recited Act, shall be and the same are hereby repealed."

The "said recited Act" is 10 Geo. 4, c. 56.

Two transcripts of rules to be submitted to a barrister, &c. by whom they are to be certified.

4. "And be it further enacted, that two transcripts, fairly written on paper or parchment, of all rules made in pursuance of the said recited Act or this Act, signed by three members, and countersigned by the clerk or secretary, (accompanied, in the case of an alteration or amendment of rules, with an affidavit of the clerk or secretary or one of the officers of the said society that the provisions of the said recited Act, or of the Act under which the rules of the society may have been enrolled, have been duly complied with,) with all convenient speed after the same shall be made, altered, or amended, and so from time to time after every making, altering, or amending thereof, shall be submitted, [in England and Wales and Berwick-upon-Tweed, to the barrister-at-law for the time being appointed to certify the rules of savings banks, and in Scotland to the Lord Advocate or any depute appointed by him for that purpose, and in Ireland to such barrister as may be appointed by his Majesty's Attorney-General in Ireland,] for the purpose of ascertaining whether the said rules of such society, or alteration or amendment thereof, are calculated to carry into effect the intention of the parties framing such rules, alterations, or amendments, and are in conformity to law and to the provisions of the said recited Act or this Act; and that the said [barrister or advocate] shall adviso with the said clerk or secretary, if required, and shall give a certificate on each of the said transcripts, that the same are in conformity to law and to the provisions of the said recited Act and this Act, or point out in what part or parts the said rules are repugnant thereto; and that the [barrister or advocate,] for advising as aforesaid, and perusing the rules, or alterations

Barrister, &c. to certify both transcripts.

Fee payable to barrister.

Sect. 4.

or amendments of the rules of each respective society, and giving such certificates as aforesaid, shall demand no further fee than that specified in the said recited Act; and one of such transcripts, when certified by the said [barrister or advocate], shall be returned to the society, and the other of such transcripts shall be [transmitted by such barrister or advocate to the clerk of the peace for the county wherein such society shall be formed, and by him laid before the justices for such county at the general quarter sessions, or adjournment thereof, held next after the time when such transcript shall have been so certified and transmitted to him as aforesaid; and the justices then and there present are hereby authorized and required, without motion, to allow and confirm the same; and such transcript shall be filed by such clerk of the peace with the rolls of the sessions of the peace in his custody, without fee or reward;] and that all rules, alterations and amendments thereof, from the time when the same shall be certified by the said barrister or advocate, shall be binding on the several members and officers of the said society, and all other persons having interest therein."

One transcript to be returned to society, the other to be sent to clerk of peace.

Justices to confirm rules.

Transcript to be filed.

Rules, &c. to be binding when certified by barrister.

By sect. 7 of the Building Societies Act, 1874, all things required to be done by or sent to the barrister or advocate and the clerk of the peace under 6 & 7 Will. 4, c. 32 must be done by or sent to the registrar of friendly societies. See the section, *post*, p. 97. The registrar, therefore, if satisfied with the rules, now sends one transcript back to the society and keeps the other himself.

Registrar substituted for barrister.

The certificate of the barrister under this Act is not conclusive as to the legality of a rule (*Laing* v. *Reed*, 21 L. T. 83; affirmed on appeal, 5 Ch. 4; 39 L. J. Ch. 1; 18 W. R. 76; 21 L. T. 773; 34 J. P. 134; *Kelsall* v. *Tyler*, 11 Ex. 513; 25 L. J. Ex. 153; 26 L. T. (O. S.) 226; 20 J. P. 150; *R.* v. *Davis*, W. N. (1866), 24; 14 W. R. 329; 13 L. T. 629; 30 J. P. 116). "It could not be contended, and it hardly was contended, that if the matter was plainly *ultra vires*, any certificate of the barrister could prevent the Court from interfering so as to prevent an abuse of power on the part of persons who have certain privileges conferred on them by

Certificate of barrister how far conclusive.

Sect. 4.

parliament. If there were such an abuse of power the certificate of the barrister could have no effect whatever. The words which render him competent to decide upon the legality of the instruments submitted to him, clearly do not apply to such a case as that before us. They probably apply to regulations affecting the engagements between the members themselves; such, for instance, as in what cases the majority might bind the minority. But if the law prohibited the raising of these sums of money, I apprehend that no certificate of the barrister could avail" (*per* Lord Hatherley, 5 Ch. p. 7).

In *Dewhurst* v. *Clarkson*, 3 El. & B. 194; 23 L. J. Q. B. 247; 18 Jur. 693; 23 L. T. (O. S.) 109; 2 C. L. R. 1143; 18 J. P. 535, however, it was held by the Court of Queen's Bench, Erle, J. *diss.*, that where an amendment of the rules of a friendly society had been certified under this section such amendment was valid, although there had been no resolution of the society in compliance with the 10 Geo. 4, c. 56, s. 9, or with the rules of the society incorporating that section.

See also as to the effect of the barrister's certificate, *Pare* v. *Clegg*, 29 Beav. 589; 30 L. J. Ch. 742; 7 Jur. N. S. 1136; 9 W. R. 795; 4 L. T. 669; 26 J. P. 53.

Murray v. *Scott.*

In a recent case one of the rules of a building society authorized the board to issue deposit or paid-up shares for 30*l.* each at 5 per cent. interest with the right of withdrawing the whole or part of the deposit upon notice in preference to all other shares. This rule was struck out by the barrister, but nevertheless the directors printed and acted upon it by issuing shares accordingly. Some years afterwards they amended this rule by altering 30*l.* into 1*l.*, and the amendment was certified by the barrister; and those who had taken 30*l.* shares exchanged them for 1*l.* shares, and others who had not before held paid-up shares took up shares of the new issue. The society was ordered to be wound up. It was held that the effect of the barrister's certificate was to make the rule which had been struck out a valid rule again, but altered by 1*l.* being substituted for 30*l.*; and that the holders of these shares, whether they became such before or after the

Sect. 4.

amendment was certified and whether they had given notice of withdrawal or not, must be paid in preference to the unadvanced members (*Murray* v. *Scott*, 9 App. Cas. 519; 53 L. J. Ch. 745; 33 W. R. 173; 51 L. T. 462, affirming *S. C.* below *nom. Re Guardian Permanent Benefit Building Society*, 23 Ch. D. 440; 52 L. J. Ch. 857; 32 W. R. 73; 48 L. T. 134).

Barrister not to be entitled to fee in respect of alterations within three years, nor for certificate to rules being copies of those already enrolled.

5. "Provided always, and be it enacted, that the said [barrister] shall be entitled to no further fee for or in respect of any alteration or amendment of any rules upon which one fee has been already paid [to the said barrister] within the period of three years: provided also, that if any rules, alterations or amendments, are sent to such [barrister or advocate], accompanied with an affidavit of being a copy of any rules, or alterations or amendments of the rules, of any other society, which shall have been already enrolled under the provisions of the said recited Act or this Act, the said [barrister or advocate] shall certify and return the same as aforesaid, without being entitled to any fee for such certificate."

See note to sect. 4, *supra*.

Sect. 6.

Sect. **6** does not apply to building societies.

If rules of society direct reference in case of dispute to arbitration, and society refuse to grant arbitrators, &c. justices may determine the dispute.

7. "And whereas in and by the said recited Act provision is directed to be made by the rules of every society whether reference of any matter in dispute shall be made to justices or to arbitrators; and whereas it is expedient that further provision should be made in case the reference is to arbitrators; be it therefore enacted, that when the rules of any society provide for a reference to arbitrators of any matter in dispute, and it shall appear to any justice of the peace, on the complaint on oath of a member of any such society, or of any person claiming on account of such member, that application has been made to such society, or the steward or other officer thereof, for the purpose of having any dispute so settled by arbitration, and that such application has not within forty days been complied with, or that the arbitrators have neglected or refused to make any award, it shall and may be lawful for such justice to summon the trustee,

Sect. 4. treasurer, steward, or other officer of the society, or any one of them against whom the complaint is made, and for any two justices to hear and determine the matter in dispute, in the same manner as if the rules of the said society had directed that any matter in dispute as aforesaid should be decided by justices of the peace, anything in the said recited Act contained to the contrary notwithstanding."

See now sect. 35 of the Building Societies Act, 1874, *post*, p. 139, which apparently extends to unincorporated societies.

Provision in case member of society is expelled.

8. "And be it further enacted, that in case any member of a friendly society established under the said recited Act or this Act shall have been expelled from such society, and the arbitrators or justices, as the case may be, shall award or order that he or she shall be reinstated, it shall and may be lawful for such arbitrators or justices to award or order, in default of such reinstatement, to the member so expelled, such a sum of money as to such arbitrators or justices may seem just and reasonable; which said sum of money, if not paid, shall be recoverable from the said society, or the treasurer, trustee, or other officer, in the same way as any money awarded by arbitrators is recoverable under the said recited Act."

Sects. 9-11.

Sects. **9** and **11** do not apply to building societies; sect. **10**, providing that members of friendly societies may be witnesses, is obsolete.

Executors, &c. of officers of friendly society to pay money due to society before any other debts.

12. "And be it further enacted, that if any person already appointed or who may hereafter be appointed to any office in a society established under the said recited Act or this Act, and being entrusted with the keeping of the accounts, or having in his hands or possession, by virtue of his said office or employment, any monies or effects belonging to such society, or any deeds or securities relating to the same, shall die, or become a bankrupt or insolvent, or have any execution or attachment or other process issued, or action or diligence raised, against his lands, goods, chattels, or effects, or property or estate, heritable or moveable, or make any

Sect. 4.

assignment, disposition, assignation, or other conveyance thereof for the benefit of his creditors, his heirs, executors, administrators, or assignees, or other persons having legal right, or the sheriff or other officer executing such process, or the party using such action or diligence, shall, within forty days after demand made in writing by the order of any such society or committee thereof, or the major part of them assembled at any meeting thereof, deliver and pay over all monies and other things belonging to such society to such person as such society or committee shall appoint, and shall pay, out of the estates, assets, or effects, heritable or moveable, of such person, all sums of money remaining due which such person received by virtue of his said office or employment, before any other of his debts are paid or satisfied, or before the money directed to be levied by such process as aforesaid, or which may be recovered or recoverable under such diligence, is paid over to the party issuing such process or using such diligence; and all such assets, lands, goods, chattels, property, estates, and effects shall be bound to the payment and discharge thereof accordingly."

No priority in bankruptcy.

A building society has no longer any priority over other creditors on the bankruptcy of one of its officers; see *Ex parte Bailey*, 5 De G. M. & G. 380; 23 L. J. Bkcy. 36; 18 Jur. 988; Bankruptcy Act, 1883, s. 40.

Priority, when allowed.

The preference given by this section is only allowed in respect of monies, &c. in the hands of an officer of the society strictly so called (*Ex parte Whipham*, 3 M. D. & De G. 564; 13 L. J. Bkcy. 8; 2 L. T. (O. S.) 426; *Ex parte Orford*, 1 De G. M. & G. 483; 16 Jur. 851; *S. C. nom. Ex parte Oxford*, 21 L. J. Bkcy. 31; *Ex parte Harris*, De G. 162; 14 L. J. Bkcy. 25); and the money must be in his hands *virtute officii* and not under any contract (*Ex parte Stamford Friendly Society*, 15 Ves. 280; *Ex parte Fleet*, 4 De G. & Sm. 52; 19 L. J. Bkcy. 10; 14 Jur. 685; *Re Shattock*, 5 L. T. 370); and see *Re Heanor Friendly Society*, 1 Beav. 508, where the money had been placed in the hands of an officer jointly with another person. But an agreement on the appointment of a treasurer that he shall pay interest on part of the sum placed in his hands will not deprive the society of their sta-

Sect. 4.

tutory priority (*Ex parte Ray*, 3 Dea. 537; 1 Mont. & Ch. 50). And where the treasurer was a partner in a banking firm and the money did not go through his hands but was paid directly to the bank to the credit of the trustees, it was held on the firm becoming bankrupt that the trustees had priority for their balance (*Ex parte Riddell*, 3 M. D. & De G. 80; 7 Jur. 21); and see *Ex parte Burge*, 1 M. D. & De G. 540; 5 Jur. 346, where the treasurer had invested money of the society upon an insufficient security.

Priority not lost by neglect of society to examine accounts.

Where the secretary of a society, the rules of which provided that the secretary's accounts should be regularly presented and audited, misappropriated the monies of the society that came to his hands and died insolvent, Jessel, M. R., held that the society was entitled to priority over the other creditors, and that the society's want of due diligence in examining the accounts was no bar to their claim (*Moors* v. *Marriott*, 7 Ch. D. 543; 47 L. J. Ch. 331; 26 W. R. 626; 42 J. P. 452); and see also as to negligence by the society *Absolom* v. *Gething*, 32 Beav. 322; 32 L. J. Ch. 786; 9 Jur. N. S. 1263; 8 L. T. 132.

Incorporated societies.

There is no priority in the case of incorporated societies.

Sects. 13—17.

The remaining sections of the Act, sects. **13—17**, contain only obsolete and formal provisions.

Receipt endorsed on mortgage to be sufficient discharge without reconveyance.

5. And be it further enacted, that it shall be lawful for the trustees named in any mortgage made on behalf of such societies, or the survivor or survivors of them, or for the trustees for the time being, to endorse upon any mortgage or further charge given by any member of such society to the trustees thereof for monies advanced by such society to any member thereof, a receipt for all monies intended to be secured by such mortgage or further charge, which shall be sufficient to vacate the same, and vest the estate of and in the property comprised in such security in the person or persons for the time being entitled to the equity of redemption, without it being necessary for the trustees of any such society to give any reconveyance of the property so mortgaged, which receipt shall be specified in a schedule to be annexed to the rules of such society, duly certified and deposited as aforesaid.

Sect. 5.

See Building Societies Act, 1874, s. 42, and note thereto, *post*, p. 143.

Not to authorize investment of funds in savings bank.

6. Provided always, and be it further enacted, that nothing herein contained shall authorize any benefit building society to invest its funds, or any part thereof, in any savings bank, or with the Commissioners for the Reduction of the National Debt.

Other investments are authorized by 10 Geo. 4, c. 56, s. 13; see this section, *ante*, p. 54.

Benefit of Act to extend to all societies established prior to June, 1836.

7. And be it further enacted, that all building societies established prior to the first day of June one thousand eight hundred and thirty-six shall be entitled to the protection and benefits of this Act, on their present rules being duly certified and deposited as directed by the said recited Acts; and no such society shall be entitled to the benefits of this Act until their rules shall have been so certified and deposited; and that no such society shall be required to alter in any manner the rules under which they are now respectively governed.

It may be doubted whether any societies established prior to June, 1836, are still in existence.

Sect. 8.

Exemption from stamp duties.

8. And be it further enacted, that no rules of any such society, or any copy thereof, nor any transfer of any share or shares in any such society, shall be subject or liable to or charged with any stamp duty or duties whatsoever.

As to exemption from stamp duty in the case of unincorporated societies see also 10 Geo. 4, c. 56, s. 37, and note thereto, *ante*, p. 78.

Public Act.

9. And be it further enacted, that this Act shall be deemed a public Act, and shall extend to Great Britain, Ireland, and Berwick-upon-Tweed, and be judicially taken notice of as such by all judges, justices, and other persons whatsoever, without the same being specially shown or pleaded.

THE BUILDING SOCIETIES ACT, 1874.

37 & 38 Vict. c. 42.

An Act to consolidate and amend the Laws relating to Building Societies. [30th July, 1874.]

Whereas it is expedient to consolidate and amend the law relating to building societies:

Be it enacted by the queen's most excellent majesty, by and with the advice and consent of the lords spiritual and temporal, and commons, in this present parliament assembled, and by the authority of the same, as follows:—

1. This Act may be cited as the Building Societies Act, 1874. Short title.

2. This Act shall commence and take effect on the second day of November one thousand eight hundred and seventy-four. Commencement of Act.

3. The registrar in this Act means (except where otherwise expressed) the registrar for the time being of friendly societies in England, Scotland, or Ireland, as the case may be, who shall, for the purposes of this Act, be the registrar of building societies. Definition of registrar.

The 10th section of the Friendly Societies Act, 1875, 38 & 39 Vict. c. 60, contains (amongst others) the following provisions:— Friendly Societies Act, 1875, s. 10.

"(1) There shall be a chief registrar of friendly societies The chief and assist-

Sect. 3.

ant registrars.

(herein termed 'the chief registrar'), and one or more assistant registrars of friendly societies for England (herein termed 'assistant registrars for England'), and such chief registrar and assistant registrars for England shall constitute the central office after mentioned. There shall be an assistant registrar of friendly societies for Scotland (herein termed 'assistant registrar for Scotland'), and an assistant registrar of friendly societies for Ireland (herein termed 'assistant registrar for Ireland').

Chief and assistant registrars to hold office during pleasure.

"(2) Every chief registrar and assistant registrar shall be appointed by and shall hold his office during the pleasure of the Treasury.

Qualification of chief and assistant registrars.

"(3) Every chief registrar shall be a barrister of not less than twelve years' standing, and one at least of the assistant registrars for England, and every assistant registrar for Ireland shall be a barrister or solicitor of not less than seven years' standing, and every assistant registrar for Scotland an advocate, writer to the signet, or solicitor of not less than seven years' standing. The central office may also, with the approval of the Treasury, have attached to it such assistants skilled in the business of an actuary and an accountant as shall from time to time be required for discharging the duties imposed on the office by this Act.

Central office to exercise functions of registrar of friendly or building societies for England, and barrister to certify savings banks.

"(4) The central office shall exercise all the functions and powers which are now by law vested in the registrar of friendly societies or the registrar of building societies for England, or as respects loan societies, building societies, and societies instituted for purposes of science, literature, or the fine arts, in the barrister appointed to certify the rules of savings banks or friendly societies, and shall be entitled to receive all statutory fees payable to such registrar or barrister, and all enactments relating to such registrar or barrister, so far as respects such societies as aforesaid, shall be construed as applying to the central office.

Chief registrar to report yearly to Parliament.

"(6) The chief registrar shall every year lay before Parliament a report of his proceedings and of those of the assistant registrars, and of the principal matters transacted by him and them, and of the valuations returned to or caused to be made by the registrar during the year preceding.

Functions of assistant registrars generally.

"(7) The assistant registrars shall, except as after provided, be subordinate to the chief registrar. They shall, within the countries for which they are respectively appointed, exercise all functions and powers by this Act given to the registrar, and may also, by the written authority of the chief registrar, exercise such of the functions and powers by this Act given to the chief registrar as he shall from time to time delegate to them.

Functions of assistant registrars for Scotland and Ireland.

"(8) Subject to any regulations to be made under this Act, the assistant registrars for Scotland and Ireland respectively shall:—

"(a) Exercise all the functions and powers now vested in the registrars of friendly or building societies for Scotland and Ireland respectively, or as respects building societies and societies instituted for purposes of science, literature, or the fine arts, vested in Scotland in the Lord Advocate or his depute appointed to certify the rules of friendly societies there, or in Ireland in the barrister appointed to certify the rules of friendly societies there, and shall be entitled to receive all fees payable to such registrar, Lord Advocate, or his depute or barrister respectively, and so that all provisions in any Acts of Parliament, not hereby repealed relating to such registrar, Lord Advocate, or his depute or barrister respectively, shall be construed as applying to such assistant registrars respectively:

"(b) Send to the central office copies of all such documents registered or recorded by them as the chief registrar shall from time to time direct:

"(c) Record all such documents and matters as shall be sent to them for record from the central office, and such other documents and matters as herein provided.

"(d) Circulate and publish, or transmit to or from societies registered within their respective countries, from or to the central office, such information and documents relating to the purposes of this Act as the

Sect. 3.

chief registrar, with the approval of the Treasury, shall from time to time direct.

"(c) Report from time to time their proceedings to the chief registrar as he shall direct.

"(9) No assistant registrar for Scotland or Ireland shall refuse to record any rules or amendments of rules which have been registered by the central office."

Definition of Court.

4. The Court in this Act means—

In England, the County Court of the district in which the chief office or place of meeting for the business of the society is situate;

In Scotland, the Sheriff's Court of the county in which such office or place of meeting is situate; and

In Ireland, the Civil Bill Court within the jurisdiction of which such office or place of meeting is situate.

Definition of terminating and permanent societies.

5. A terminating society in this Act means a society which by its rules is to terminate at a fixed date, or when a result specified in its rules is attained; a permanent society means a society which has not by its rules any such fixed date or specified result at which it shall terminate.

Application to Scotland.

6. In the application of this Act to Scotland the following words and expressions shall have the meanings hereby assigned to them; viz., "freehold estate" shall mean "heritable estate"; "mortgage" shall mean "conveyance or bond and disposition in security"; "letters of administration" shall mean "confirmation."

Sect. 7.

Repeal of 6&7 Will. 4, c. 32.

7. The Act of the sixth and seventh years of his late Majesty King William the Fourth, chapter thirty-two, intituled "An Act for the Regulation of Benefit Building Societies," is hereby repealed, but this repeal shall not affect any subsisting society certified under the said Act, until such society shall have obtained a certificate of incorporation under this Act; and this repeal shall not affect the past operation of the said Act, or the force or operation, validity or invalidity, of anything done or suffered, or any bond or security given, or any right, title, obligation, or liability accrued, or any proceedings taken thereunder, or under the rules of any society which has been certified thereunder: provided that with regard to such subsisting societies as may not obtain certificates of incorporation under this Act, all things required to be done by or sent to the barrister or advocate and the clerk of the peace under the provisions of the said repealed Act shall be done by or sent to the registrar.

Societies established under the Act of 1836 how affected by the Act of 1874.

The following appears to be the effect of this and the next section, as amended by the Act of 1875. Every society in existence on November 2nd, 1874, and certified under the Act of 1836 (the Act here referred to), may adopt either of two courses. It may (1) obtain a certificate of incorporation under the Act of 1874; it will then be deemed to be a society under that Act, and its rules will, so far as they are not contrary to any express provisions of the Act, continue in force until altered or rescinded; or (2) it may prefer to remain under the old law, in which case it will simply *not* obtain a certificate of incorporation, and the only sections of the Act of 1874 that will affect it (excepting those that relate to the mode of obtaining a certificate of incorporation) will be sects. 7, 10, 35, 36 and 39. It should be remembered however, that owing to an error that crept into the next section

Sect. 7. of this Act all societies the rules of which had been certified under the repealed Act were for a few months brought within this Act even though they had not been incorporated; see sect. 8 and note thereto, *infra*.

Societies under former Act to continue.

8. *Every society the rules of which have been certified under the said repealed Act shall be deemed to be a society under this Act, and may obtain a certificate of incorporation under this Act, and thereupon its rules shall, so far as the same are not contrary to any express provisions of this Act, continue in force until altered or rescinded as hereinafter mentioned.*

This section, it will be observed, provides that every society certified under the Act of 1836 shall be deemed to be a society under the present Act *whether it has obtained a certificate of incorporation or not*, which was never intended. The mistake is said to have arisen from the words "shall be deemed to be a society under this Act" getting accidentally transposed while the bill was in the House of Lords. The section was accordingly repealed as from the 2nd of November, 1874, by the Building Societies Act, 1875, which provides, instead, that from and after the 22nd of April, 1875, every society the rules of which have been certified under the Act of 1836 may obtain a certificate of incorporation under the Act of 1874, *and thereupon* shall be deemed to be a society under that Act; but the repeal of sect. 8 is not to affect any certificate of incorporation given or any other thing done or suffered in pursuance of the section prior to the 22nd of April, 1875. See the Building Societies Act, 1875, 38 Vict. c. 9, s. 1, *infra*, p. 155.

The effect of these sections was considered in some of the cases which arose in the winding-up of the Guardian Permanent Benefit Building Society, which was a society certified under the Act of 1836, but not incorporated under the Act of 1874. The 32nd rule of that society gave the directors a general power of borrowing money as occasion might require, under which they obtained loans from different persons, in some instances with and in others without security, and questions arose as to the position of the persons who had made the advances. In *Calvert's Case*, the loans had been made in June, 1874, and July, 1875. The Vice-Chancellor of the Duchy of Lancaster held that the Acts of 1874 and 1875 did not affect the question at all, and therefore that the lender could not have the benefit of sect. 15 of the former Act; but he decided in her favour on other grounds. The Court of Appeal, on the contrary, held that the rule was altogether void, and that the loan created no debt either at law or in equity, but apparently agreed with the Vice-Chancellor that the Acts of 1874 and 1875 did not affect the question; see *Re Guardian Permanent Benefit Building Society, Calvert's Case*, 23 Ch. D. 440, 445; 52 L. J. Ch. 857; 32 W. R. 73; 48 L. T. 134. On appeal to the House of Lords this decision of the Court of Appeal was reversed, their Lordships holding that the rule was valid, and it therefore became unnecessary to consider the effect of the two Acts of Parliament; see *Agnew* v. *Murray*, 9 App. Cas. 519, 525; 53 L. J. Ch. 745; 33 W. R. 173; 51 L. T. 462, where the loans had been made subsequently to April, 1875; *Brimelow* v. *Murray*, 9 App. Cas. 519, 529; 53 L. J. Ch. 745; 33 W. R. 173; 51 L. T. 462, where the loans had been made in May and June, 1874. These two cases were in substance, though not in form, appeals from the decision in *Calvert's Case*. *Agnew* v. *Murray* raised only the question of the validity of rule 32; *Brimelow* v. *Murray* raised in addition the question of the effect of the Acts of 1874 and 1875, the contention being that the lending was made valid by the former Act (ss. 8, 15) and not invalidated by the latter.

Sect. 8.

In *Hawkins' Case*, 23 Ch. D. 440, which arose in the same winding-up, the loans were made between November 2, 1874, and April 22, 1875, *i.e.* while sect. 8 of the Act of 1874 was in force. It was accordingly argued for the lender that the loans were made under the borrowing powers conferred by that Act, and must therefore be valid on this ground at least. The Vice-Chancellor held that the argument failed because the provisions of sect. 15, sub-sect. 5 of the Act had not been complied with; but the Court of Appeal reversed this decision,

Sect. 8.

being of opinion that the sub-section referred to was only directory, and did not affect the validity of the security.

Incorporation of societies.

9. Every society now subsisting or hereafter established shall, upon receiving a certificate of incorporation under this Act, become a body corporate by its registered name, having perpetual succession, until terminated or dissolved in manner herein provided, and a common seal.

Certificate of incorporation.

As to the mode of applying for a certificate of incorporation, see sect. 12 and note thereto, *infra*, p. 102; and as to the vesting of the property of the society on its incorporation, see sect. 27 and note thereto, *infra*, p. 122. The form of the certificate of incorporation is given in the schedule to the Building Societies Act, 1877, *infra*, p. 160.

Court cannot declare certificate void.

When once the registrar has given his certificate of incorporation the Court has no power to declare it void on the ground that it was irregularly obtained; see *Glover* v. *Giles*, 18 Ch. D. 173; 50 L. J. Ch. 568; 29 W. R. 603; 45 L. T. 344. In that case (in which the society was not a party to the action) Mr. Justice Fry, in delivering judgment, said:—

"It appears to me clear that before the certificate was granted by the registrar it was his duty to satisfy himself whether the application was made by authority of a general meeting of the society specially called for the purpose, and he was at liberty to require the person making the application to verify that authority by a statutory declaration, and, upon this being done, and the certificate being granted according to the terms of the Act, the society became incorporated.

"Now, it is said, I can declare that incorporation to be void, on the ground that no proper meeting was held, and it is said that the meeting which was held on the 10th of April, 1879, was not a proper meeting within the meaning of the 12th section of the Act, because it was not summoned in compliance with certain rules of the society with regard to the summoning of general meetings. In my view, I have

Sect. 9.

no power to inquire into that at all, and I cannot declare the incorporation to be void. The incorporation of persons into bodies corporate is a prerogative of the Crown, and although in this case the prerogative is exercised under certain statutory provisions, the incorporation is none the less an exercise of the prerogative. There is a perfectly well-known method by which an incorporation may be recalled or made void. Moreover, it is competent to proceed by *quo warranto*, and to show that persons who represent themselves as members or officers of a corporation are not so. But it is quite new to me to hear that some of the individual corporators of a corporation can come to this Court and ask to have it declared, as against other members of the corporation, that the incorporation was obtained by fraud or irregularity. And there is in this case, as it appears to me, this further fatal objection, that the declaration that the incorporation is void is sought for in the absence of the corporation itself, which is not made a defendant to this action. I am in effect asked to declare an incorporation void in the absence of the corporation itself, a step which in common fairness it is impossible for me to take."

Penalty for acting without certificate.

If any society formed under the Act after November 2nd, 1874, or any persons representing themselves to be a society under the Act, commence business without first obtaining a certificate of incorporation, they become liable to a penalty not exceeding five pounds; see sect. 43, *infra*, p. 151.

Termination of society.

As to the modes in which a society under the Act may be terminated or dissolved see sect. 32 and note thereto, *infra*, p. 126.

Enrolments to be sent to registrar.

10. On the commencement of this Act all transcripts of the rules of societies certified and enrolled under the said repealed Act which are now filed with the rolls of the sessions of the peace of any county, riding or division, city or borough, liberty or place, shall, on a proper application made for that purpose, be taken off the file and transmitted by the

Sect. 10. clerk of the peace to the registrar, to be by him kept and registered; and upon such registration every such subsisting society shall be entitled to a certificate of incorporation on application to the registrar.

The "said repealed Act" is the Act of 1836, 6 & 7 Will. 4, c. 32. The section does not say by whom the "proper application" should be made, but as a matter of fact it was made by the registrar on the commencement of the Act to the various clerks of the peace and was complied with by most of them (Scratchley & Brabrook on Building Societies, p. 30, note *a*).

Where enrolled transcript of rules not transmitted.

11. Any society now subsisting, the transcript of the rules of which is not transmitted to the registrar by the clerk of the peace, shall, upon furnishing the registrar with a copy of its rules, purporting to be certified or to be a true copy of rules certified by the barrister under the said repealed Act, authenticated by statutory declaration of the secretary or other officer of the society, as the registrar may require, be entitled to a certificate of incorporation, and such copy of rules shall be by him kept and registered.

Certificate of incorporation how to be granted.

12. A certificate of incorporation under this Act shall not be granted to an existing society except upon application to the registrar made by authority of a general meeting of the society specially called for the purpose; and the registrar may require of the person making the application a statutory declaration that such authority was duly given.

Application for certificate

An application for the grant of a certificate of incorporation to a society *in existence on November 2nd*, 1874, can only be made by a person authorized by a general meeting of the society specially called for the purpose. The application must be made in a prescribed form, and must be accompanied by (1) a copy of the rules of the society at the date of the application; (2) a statutory declaration by the applicant, also in a prescribed form. If the registrar on receiving the application for a certificate has not already received the rules from the clerk of the peace he must make application for them to the latter, and if he does not then receive them within seven days he must inform the applicant of the fact. The applicant will then be required to prove that the rules are certified as provided by sect. 11 before the society can be incorporated. See Treasury Regulations, 1884, r. 1, *infra*, p. 164.

Sect. 12. of incorporation:— 1. Where society in existence on November 2nd, 1874:

An application for the grant of a certificate of incorporation to a society *to be established after* November 2nd, 1874, must be in a prescribed form, and must be accompanied by two printed copies of the rules marked and signed in a particular way. See Treasury Regulations, 1884, r. 2, *post*, p. 165.

2. Where society established since November 2nd, 1874.

The Court cannot declare a certificate of incorporation void on the ground that it was irregularly obtained; see *Glover* v. *Giles*, cited in note to sect. 9, *ante*, p. 100.

Avoiding certificate.

As to the certificate of incorporation being evidence, see sect. 20, *post*, p. 115.

Evidence.

A fee of one pound is payable for the certificate of incorporation (Treasury Regulations, 1884, r. 25, *infra*, p. 170).

Fee.

13. Any number of persons may establish a society under this Act, either terminating or permanent, for the purpose of raising by the subscriptions of the members a stock or fund for making advances to members out of the funds of the society upon security of freehold, copyhold, or leasehold estate, by way of mortgage; and any society under this Act shall, so far as is necessary for the said purpose, have power to hold land with the right of foreclosure, and may from time to time raise funds by the issue of shares

Purpose for which societies may be established.

Sect. 13.

of one or more denominations, either paid up in full or to be paid by periodical or other subscriptions, and with or without accumulating interest, and may repay such funds when no longer required for the purposes of the society: provided always, that any land to which any such society may become absolutely entitled by foreclosure, or by surrender, or other extinguishment of the right of redemption, shall as soon afterwards as may be conveniently practicable be sold or converted into money.

The number of persons establishing the society cannot be less than three; see sect. 17, *post*, p. 111.

The general power of a society to hold land is strictly limited by sect. 37, *post*, p. 140.

Limitation of liability of members.

14. The liability of any member of any society under this Act in respect of any share upon which no advance has been made shall be limited to the amount actually paid or in arrear on such share, and in respect of any share upon which an advance has been made shall be limited to the amount payable thereon under any mortgage or other security or under the rules of the society.

Limit of liability cannot be exceeded.

The limit of liability prescribed by this section cannot be exceeded. In a recent case the rules of a society provided that the shares should be of the value of 25*l*. each, payable by certain instalments, and should be treated as paid-up shares when the amounts to be credited to the member had arrived at the full sum of 25*l*. A member took twenty-eight shares on which he obtained an advance of 700*l*. secured by mortgage in the usual way; when he had repaid instalments of principal to the amount of 414*l*. the society was ordered to be wound up. There were no outside creditors. The member having subsequently given notice of withdrawal under the rules, questions arose as to the terms on which he was

Sect. 14.

entitled to withdraw. The Lord Chancellor (Earl of Selborne) in giving judgment in favour of the member said :—

"Then the next thing which I observe (and it is so far common to both classes of members) is that this is a society in which the liability of each member is strictly limited in point of amount. The rules say that the shares shall be of the value of 25*l*. each, payable by certain instalments; and under the 5th rule they are to be treated as paid-up shares when the amounts to be credited to the member have arrived at the full sum of 25*l*. If there were nothing but the rules, I should say that this is a clear case of a liability limited to the amount of 25*l*. per share. But over and above the rules the Act of 1874, under which the society is governed, says expressly, 'the liability of any member of any society under this Act in respect of any share upon which no advance has been made, shall be limited to the amount actually paid or in arrear on such share.' In favour, therefore, of the unadvanced member, the statute reduces the liability to a lower point than the full 25*l*.—he is only to be liable (which I think means either to creditors or to anybody else) for that which is actually in arrear at the time when the liability is to be enforced, in addition to what he has actually paid. The clause then goes on to state, 'And in respect of any share upon which an advance has been made, the liability of any member shall be limited to the amount payable thereon under any mortgage or other security or under the rules of the society.' Now, under the rules of this society, no share is to be more than 25*l*. The liability, if it depended upon the rules alone, would be only 25*l*. per share, whether it was advanced or unadvanced. The mortgage in this case is given for the full amount which is advanced, namely, 25*l*. upon each of the twenty-eight shares held by the present respondent, making in the whole 700*l*.; and there is nothing whatever in the rules to increase the liability beyond the mortgage. The result is that 25*l*. per share, or 700*l*. in the whole, having been advanced upon these shares, 414*l*. had been actually repaid by the instalments required under the rules before the winding-up order was made, and there remained to be made up in some way or other (that is, there remained payable) 286*l*.

Sect. 14. at that time. . . . Therefore, the maximum sum required in order to reach the full limit of liability in respect of these shares was, at the date of the winding-up order, 286*l*" (*Brownlie* v. *Russell*, 8 App. Cas. 235, 249; 48 L. T. 881; 47 J. P. 757).

Power to borrow money.

15. With respect to the borrowing of money by societies under this Act, the following provisions shall have effect:

(1.) Any society under this Act may receive deposits or loans, at interest, within the limits in this section provided, from the members or other persons, or from corporate bodies, joint stock companies, or from any terminating building society, to be applied to the purposes of the society:

(2.) In a permanent society the total amount so received on deposit or loan and not repaid by the society shall not at any time exceed two-thirds of the amount for the time being secured to the society by mortgages from its members:

(3.) In a terminating society the total amount so received and not repaid may either be a sum not exceeding such two-thirds as aforesaid, or a sum not exceeding twelve months subscriptions on the shares for the time being in force:

(4.) Any deposits with or loans to a society under this Act, made before the commencement of this Act in accordance with its certified rules, are hereby declared to be valid and binding on the society, but no further deposits or loans shall be received by such

Sect. 15.

society, except within the limits provided by this section:

(5.) Every deposit book or acknowledgment or security of any kind given for a deposit or loan by a society shall have printed or written therein or thereon the whole of the fourteenth and fifteenth sections of the present Act.

Limits of borrowing power:— In permanent society; In terminating society.

This section confers upon all societies under the Act a power to borrow money within certain prescribed limits. In the case of a *permanent* society the sum lent must not exceed two-thirds of the amount for the time being secured to the society by mortgages from its members; in the case of a *terminating* society it may be either (1) a sum not exceeding such two-thirds, or (2) a sum not exceeding twelve months' subscriptions on the shares for the time being in force. In the case of a society established after the 2nd of November, 1874, the rules must state whether the society intends to avail itself of the borrowing powers contained in the Act, and if so within what limits, not exceeding those prescribed by the Act (sect. 16, sub-sect. 2); and the same rule applies in the case of a complete alteration of the rules of a society previously established (Treasury Regulations, 1884, r. 5, *infra*, p. 166).

The limit prescribed by the rules cannot be exceeded.

Whichever of the two alternative limits allowed by sect. 15 the rules of a terminating society adopt the directors will be bound by; and if they exceed such limit they will be personally liable for the excess, even though the borrowing be not in excess of the other alternative limit allowed by sect. 15; see sect. 43, *infra*, p. 151; *Looker* v. *Wrigley*, *Leigh* v. *Wrigley*, 9 Q. B. D. 397; 46 J. P. 758.

Overdrawing banking account is borrowing.

A loan to a society from its bankers secured by deposit of title deeds and made by allowing the society to overdraw its account is a "loan" within sect. 15; see *Looker* v. *Wrigley*, *Leigh* v. *Wrigley*; *Cunliffe Brooks & Co.* v. *Blackburn Benefit Building Society*, 9 App. Cas. 857; 54 L. J. Ch. 376; 33 W. R. 309; 52 L. T. 225. A distinction has been taken in some cases between overdrawing a banking

Sect. 15. account, or (as it is called) "taking advantage of banking facilities," and other kinds of borrowing; see *Re Cefn Cilcen Mining Co.*, 7 Eq. 88; 38 L. J. Ch. 78; 19 L. T. 593; *Waterlow v. Sharp*, 8 Eq. 501; 20 L. T. 902, both decided by Stuart, V.-C.; but this distinction is now exploded.

As to loans to an unincorporated society made in the interval between November 2nd, 1874, and April 22nd, 1875, see Building Societies Act, 1874, s. 8; Building Societies Act, 1875, s. 1, *infra*, p. 155; *Re Guardian Permanent Benefit Building Society, Hawkins' Case*, 23 Ch. D. 440, 452; 52 L. J. Ch. 857; 32 W. R. 73; 48 L. T. 134, cited *ante*, p. 99.

Sub-sect. 5 is directory only.

The enactment in the fifth sub-section is directory only, and non-compliance with it does not affect the validity of any security given for a loan (*Re Guardian Society, Hawkins' Case*); the directors, however, or other person or persons in fault become liable to a penalty not exceeding five pounds; see sect. 43, *infra*, p. 151.

Unincorporated society.

As to the power of an unincorporated society to borrow money, see *ante*, p. 21.

Matters to be set forth in the rules.

16. The rules of every society hereafter established under this Act shall set forth—

1. The name of the society, and chief office or place of meeting for the business of the society:
2. The manner in which the stock or funds of the society are to be raised, the terms upon which paid-up shares (if any) are to be issued and repaid, and whether preferential shares are to be issued, and, if so, within what limits, if any; and whether the society intends to avail itself of the borrowing powers contained in this Act, and, if so, within what limits, not exceeding the limits prescribed by this Act:
3. The purposes to which the funds of the society

are to be applied, and the manner in which they are to be invested: Sect. 16.

4. The terms upon which shares may be withdrawn, and upon which mortgages may be redeemed:
5. The manner of altering and rescinding the rules of the society, and of making additional rules:
6. The manner of appointing, remunerating, and removing the board of directors or committee of management, auditors, and other officers:
7. The manner of calling general and special meetings of the members:
8. Provision for an annual or more frequent audit of the accounts and inspection by the auditors of the mortgages and other securities belonging to the society:
9. Whether disputes between the society and any of its members, or any person claiming by or through any member, or under the rules, shall be settled by reference to the Court, or to the registrar, or to arbitration:
10. Provision for the device, custody, and use of the seal of the society, which shall in all cases bear the registered name thereof:
11. Provision for the custody of the mortgage deeds and other securities belonging to the society:
12. The powers and duties of the board of directors or committee of management and other officers:
13. The fines and forfeitures to be imposed on members of the society:
14. The manner in which the society, whether ter-

Sect. 16.

minating or permanent, shall be terminated or dissolved.

Alteration of rules.

On a complete alteration of the rules of any society under this Act the registrar is bound to see that the matters mentioned in this section are provided for (Treasury Regulations, 1884, r. 5, *infra*, p. 166). A "complete alteration" is the substitution of an entire set of rules for an existing set (Treasury Regulations, 1884, r. 3, *infra*, p. 165).

Name of society.

The last words in the name of any society established and incorporated under this Act must be "Building Society," and the registrar may refuse to allow the insertion in the name of any society about to be established and applying for incorporation of any words implying that the society is other than a building society (Treasury Regulations, 1884, r. 7, *infra*, p. 166).

No society can be registered in a name identical with or closely resembling that of a subsisting society, unless the latter is being terminated or dissolved and consents to such registration: see sect. 17, *infra*, p. 111.

Change of name.

As to the power of a society to change its name, see sect. 22 and note thereto, *infra*, p. 116.

Change of chief office.

A society may change its chief office: see the Building Societies Act, 1877, s. 2, *infra*, p. 157.

Borrowing powers.

The limits of the borrowing powers of a society under the Act are those fixed by sect. 15. In the case of a *permanent* society the rules can only prescribe one limit, viz. two-thirds of the amount for the time being secured to the society by mortgages from its members (sect. 15, sub-s. 2); in the case of a *terminating* society they may prescribe *one of two* limits, viz. either of those mentioned in sect. 15, sub-s. 3; but whichever limit the rules adopt the directors must observe: see *Looker* v. *Wrigley*, *Leigh* v. *Wrigley*, 9 Q. B. D. 397; 46 J. P. 759, cited in note to sect. 15, *supra*, p. 107.

Investment of surplus funds.

As to the investment of surplus funds of the society, see sect. 25, *infra*, p. 120.

Alteration of rules.

As to the power of a society to alter its rules, see sect. 18 and note thereto, *infra*, p. 112.

Settlement of disputes.

As to the settlement of disputes between the society and a

member or any person claiming under a member, see sects. 34, 35 and 36, and note to sect. 34, *infra*, pp. 134—140. Sect. 16.

Termination of society.

As to the proceedings necessary for the termination or dissolution of a society under the Act, see sect. 32 and notes thereto, *infra*, p. 126.

Rules to be made.

17. The persons intending to establish a society under this Act shall transmit to the registrar two copies of the rules agreed upon by them for the government of the society, signed by three of such persons and by the intended secretary or other officer; and the registrar, if he find that the rules contain all the provisions set forth in section sixteen of this Act, and that they are in conformity with this Act, shall return one copy of the rules to the secretary or other officer of the society, with a certificate of incorporation, and shall retain and register the other copy; provided that no society shall be registered under this Act in a name identical with that in which a subsisting society is already registered, or so nearly resembling the same as to be calculated to deceive, unless such subsisting society is in course of being terminated or dissolved, and consents to such registration. The society shall supply to any person requiring the same a complete printed copy of the rules, with a copy of the certificate of incorporation appended thereto, and shall be entitled to charge for every such printed copy of rules a sum not exceeding one shilling.

Registration of rules.

Certificate of incorporation.

The form of the certificate of incorporation is given in the schedule to the Building Societies Act, 1877, *infra*, p. 160. See also as to the grant of the certificate s. 12 and note thereto, *supra*, p. 102.

Name in which society

The restriction in this section as to the name in which a society may be registered is similar to that contained in

Sect. 17.

may be registered.

s. 20 of the Companies Act, 1862. In the following cases injunctions to restrain the defendants from using the name they had adopted, on account of its similarity to that of the plaintiffs, were refused: *Colonial Life Assurance Co.* v. *Home and Colonial Assurance Co. Limited*, 33 Beav. 548; 33 L. J. Ch. 741; 10 Jur. N. S. 967; 12 W. R. 783; 10 L. T. 448; *London Assurance* v. *London and Westminster Assurance Corporation, Limited*, 32 L. J. Ch. 664; 9 Jur. N. S. 843; *London and Provincial Law Assurance Society* v. *London and Provincial Joint Stock Life Assurance Co.*, 17 L. J. Ch. 37; *Merchant Banking Co. of London* v. *Merchants' Joint Stock Bank*, 9 Ch. D. 560; 47 L. J. Ch. 828; 26 W. R. 847; *London and County Banking Co.* v. *Capital and Counties Bank*, 9 Ch. D. p. 567; *Australian Mortgage Land and Finance Co.* v. *Australian and New Zealand Mortgage Co.*, W. N. (1880), 6.

On the other hand an injunction was granted on this ground in *Accident Insurance Co.* v. *Accident Disease and General Insurance Corporation*, W. N. (1884), 176; and would have been granted in *Guardian Fire and Life Assurance Co.* v. *Guardian and General Insurance Co. Limited*, 50 L. J. Ch. 253; 43 L. T. 791, had not the defendants agreed to change their name.

Where a trade union divided into two sections and each applied to register in the name which the society had always gone by, the registrar was held to have acted rightly in refusing to register either (*R.* v. *The Registrar of Friendly Societies*, L. R. 7 Q. B. 741; 41 L. J. Q. B. 366; 27 L. T. 229).

Change of name.

As to the power of a society to change its name, see sect. 22 and note thereto, *infra*, p. 116.

Alteration of rules.

18. Any society under this Act, certified previously to the passing of this Act, may alter or rescind any rule or make any additional rule by the vote of three-fourths of the members present at a special meeting called for the purpose, of which meeting notice, specifying the proposed alteration, rescission, or addition shall be given to the members in the manner provided by the rules of the society, or in the absence of such rules by letters sent through the post seven days previous to such meeting; and any society hereafter established may alter or rescind any rule, or make an additional rule, in the manner its rules direct; and every society under this Act altering or rescinding any rule, or making an additional rule, shall forward two copies of every resolution for rescission of a rule, and of every alteration of or addition to its rules, signed by three members and the secretary, and a statutory declaration of an officer of the society that the provisions of this section have been complied with, to the registrar, who, if he find that such alteration, addition, or rescission is in conformity with this Act, shall return one of the copies to the secretary or other officer of the society with a certificate of registration, and retain and register the other copy. **Sect. 18.**

This section it will be observed divides itself into three parts. First, it provides how a society under the Act *but certified previously to the passing thereof* may alter its rules. Secondly, it provides how a society *established after* the passing of the Act may alter its rules. Thirdly, it directs that *every society under the Act*, whenever established, must on altering or adding to its rules send certain documents to the registrar in order that the alteration may be registered. The certificate of registration of an alteration of rules is in the form given in the schedule to the Building Societies Act, 1877, *infra*, p. 160.

Partial and complete alteration.

An alteration of the rules of a society may be either (1) a partial alteration; or (2) a complete alteration. For the difference between them and the mode in which application is made to register an alteration of each kind, see Treasury Regulations, 1884, rr. 3—6, *infra*, p. 165.

Sect. 18.

"Special meeting." As to the meaning of "a special meeting" see *Cutbill* v. *Kingdom*, 1 Ex. 494; 17 L. J. Ex. 177, cited *ante*, p. 50.

Change of chief office. A society may change its chief office without any alteration of rule being necessary; but notice of the change must be given to the registrar; see Building Societies Act, 1877, s. 2, *infra*, p. 157. His certificate of the change is given in the form prescribed by the schedule to that Act.

Fee. The fee for the certificate of registry of an alteration of rules is ten shillings (Treasury Regulations, 1884, r. 25, *infra*, p. 170).

Sinclair v. *Mercantile Building Society.* By the rules of a building society prior to January 1882 unadvanced members were entitled on withdrawal to receive back all instalments paid by them to the society with interest at 4 per cent., but without receiving any of the profits which had been allocated to their shares. In January 1882 the society passed the following rules :—"15. Members may withdraw their shares on which no advances have been granted, with one half of the profits allocated thereon till the 31st day of January preceding repayment, and interest on said instalments for the period between the last-named date and said repayment, at a rate per annum equal to one-half of the profits allocated for the previous financial year, on giving one month's written notice to the manager. . . . Such repayments to withdrawing members holding shares subscribed for prior to 31st January 1881 shall be under deduction of 15 per cent. of the instalments due on, and the profits allocated to, said shares as at last-named date." "17. The books are to be balanced and the profits or losses declared at the end of January in each year. At the close of the years during which there have been profits declared, 5 per cent. thereof shall be carried to the reserve account to meet contingent losses, and the balance allocated amongst the shares in proportion to the instalments due thereon, each member's profit being credited to his account and at the end of his pass-book. At the close of the year during which there have been losses declared, these shall be allocated amongst the shares, each member's loss being debited to his account, and at the end of his pass-book, in the proportion aforesaid." A shareholder who had been a member since 1874, in March 1882 gave notice of withdrawal under the old rules, maintaining that the new rules 15 and 17 were *ultra vires*. The Court of Session held that under the circumstances the member was barred by acquiescence from disputing the validity of r. 15, and that r. 17 was not *ultra vires* (*Sinclair* v. *Mercantile Building Investment Society*, 12 R. 1243; 22 Sc. L. R. 820).

Sect. 18.

19. Any society under this Act, in a schedule to its rules, may describe the forms of conveyance, mortgage, transfer, agreement, bond, security for deposit or loan, or other instrument necessary for carrying its purposes into execution.

Rules may be made to provide forms of conveyance, &c.

Forms of the bond to be given by the officers of the society under sect. 23, and of the statutory receipt under sect. 42, are given in the schedule to the Act, *infra*, p. 152. Forms of various certificates to be given by the registrar are contained in the schedule to the Act of 1877, *infra*, p. 160; and various other forms are appended to the Treasury Regulations, 1884, *infra*, p. 173.

Forms.

As to mortgages to building societies, see *ante*, p. 38 *et seq*.

Mortgages.

20. Any certificate of incorporation or of registration, or other document relating to a society under this Act, purporting to be signed by the registrar, shall, in the absence of any evidence to the contrary, be received by the Court, and by all Courts of law and equity and elsewhere, without proof of the signature; and a printed copy of the rules of a society, certified by the secretary or other officer of the society to be a true copy of its registered rules, shall, in the absence of any evidence to the contrary, be received as evidence of the rules.

Evidence of registration.

Sect. 39 of the Friendly Societies Act, 1875, 38 & 39 Vict.

Friendly Societies

Sect. 20.

Act, 1875, s. 39.

c. 60, provides that every instrument or document, copy or extract of an instrument or document, bearing the seal or stamp of the Central Office, shall be received in evidence without further proof; and that every document purporting to be signed by the chief or any assistant registrar shall, in the absence of any evidence to the contrary, be received in evidence without proof of the signature. And rule 26 of the Treasury Regulations, 1884 (*infra*, p. 172), provides that every document under the Building Societies Acts bearing the seal of the Central Office for registry of Friendly Societies, or the signature of the Assistant-Registrar of Friendly Societies for Scotland or Ireland, as the case may require, shall be deemed to be duly authenticated for the purposes of those Acts and the regulations made thereunder.

"The Court." For the definition of "the Court" see sect. 4 of the Act, *supra*, p. 96.

Rules to be binding on members and others.

21. The rules of a society under this Act shall be binding on the several members and officers of the society, and on all persons claiming on account of a member, or under the rules, all of whom shall be deemed and taken to have full notice thereof.

Advanced member. An advanced member is not bound by an alteration in the rules made after he has received his advance and executed a mortgage for the amount; see *Smith's Case*, 1 Ch. D. 481; 45 L. J. Ch. 143; 24 W. R. 103, cited *ante*, p. 43, where the society was under the old law.

Change of name.

22. A society under this Act may change its name by resolution of three-fourths of the members present at a meeting called for the purpose, provided that the new name is not identical with that of any society previously registered and still subsisting, or so nearly resembling the same as to be calculated to deceive, unless such subsisting society is in course of being terminated or dissolved, and consents to such registration. Notice of the change of name shall be sent to the registrar and registered by him, and he shall give a certificate of registration. Such change of name shall not affect any right or obligation of the society, or of any member thereof, or other person concerned. Sect. 22.

Identity of name.

As to identity or similarity of names, see note to sect. 17, *ante*, p. 111.

Form of notice.

The notice to be given to the registrar must be in a prescribed form and accompanied by a statutory declaration, also in a prescribed form; and the registrar before issuing a certificate of registration of change of name is bound to ascertain that there is no such identity or resemblance of name as is mentioned in this section; see Treasury Regulations, 1884, r. 8, *infra*, p. 167.

No change of name can be registered unless the new name ends with the words "Building Society"; and the registrar may refuse to allow the retention in the name of any society which seeks to change its name of any words implying that the society is other than a building society (Treasury Regulations, 1884, r. 7, *infra*, p. 166).

Fee.

A fee of ten shillings is payable for the certificate of registry of a change of name (Treasury Regulations, 1884, r. 25, *infra*, p. 171).

Form of certificate.

The certificate of registration of a change of name is in the form given in the schedule to the Building Societies Act, 1877, *infra*, p. 160.

Officers to give security.

23. Every officer of a society under this Act having the receipt or charge of any money belonging to the society shall, before taking upon himself the execution of his office, become bound with one sufficient surety at the least, in a bond according to the form set forth in the schedule to this Act, or give the security of a guarantee society, or such other security

Sect. 23. as the society direct, in such sum as the society require, conditioned for rendering a just and true account of all moneys received and paid by him on account of the society, and for payment of all sums of money due from him to the society, at such times as its rules appoint, or as the society require him to do so.

Form of bond. For the form of bond, see *post*, p. 152.

Remuneration of officers. In the absence of a special contract the officers of a society can only look to the funds of the society for their remuneration, and if the funds fail the officers must remain unpaid; see *Alexander* v. *Worman*, 6 H. & N. 100; 30 L. J. Ex. 198; 3 L. T. 477; 25 J. P. 312, cited *ante*, p. 52.

Liability of officers. As to the liability of officers generally, see *ante*, pp. 62—66.

Officers to account. **24.** Every such officer, his executors or administrators, shall, upon demand made, or notice in writing given or left at his last or usual place of residence, give in his account as may be required by the board of directors or committee of management of the society, to be examined and allowed or disallowed by them, and shall, on the like demand or notice, pay over all the moneys remaining in his hands, and deliver all securities and effects, books, papers, and property of the society in his hands or custody, to such person as the society appoint; and in case of any neglect or refusal to deliver such account, or to pay over such moneys, or to deliver such securities and effects, books, papers, and property, in manner aforesaid, the society may sue upon the bond, or may apply to the Court, who may proceed thereupon in a summary way, and make such order thereon as to the Court in its discretion shall seem just, which order shall be final and conclusive.

Remedy of the society The remedy of the society against an officer under this rule is twofold. It may either (1) sue him on his bond; or (2) apply (in England) to the County Court of the district in which the chief office or place of meeting for the business of the society is situated (sect. 4, *ante*, p. 96), and the Court may proceed in a summary way and make such order as it thinks just, from which order there will be no appeal. **Sect. 24.** against its officers.

1. An action on the bond may be brought in any Court apparently. The society will sue in its registered name (sects. 9, 27), and the proceedings will be the same in all respects as in any other action of a similar nature. Suing on the bond.

2. If the society prefers to apply to the County Court the proceeding must, it is conceived, be by plaint or petition; see Ord. XL of the County Court Rules, 1875, which provides that where by any Act *not before mentioned in the rules* proceedings are directed to be taken in the County Court, they shall be commenced by plaint or petition, and the previous rules, so far as applicable, shall apply to such proceedings. A difficulty is caused by the fact that the Building Societies Act, 1874, *is* previously mentioned in the rules, viz. in Ord. XXXIX; but as this order relates only to winding-up, and the rules contain no other direction whatever as to proceedings under the Building Societies Act, it would seem that all proceedings under the Act, except proceedings for winding-up, must be governed by Ord. XL. Assuming this to be so, then the proceedings under the plaint or petition will be similar to those in other cases, and the general rules and practice of the County Court as laid down by the Rules of 1875 will apply. Proceeding in County Court.

It may be observed that sect. 20 of the Friendly Societies Act, 1875, 38 & 39 Vict. c. 60, contains very similar provisions to those in sects. 23 and 24 of this Act. Proceedings under this section so far as they differ from ordinary County Court practice are regulated by Ord. XXXV of the County Court Rules, 1875; and Mr. Pitt-Lewis considers that in proceedings against officers under the Building Societies Act it would be prudent to follow the rules laid down by Ord. XXXV with respect to proceedings against officers of friendly societies; see Pitt-Lewis on County Courts, 2nd ed. p. 1063.

Sect. 24.

Scotland and Ireland.

As to the meaning of "the Court" in Scotland or Ireland, see sect. 4, *ante*, p. 96.

Dismissed officer.

An officer who has been dismissed may be ordered forthwith to deliver up property belonging to the society without regard to the question whether the dismissal was wrongful or not, and from such an order there is no appeal (*First Edinburgh &c. Starr-Bowkett Building Society* v. *Munro*, 11 R. 5).

Investment of surplus funds.

25. Any society under this Act may from time to time, as the rules permit, invest any portion of the funds of the society, not immediately required for its purposes, upon real or leasehold securities, or in the public funds, or in or upon any parliamentary stock or securities, or in or upon any stock or securities payment of the interest on which is guaranteed by authority of parliament, or in the case of terminating societies, with other societies under this Act; and for the purpose of investments in the public funds or upon security of copyhold or customary estate, the society, or the board of directors or committee of management thereof, may from time to time appoint and remove trustees.

Unauthorized investment.

In a late case the trustees of a friendly society advanced 300*l*. on a joint and several promissory note, this not being one of the modes of investment authorized by the Friendly Societies Act, 1875. The Court of Appeal held, reversing the decision of Fry, J., that though the loan was unauthorized, and was a breach of trust, there was nothing illegal in the transaction so as to prevent the trustees from recovering the money against the estate of one of the makers of the note who had died (*Re Coltman, Coltman* v. *Coltman*, 19 Ch. D. 64; 51 L. J. Ch. 3; 30 W. R. 342; 45 L. T. 392); see also *Hardy* v. *Metropolitan Land and Finance Co.*, 7 Ch. 427; 41 L. J. Ch. 257; 20 W. R. 425; 26 L. T. 407, reversing the decision of Romilly, M. R., 12 Eq. 386, cited *ante*, p. 56.

Sect. 26.

When trustees are absent, &c. registrars may order stock to be transferred.

26. When any person in whose name any stock transferable at the Bank of England or Bank of Ireland is standing, either jointly with another or others, or solely, as a trustee for any society under this Act, is absent from England or Ireland respectively, or becomes bankrupt, or files any petition or executes any deed for liquidation of his affairs by assignment or arrangement, or for composition with his creditors, or becomes a lunatic, or is dead, or if it be unknown whether such person is living or dead, the registrar, on application in writing from the secretary or other officer of the society and three members of the board of directors or committee of management thereof, and on proof satisfactory to him, may direct the transfer of the stock into the name of any other person or persons as trustee or trustees for the society; and such transfer shall be made by the surviving or continuing trustee or trustees, and if there be no such trustee, or if such trustee or trustees shall refuse or be unable to make such transfer, and the registrar shall so direct, then by the accountant general or deputy or assistant accountant general of the Bank of England or Bank of Ireland, as the case may be; and the Governors and Companies of the Bank of England and Bank of Ireland respectively are hereby indemnified for anything done by them or any of their officers in pursuance of this section against any claim or demand of any person injuriously affected thereby.

Application to transfer stock.

An application to the registrar to direct a transfer of stock must be made in a prescribed form, and must be accompanied by a statutory declaration (also in a prescribed form) and by the certificate of the stock in respect of which the application

Sect. 26. is made. A copy of the proposed application and declaration must be submitted to the registrar before the application is made; and the registrar, before directing a transfer, may require further proof of any statement in the application. The registrar gives his direction in a specified form so framed as to suit the particular circumstances of the case; and the direction is then registered and delivered to the applicants endorsed with the word "Registered" and duly authenticated; see Treasury Regulations, 1884, rr. 9—12, 26, *infra*, pp. 167, 172.

Fee. A fee of one pound is payable on a direction to transfer stock (Treasury Regulations, 1884, r. 25, *infra*, p. 171).

Property of the society vested without conveyance.

27. All rights of action and other rights, and all estates and interests in real and personal estate whatsoever, *now* belonging to or held in trust for any society certified under the said repealed Act, shall, on the incorporation of the society under this Act, vest in the society without any conveyance or assignment whatsoever, save and except in the case of stocks and securities in the public funds of Great Britain and Ireland, and estates in copyhold or customary hereditaments, the title to which cannot be transferred without admittance.

Vesting of property of society on incorporation.

This section is to be read as if the word "now" were omitted; see the Building Societies Act, 1877, s. 3, *infra*, p. 158; and see also sect. 4 of that Act and note thereto, *infra*, p. 158.

Conveyance of property on union or transfer.

As to the conveyance of the property of a society uniting with or transferring its engagements to another society under sect. 33, see sect. 5 of the Act of 1877, *infra*, p. 159.

As to copyholds.

28. Where any society under this Act is entitled in equity to any hereditaments of copyhold or customary tenure by way of mortgage, the lord of the manor of which the same are held shall from time to time, if required by the society, admit such persons, not more than three, as the society appoints, to be trustees on its behalf as tenants in respect of such hereditaments, on payment of the usual fines, fees, and other dues payable on the admission of a single tenant, or may admit the society as tenant in respect of the same, on payment of such special fine, or compensation in lieu of fine, and fees as may be agreed upon.

Sect. 28.

Mortgages of copyholds.

It is not the practice for a mortgagee of copyholds to be admitted in the first instance, as upon admittance a fine becomes due to the lord. The mortgagee, however, incurs no risk by adopting this course, as the admittance when made relates back to the surrender, and he cannot therefore be prejudiced by the previous admittance of any subsequent surrenderee.

Payment of sums not exceeding 50*l.* when members or depositors die intestate.

29. If any member of or depositor with a society under this Act having in the funds thereof a sum of money not exceeding fifty pounds shall die intestate, then the amount due may be paid to the person who shall appear to the directors or committee of management of the society to be entitled under the Statute of Distributions to receive the same, without taking out letters of administration, upon the society receiving satisfactory evidence of death and a statutory declaration that the member or depositor died intestate, and that the person so claiming is entitled as aforesaid: Provided that whenever the society after the decease of any member or depositor has paid any such sum of money to the person who at the time appeared to be entitled to the effects of the deceased under the belief that he had died intestate

Payment to persons appearing to be next of kin declared valid.

Sect. 29. the payment shall be valid and effectual with respect to any demand from any other person as next of kin or as the lawful representative of such deceased member or depositor against the funds of the society, but nevertheless such next of kin or representative shall have his lawful remedy for the amount of such payment as aforesaid against the person who has received the same.

The provisions of this section, it will be observed, are not limited to members; they extend also to the case of any *depositor* who dies intestate having in the funds of the society a sum not exceeding fifty pounds.

Provision for the case of a member dying intestate leaving an infant heir.

30. Whenever a member of a society under this Act, having executed a mortgage to the society, shall die intestate, leaving an infant heir or infant coheiress, it shall be lawful for the said society, after selling the premises so mortgaged to them, to pay to the administrator or administratrix of the deceased member any money, to the amount of one hundred and fifty pounds, which shall remain in the hands of the said society after paying the amount due to the society and the costs and expenses of the sale, without being required to pay the same into the Post Office Savings Bank, as provided by the Trustees Relief Act, and the Acts amending or extending the same. The said sum of one hundred and fifty pounds to be considered as personal estate, and liable to duty accordingly.

This section applies only where the four following conditions are fulfilled:—(1) The deceased member must have executed a mortgage to the society; (2) he must have died intestate; (3) his heir must be an infant; (4) the surplus sale monies must not exceed 150*l*. In such a case the society must pay the administrator instead of paying the money into Court; and if they perversely adopted the latter course they would no doubt have to pay the costs of getting the money out again.

Sect. 30.

Punishment of fraud in withholding money, &c.

31. If any person whosoever, by false representation or imposition, obtains possession of any monies, securities, books, papers, or other effects of a society under this Act, or, having the same in his possession, withholds or misapplies the same, or wilfully applies any part thereof to purposes other than those expressed or directed in the rules of the society and authorized by this Act, he shall be liable on summary conviction to a penalty not exceeding twenty pounds, with costs not exceeding twenty shillings, and to be ordered to deliver up to the society all such monies, securities, books, papers, or other effects to* the society, and to repay the amount of money applied improperly, and in default of such delivery of effects, or repayment of such amount of money, or payment of such penalty and costs aforesaid, to be imprisoned, with or without hard labour, for any time not exceeding three months; but nothing herein contained shall prevent any such person from being proceeded against by way of indictment if a conviction has not been previously obtained against him for the same offence under the provisions of this Act.

* Qy. "of."

"Withholds or misapplies."

In a case under the Friendly Societies Act, 1855, 18 & 19 Vict. c. 63, s. 24, which contained provisions very similar to those in the text, it was held that to render the treasurer of a society liable to penalties for "withholding or misapplying" monies of the society which had come to his hands as treasurer it must be shown that he had been guilty of some fraud or misrepresentation, and that mere inability to pay over the

Sect. 31.

money to the trustees was not enough (*Barrett* v. *Markham*, L. R. 7 C. P. 405; 41 L. J. M. C. 118; 27 L. T. 313; 36 J. P. 535); and see also *Ex parte O'Donnell*, L. R. 1 Q. B. 274; 35 L. J. M. C. 99; 14 W. R. 83; 30 J. P. 279.

As to procedure, see the Summary Jurisdiction Act, 1879, 42 & 43 Vict. c. 49.

Proceedings necessary for the termination or dissolution of a society.

32. A society under this Act may terminate or be dissolved—

1. Upon the happening of any event declared by its rules to be the termination of the society.
2. By dissolution in manner prescribed by its rules.
3. By dissolution with the consent of three-fourths of the members, holding not less than two-thirds of the number of shares in the society, testified by their signatures to the instrument of dissolution. The instrument of dissolution shall set forth—
    (*a*.) the liabilities and assets of the society in detail;
    (*b*.) the number of members, and the amount standing to their credit in the books of the society;
    (*c*.) the claims of depositors and other creditors, and the provision to be made for their payment;
    (*d*.) the intended appropriation or division of the funds and property of the society;
    (*e*.) the names of one or more persons to be appointed trustees for the special purpose, and their remuneration.

Alterations in the instrument of dissolution may

Sect. 32.

be made with the like consent, testified in the same manner. The instrument of dissolution and all alterations therein shall be registered in the manner provided for the registration of rules, and shall be binding upon all the members of the society.

4. By winding-up, either voluntarily under the supervision of the Court or by the Court, if the Court shall so order, on the petition of any member authorized by three-fourths of the members present at a general meeting of the society specially called for the purpose to present the same on behalf of the society, or on the petition of any judgment creditor for not less than fifty pounds, but not otherwise. General orders for regulating the proceedings of the Court under this section may be from time to time made by the authority for the time being empowered to make general orders for the Court.

Notice of the commencement and termination of every dissolution or winding-up shall be sent to the registrar and registered by him.

Modes in which society may come to an end.

This section enumerates four ways in which a society under the Act, *i.e.* a society originally constituted under the Act or a society formed under the Act of 1836 but incorporated under the present Act—may come to an end:—

Termination.

1. The society may be determined by the happening of any event which its rules declare shall be the termination of the society. This applies only to the case of a terminating society; see sect. 5, *ante*, p. 96.

Dissolution in manner prescribed

2. The society may be dissolved in the manner prescribed by its rules; and by sect. 16, sub-sect. 14, *ante*, p. 109, the rules of every society *must* set forth the manner in which the

Sect. 32. by rules.

society, whether terminating or permanent, is to be terminated or dissolved. In a dissolution of this kind no instrument of dissolution is required, but notice in duplicate of the commencement and termination of the dissolution must be given to the registrar, who will return one copy of each to the society, endorsed with the word "Registered" and duly authenticated (Treasury Regulations, 1884, rr. 16, 17, 26, *infra*, pp. 168, 172). A fee of two shillings and sixpence is payable for registering a notice of the commencement or termination of a dissolution (Treasury Regulations, 1884, r. 25, *infra*, p. 171).

Dissolution by instrument of dissolution.

3. The society may be dissolved by an instrument of dissolution signed by three-fourths of the members holding not less than two-thirds of the whole number of shares in the society. The instrument of dissolution must be in a prescribed form, and must be sent to the registrar signed in duplicate and accompanied by a statutory declaration; and the registrar will return one of the duplicates to the society with a certificate of registration (Treasury Regulations, 1884, rr. 13, 14, *infra*, p. 168).

Statement of liabilities and assets.

As to what is a sufficient statement in the instrument of dissolution of the liabilities and assets of the society, see *Glover* v. *Giles*, 18 Ch. D. 173; 50 L. J. Ch. 568; 29 W. R. 603; 45 L. T. 344.

Alterations in instrument of dissolution.

Alterations (which will require registration) may be made in the instrument of dissolution in the manner mentioned in the section; and all alterations must be signed, declared to and certified in the same way as the original instrument; see Treasury Regulations, 1884, r. 15, *infra*, p. 168.

Notice.

Notice in duplicate of the termination of the dissolution must be given to the registrar, who will return one copy to the society endorsed with the word "Registered," and duly authenticated (Treasury Regulations, 1884, r. 17, *infra*, p. 169).

Fee.

A fee of ten shillings is payable for the certificate of registry of an instrument of dissolution, or any alteration therein; and a fee of two shillings and sixpence for registry of notice of the termination of the dissolution (Treasury Regulations, 1884, r. 25, *infra*, p. 171).

Sect. 32.

Winding-up.

4. The remaining method of putting an end to a society under the Act is by winding-up, and sub-sect. 4 is worded in such a way as to cause some difficulty on this point. In the first place, does it specify *three* ways of winding-up—(1) voluntary, (2) under supervision, and (3) compulsory; or only *two*—(1) under supervision, (2) compulsory? Mr. Buckley takes one view, Mr. Pitt-Lewis the other; see Buckley on the Companies Acts, 4th ed. p. 203; Pitt-Lewis on County Courts, 2nd ed. p. 1067. It is submitted that the true construction of the sub-section is this; it contemplates only two ways of winding-up—(1) compulsory, and (2) under supervision. In either case an order of the Court is requisite, and such order can only be made either on the petition of a member specially authorized by the society, or of a *judgment* creditor for not less than fifty pounds. The subsection does not contemplate a purely voluntary winding-up; if the society wishes to settle its affairs without the interference of the Court it must proceed in the manner pointed out by the previous sub-sections. See Treasury Regulations, 1884, rr. 13—17a, *infra*, p. 168.

Court.

In the next place, with regard to the mode of proceeding it will be remembered that sect. 4 defines the Court to mean in England the County Court of the district in which the chief office or place of meeting for the business of the society is situate. The Act itself does not specify any mode of procedure, but authorizes (sect. 32, sub-sect. 4) the making of general orders for regulating the proceedings of the Court under sect. 32. Accordingly Ord. XXXIX of the County Court Rules, 1875, provides as follows:—

County Court Rules, 1875, Ord. XXXIX.

"The general orders, rules, and forms of the Chancery Division of the High Court of Justice regulating for the time being the mode of proceeding under 'The Companies Acts, 1862 and 1867,' shall be the orders, rules, and forms in all proceedings in the County Courts for the winding-up of a society registered under 'The Industrial and Provident Societies Act, 1862,' 'The Building Societies Act, 1874,' or for the winding-up of a company under 'The Companies Acts, 1862 and 1867,' so far as the same are applicable. Provided that where it shall appear to the Court inconve-

Sect. 32. nient that the Bank of England should be the bank used for the purposes mentioned in the Order and Rules, it shall be competent for the Court to name some bank to be used in lieu of the Bank of England."

Jones v. Swansea, &c. Building Society. The effect of this provision was considered in *Jones* v. *Swansea Cambrian Benefit Building Society*, 29 W. R. 382; S.C. *nom. Andrew* v. *Swansea Cambrian Benefit Building Society*, 50 L. J. Q. B. 428; 44 L. T. 106; 45 J. P. 507. In that case the plaintiff claimed to be a mortgagee of the society and brought an action for foreclosure. While the action was pending a winding-up order was made by the county court judge. The plaintiff applied for leave to continue his action, which the judge refused; and an appeal by the plaintiff to a Divisional Court (Denman and Lindley, JJ.) was dismissed. In the course of his judgment, Lindley, J., said:—

"Now, the first question is whether the Companies Act of 1862 applies at all. If it does not, then the logical consequence would be that there was no necessity for going to the County Court judge to stay the action. He had no right to entertain the case, and leave to appeal would not be competent to him, either to grant or refuse. They would have gone to the wrong place; an appeal in that point of view would be wrong. Now, is that so? A question arises which is not altogether free from difficulty, in consequence of the mode in which the 32nd section of 37 & 38 Vict. c. 42, is worded. Thus it says, 'A society may terminate or be dissolved,' among other things, and other ways, in this way (sub-section 4), by winding-up either voluntarily under the supervision of the Court, or by the Court—under the Act which I am now reading, 'the Court,' meaning the County Court, that is clear. Therefore, it may be by winding-up voluntarily under the supervision of the Court, or by the Court, if the Court shall so order by a petition—I need not read that. There are 'general orders' for regulating the proceedings of the Court which, under this order, may from time to time be made. Nothing is found under the terms of that section, either incorporating or referring to, or in any way embodying what I may refer to as the winding-up provisions of the Companies Acts of 1862 and 1867. Perhaps it is a pity that was not done, as it would have saved all controversy. The expression which is wanted there to make the thing plain is found in the Industrial [and] Provident Societies Act, (39 & 40 Vict. c. 45), s. 17, which expressly makes the provisions of the Companies Act of 1862 applicable to them. Whether they thought there had been a slip or blunder I do not know, but at all events it is plain enough that this Building Act has not got that language.

"Therefore, the argument is this: the company is to be wound up by the County Court, and any rules which the County Court may make would be applicable to the winding-up, and the County Court has made rules, and adopts the Orders and Rules in Chancery under the Acts of 1862 and 1867, but the argument is this: the Building Act (37 & 38 Vict.) says nothing at all about the Companies Acts of 1862 and 1867, and does not incorporate them, and, therefore, it is said the Companies Acts of 1862 and 1867 did not apply at all, but all that does apply is the 32nd section of the Building Societies Act, which applies to the Orders and Rules of Chancery made by the Acts of 1862 and 1867. If that argument were to prevail, the consequence would be somewhat curious. The Rules and Orders of Chancery made under the Companies Acts of 1862 and 1867 are utterly unworkable without the Acts themselves; they are based upon those Acts, and the Acts and Orders make a sort of code for winding-up, the one quite unworkable without the other. If you want to wind up a company under the Acts there are certain rules; if you try to do without them, all I can say is, you will soon find you can do nothing of the sort. However, the result is one which is to be arrived at by a proper method of interpretation, and it appears to me the proper interpretation is that pointed to by Mr. Cave. In point of fact, though there are Building Societies Acts passed, building societies can be put under the Acts of 1862 and 1867 by virtue of clauses in those Acts relating to industrial companies; *and the true effect, to my mind, of this 32nd section of the Building Societies Act is simply this, to substitute the County Court for the Court of Chancery.* I think that is the true effect, and it does in effect indirectly do that, although not expressly incorporating

Sect. 32. the winding-up under the Companies Act of 1862; there is no line to be drawn between them. Then it follows, if that is so, that this action is stayed by sect. 87 of the Companies Act, 1862, and that they cannot go on without leave of the County Court judge. They applied for leave, and were refused that leave. Then next, it is said, there is no appeal given, on the ground that there is no appeal from that Court to this; and, secondly, there is no appeal because he has no discretion in the matter.

"As to the point that there is no appeal, I think that is plainly answered by the 43rd section of the Companies Act, 1867. That section was inserted in order to give appeals from the County Court in matters of winding-up to the then Court of Chancery. It had been decided before that there was no appeal to a Court of law from a County Court decision in a winding-up; that will be found in the case of *Henderson* v. *Bamber*, 35 L. J. C. P. 65. That defect was cured by the 43rd section of the Companies Act, 1867, which gave an appeal in winding-up matters to the Court of Chancery, which, in those days, knew much more about those things than the Common Law Courts. Therefore, an appeal lay from them under the 43rd section. The Judicature Act transfers the appeal to us, and, therefore, I feel no difficulty in saying there is an appeal. Then, with respect to its being discretionary, in one sense it is, of course, discretionary; it is not like an order as to costs, and this was so decided by the Court of Chancery itself more than once; and they used to revise and reverse the decisions of the Vice-Chancellor in this very same subject, and several cases may be found. Indeed, I rather think that it is not a new section, but that it is taken from an old section of the Act of 1856, and there are a great number of cases to be found in the books in which orders under this section have been appealed from, and sometimes successfully. It is, therefore, not such a matter of discretion as in other matters from which there is no appeal at all. It appears to me the appeal is competent."

It is clear, therefore, from this decision that all the winding-up provisions of the Companies Acts, 1862 and 1867, as well as the Orders made under those Acts, apply in the case of

Sect. 32.

incorporated building societies, the only difference being that the proceedings take place in the County Court of the district where the society is situate instead of in the Chancery Division of the High Court. In the case of a compulsory winding-up there will be no difficulty. In the case of a winding-up under supervision, however, which necessarily pre-supposes a voluntary liquidation, it must be admitted that it is far from easy to say what is the precise course to be adopted. It is suggested that a possible construction of the Act is that it enables a building society to initiate proceedings for a voluntary liquidation, but only with a view to the presentation of a petition for a supervision order, either by the society or a judgment creditor.

Notice of the commencement and termination of every winding-up, subject to the supervision of the Court, or by the Court, must be given to the registrar in duplicate, and he will return one copy to the society endorsed with the word "Registered," and duly authenticated (Treasury Regulations, 1884, rr. 16a, 17a, *post*, p. 168).

In Scotland there is no difficulty, apparently, in the sheriff making an order to wind up under the supervision of the Court; see for an instance *Scottish Property Investment Company Building Society* v. *Boyd*, 12 R. pp. 129, 131.

It is beyond the scope of this treatise to enter into the general law of winding-up, or the practice of the County Court; they will be found in treatises which are in the hands of every practitioner.

Unincorporated societies.

As to the winding-up of unincorporated societies, see *ante*, p. 28.

Societies may unite with others, or one society may transfer its engagements to another.

33. Two or more societies under this Act may unite and become one society, with or without any dissolution or division of the funds of such societies or either of them, or a society under this Act may transfer its engagements to any other such society, upon such terms as shall be agreed upon by three-fourths of the members (holding not less than two-thirds of the whole number of shares) of each of

Sect. 33. such societies present at general meetings respectively convened for the purpose; but no such transfer shall prejudice any right of any creditor of either society. Notice of every such union or transfer shall be sent to the registrar and registered by him.

Notice of union or transfer.

Notice in duplicate of the proposed union must be given to the registrar, who will return one copy to the united society endorsed with the word "Registered," and duly authenticated; and a similar notice must be given on a transfer of its engagements from one society to another. See Treasury Regulations, 1884, rr. 18, 19, 26, *infra*, p. 169.

Fee.

A fee of ten shillings must be paid for registry of a union or transfer (Treasury Regulations, 1884, r. 25, *infra*, p. 171).

Conveyance of property on union or transfer.

The registration of the notice of union or transfer operates as an effectual conveyance from the uniting societies to the united society, or from the transferring to the transferee society, as the case may be, of the property specified in the instrument of union or transfer, except in the case of public stocks and estates in copyhold and customary hereditaments where admittance is requisite; but no union or transfer will affect the rights of any creditor of any society uniting or transferring its engagements; see Building Societies Act, 1877, s. 5, *infra*, p. 159. It will be observed that the saving of the rights of creditors in that section is worded somewhat differently from the provision to that effect in the text.

Determination of dis- (*Sic.*) arbitration.

34. Where the rules of a society under this Act direct disputes to be referred to arbitration, arbitrators shall be named and elected in the manner such rules provide, or, if there be no such provision, at the first general meeting of the society, none of the said arbitrators being beneficially interested, directly or indirectly, in its funds; of whom a certain number, not less than three, shall be chosen by ballot in each such case of dispute, the number of the said arbitra-

Sect. 34.

tors and mode of ballot being determined by the rules of the society; the names of such arbitrators shall be duly entered in the minute book of the society, and, in case of the death or refusal or neglect of any of the said arbitrators to act, the society, at a general meeting, shall name and elect an arbitrator to act in the place of the arbitrator dying, or refusing or neglecting to act; and whatever award shall be made by the arbitrators or the major part of them, according to the true purport and meaning of the rules of the society, shall determine the dispute; and should either of the parties to the dispute refuse or neglect to comply with or conform to such award within a time to be limited therein, the court, upon good and sufficient proof being adduced of such award having been made, and of the refusal of the party to comply therewith, shall enforce compliance with the same upon the petition of any person concerned. Where the parties to any dispute arising in a society under this Act agree to refer the dispute to the registrar, or where the rules of the society direct disputes to be referred to the registrar, the award of the registrar shall have the same effect as that of arbitrators.

Court may order compliance with the decision of arbitrators.

Determination of disputes by registrar.

This and the two following sections deal with the important question of the settlement of disputes between a society and its members. In the first place it is to be observed that the meaning of the word "disputes" has been the subject of much controversy, and particularly whether it included questions arising out of mortgages made to a society by its members, so as to oust the ordinary jurisdiction of the Courts. In the case of societies under the *old* law it was finally decided by the House of Lords in the case of *Mulkern* v. *Lord*, 4 App. Cas. 182; 48 L. J. Ch. 745; 27 W. R. 510;

Settlement of disputes between society and its members.

Sect. 34. 40 L. T. 594, that a rule to the effect that any dispute between the society and a member should be referred to arbitration did not prevent a member who had executed a mortgage to the society from bringing an action in the Chancery Division for an account and general relief. But the late Master of the Rolls, Sir George Jessel, held that this did not apply in the case of a society under the Act of 1874, and that where the rules of such a society directed a reference of disputes to arbitration the Court had no jurisdiction (*Wright* v. *Monarch Investment Building Society*, 5 Ch. D. 726; 46 L. J. Ch. 649). This decision was followed in the Court of Appeal, under his Lordship's presidency, in *Hack* v. *London Provident Building Society*, 23 Ch. D. 103; 52 L. J. Ch. 541; 31 W. R. 392; 48 L. T. 247; and was finally approved and adopted by the House of Lords (Lords Blackburn and Watson, the Earl of Selborne, L. C., *diss.*) in *Municipal Permanent Investment Building Society* v. *Kent*, 9 App. Cas. 260; 53 L. J. Ch. 290; 32 W. R. 681; 51 L. T. 6; 48 J. P. 532. In consequence of this decision the law was altered by the Building Societies Act, 1884, which provides (sect. 2) that the word "disputes" in the Building Societies Acts, 1874 to 1884, or in the rules of any society thereunder, shall be deemed to refer only to disputes between the society and a member, or any representative of a member in his capacity of a member of the society, *unless by the rules for the time being it shall be otherwise expressly provided:* and, in the absence of such express provision, shall not apply to any dispute between any such society and any member thereof, or any person whatever, as to the construction or effect of any mortgage deed, or any contract contained in any document, other than the rules of the society, and shall not prevent any society, or any member thereof, or any person claiming through or under him, from obtaining in the ordinary course of law any remedy in respect of any such mortgage or other contract to which he or the society would otherwise be by law entitled; but the section contains the usual saving clause. See the section, *infra*, p. 162.

With regard to the mode in which disputes are to be decided, sect. 16, sub-sect. 9 (*ante*, p. 109), provides that the rules of every society established since November 2nd, 1874, must set forth whether disputes between the society and any of its members, or any person claiming by or through any member, or under the rules, shall be settled by reference to the Court, or to the registrar, or to arbitration—"the Court" meaning in England the County Court of the district in which the chief office or place of meeting for the business of the society is situate (sect. 4, *ante*, p. 96). In the case of societies established prior to November 2nd, 1874, the old law required that the rules should specify whether disputes should be referred to justices of the peace or to arbitrators; see *ante*, p. 68. Sect. 34.

Where the rules direct disputes to be referred to arbitration the arbitrators must be chosen in the manner directed by the rules; or, if the rules contain no provision to this effect, then in the manner pointed out in sect. 34. The award of the arbitrators or the majority of them will determine the dispute (sect. 34), and there is no appeal from their decision (sect. 36); but the arbitrators may, on request, state a case for the opinion of the Supreme Court on any question of law, and may make an order for discovery (*ibid.*). For the form of an order for discovery see Treasury Regulations, 1884, r. 23, *infra*, p. 170; a fee of ten shillings is payable for the order (Treasury Regulations, 1884, r. 25, *infra*, p. 171). Reference to arbitration.

The award need not be in any particular form, except that it must limit a time within which it is to be complied with (sect. 34); but the form prescribed by sect. 27 of the Act 10 Geo. 4, c. 56, *ante*, p. 82, may conveniently be adopted. The award may be enforced by the County Court on the petition of any person concerned (sect. 34). If either party to the dispute declines to arbitrate, or the arbitrators fail to make any award, application must be made to the County Court (sect. 35, sub-sect. 1). Award.

2. The registrar may determine a dispute in the following cases:— Determination of disputes by registrar.

(a) Where the parties to the dispute agree to refer it to him (sect. 34).

(b) Where the rules of the society direct disputes to be referred to the registrar (sect. 34).

Sect. 34.

The submission of a dispute to the registrar must be in duplicate in the form given in the Treasury Regulations, 1884, see r. 20, *post*, p. 170. Where the rules of the society provide that disputes shall be submitted to the registrar, and either party to the dispute refuses or neglects to fill up and sign the portion of the submission relating to his case, the other party may send the submission to the registrar. The registrar may require either party to support any statement in the submission by statutory declaration; and if he requires the parties to appear he must give them notice of the time and place of hearing (Treasury Regulations, 1884, rr. 20, 21, *infra*, p. 170). The registrar's award will have the same effect as that of arbitrators (sect. 34); it must be in a prescribed form (Treasury Regulations, 1884, r. 22, *infra*, p. 170), and a fee of one pound will be payable for it (Treasury Regulations, 1884, r. 25). If more than one hearing or an adjournment becomes necessary, an additional pound will be payable for every hearing after the first, and for every adjournment (*ibid.*).

The decision of the registrar is final (sect. 36), but he may state a case for the opinion of the Supreme Court on any question of law and may grant discovery (*ibid.*). For the form of an order for discovery and the fee payable on it see Treasury Regnlations, 1884, rr. 23, 25, *infra*, p. 170.

Determination of disputes by County Court.

3. A dispute may be determined by the County Court in the following cases:—

(a) Where application has been made by either party to the other to have the dispute settled by arbitration, and such application has not been complied with within forty days (sect. 35, sub-sect. 1).

(b) Where arbitrators have refused or have for twenty-one days neglected to make any award (sect. 35, sub-sect. 1).

(c) Where the rules direct disputes to be referred to the Court (sect. 35, sub-sect. 2).

(d) Where the rules direct disputes to be referred to justices (sect. 35, sub-sect. 2).

In the first two cases the proceeding is expressly directed to be by petition; in cases (c) and (d) proceedings should be commenced by plaint and summons in the ordinary way, and the usual County Court practice will apply (Pitt-Lewis on County Courts, Vol. II. p. 1065, 2nd ed.). **Sect. 34.**

The decision of the County Court judge will be final (s. 36), but he may state a case for the Supreme Court on any question of law, and may grant discovery (*ibid.*). For the form of an order for discovery and for the fee payable on it see Treasury Regulations, 1884, rr. 23, 25, *infra*, p. 170.

35. The court may hear and determine a dispute in the following cases: Determination of disputes by Court.

1. If it shall appear to the court, upon the petition of any person concerned, that application has been made by either party to the dispute to the other party, for the purpose of having the dispute settled by arbitration under the rules of the society, and that such application has not within forty days been complied with, or that the arbitrators have refused or for a period of twenty-one days have neglected to make any award.
2. Where the rules of the society direct disputes to be referred to the court or to justices.

See note to sect. 34, *ante*, p. 135.

As to what amounts to an "application" under sub-sect. 1, see *Sinclair* v. *Mercantile Building Investment Society*, 12 R. 1243; 22 Sc. L. R. 820.

36. Every determination by arbitrators or by the court or by the registrar under this Act of a dispute shall be binding and conclusive on all parties, and shall be final to all intents and purposes, and shall not be subject to appeal, and shall not be removed or removable into any court of law, or restrained or restrainable by the injunction of any court of equity; Determination to be final.

Sect. 36. provided always, that the arbitrators, or the registrar, or the court, as the case may be, may, at the request of either party, state a case for the opinion of the Supreme Court of Judicature on any question of law, and shall have power to grant to either party to the dispute such discovery, as to documents and otherwise, as might now be granted by any court of law or equity, such discovery to be made on behalf of the society by such officer of the society as the arbitrators, registrar, or court may determine.

See note to sect. 34, *ante*, p. 135.

Buildings for the purpose may be purchased or leased.

37. A society under this Act may purchase, build, hire, or take upon lease any building for conducting its business, and may adapt and furnish the same, and may purchase or hold upon lease any land for the purpose only of erecting thereon a building for conducting the business of the society, and may sell, exchange, or let such building, or any part thereof.

A society has no other power to hold land than that conferred by this section. Land acquired by foreclosure, surrender, or other extinguishment of the right of redemption, must be sold as soon as can conveniently be done; see sect. 13, *ante*, p. 103.

Minors may be elected members.

38. Any person under the age of twenty-one years may be admitted as a member of any society under this Act, the rules of which do not prohibit such admission, and may give all necessary acquittances; but during his nonage he shall not be competent to vote or hold any office in the society.

Married women.

As to married women holding shares in a building society see Married Women's Property Act, 1882, ss. 6—10.

As to an executor becoming a member see *Cruikshank* v. *Duffin*, cited *ante*, p. 77. Executor.

39. Two or more persons may jointly hold a share or shares in any society under this Act; and all shares held jointly by any two or more persons in any society subsisting at the time appointed for the commencement of this Act, the rules whereof shall not prohibit such joint holding, shall be deemed to be lawfully so held. Shares may be held by two or more persons.

The latter part of this section applies to all societies in existence on November 2nd, 1874, whether they have obtained a certificate of incorporation under the Act of 1874 or not. It had been decided in the case of *Dobinson* v. *Hawks*, 16 Sim. 407; 12 Jur. 1037; 12 L. T. (O. S.) 238, that in the absence of an express provision in the rules authorizing a joint holding of shares such a holding was illegal.

40. The secretary or other officer of every society under this Act, shall, once in every year at least, prepare an account of all the receipts and expenditure of the society since the preceding statement, and a general statement of its funds and effects, liabilities and assets, showing the amounts due to the holders of the various classes of shares respectively, to depositors and creditors for loans, and also the balance due or outstanding on their mortgage securities (not including prospective interest), and the amount invested in the funds or other securities; and every such account and statement shall be attested by the auditors, to whom the mortgage deeds and other securities belonging to the society shall be produced, and such account and statement shall be countersigned by the secretary or other officer; and every Societies shall make annual audits and statements of the funds to the members.

Sect. 40. member, depositor, and creditor for loans shall be entitled to receive from the society a copy of such account and statement, and a copy thereof shall be sent to the registrar within fourteen days after the annual or other general meeting at which it is presented, and another copy thereof shall be suspended in a conspicuous place in every office of the society under this Act.

The rules must contain provisions for an annual or more frequent audit of the accounts and inspection by the auditors of the mortgages and other securities belonging to the society (sect. 16, sub-sect. 8, *ante*, p. 109).

Impeaching audited account.

As to impeaching audited accounts on the ground of fraud, see *Holgate* v. *Shutt*, cited *ante*, p. 77, where the society was under the old law.

Exemption from stamp duties.

41. No rules of any society under this Act, nor any copy thereof, nor any power, warrant, or letter of attorney granted or to be granted by any person as trustee for the society for the transfer of any share in the public funds standing in his name, nor any receipts given for any dividend in any public stock or fund, or interest of exchequer bills, nor any receipt, nor any entry in any book of receipt, for money deposited in the funds of the society, nor for any money received by any member, his executors, or administrators, assigns, or attorneys, from the funds of the society, nor any transfer of any share, nor any bond or other security to be given to or on account of the society, or by any officer thereof, nor any order on any officer for payment of money to any member, nor any appointment of any agent, nor any certificate or other instrument for the revocation of any such appointment, nor any other instrument or document whatever required or authorised to be given, issued, signed, made, or produced in pursuance of this Act, or of the rules of the society, shall be subject or liable to or charged with any stamp duty or duties whatsoever, provided that the exemption shall not extend to any mortgage. Sect. 41.

This section is taken from sect. 37 of the Act 10 Geo. 4, c. 56, but with certain alterations, the most important of which is that relating to mortgages. The law with respect to the stamps on mortgages now stands thus: In the case of societies *under the Act of* 1874, *i.e.* societies established in the first instance under that Act, or societies established under the Act of 1836 but incorporated under the Act of 1874, mortgages to a building society must be stamped in the ordinary way. In the case of societies *governed exclusively by the Act of* 1836 mortgages to the society by a *member* for a sum *not exceeding five hundred pounds*, but no others, are exempt from stamp duty; see *ante*, p. 79. Stamp duty on mortgages.

As to the meaning of the word "receipt" see *Attorney-General* v. *Phillips*, 24 L. T. 832; 19 W. R. 1146, cited *ante*, p. 79, where a receipt for rent was held liable to duty. "Receipt."

As to the meaning of "bond or other security" see *Re Royal Liver Friendly Society*, L. R. 5 Ex. 78, cited *ante*, p. 80. "Bond or other security."

42. When all moneys intended to be secured by any mortgage or further charge given to a society under this Act in England or Ireland have been fully paid or discharged, the society may endorse upon or annex to such mortgage or further charge a reconveyance of the mortgaged property to the then owner of the equity of redemption, or to such persons and to such uses as he may direct, or a receipt under the seal of the society, countersigned by the secretary or manager, in the form specified in the schedule to this Act, and such receipt shall vacate the mortgage or Receipt endorsed on mortgage to be sufficient discharge without reconveyance.

Sect. 42.

further charge or debt, and vest the estate of and in the property therein comprised in the person for the time being entitled to the equity of redemption, without any re-conveyance or re-surrender whatever; and if the said mortgage or further charge has been registered under any Act for the registration or record of deeds or titles, the registrar under such Act, or his deputy or assistant registrar, or the recording officer, as the ease may be, or, in the case of copyholds or lands of customary tenure, if the mortgage or further charge has been entered on any court rolls, the steward of the manor or his deputy respectively shall, on production of such receipt, verified by oath of any person, make an entry opposite the entry of the charge or mortgage, to the effect that such charge or mortgage is satisfied, and shall grant a certificate, either on the said mortgage or charge or separately, to the like effect, which certificate shall be received in evidence in all courts and proceedings without any further proof, and which entry shall have the effect of clearing the register or record of such mortgage; and the registrar or recording officer shall be entitled to a fee of two shillings and sixpence for making the said entry and granting the said certificate, and such fee shall in Ireland be paid by stamps, and applied as the other fees of the Registry of Deeds Office and Record of Title Office are now by law directed to be paid and applied.

Discharge of mortgages to a building society.

This section, which is taken from sect. 5 of the Building Societies Act, 1836, 6 & 7 Will. 4, c. 32, *ante*, p. 90, prescribes two methods by which, on the discharge of a mortgage to a society under this Act in England or Ireland, the property comprised in the security may again become vested

Sect 42.

in the mortgagor or those claiming under him—(1) a reconveyance; (2) a statutory receipt.

Reconveyance.

If a society *under the Act of* 1874 executes a reconveyance it must, by the express terms of the section, be to the *then owner of the equity of redemption, or to such persons and to such uses as he may direct.* "I do not think any lawyer would say that the reconveyance authorized by the Act is authorized to be made to anybody but the person who at law is entitled to call for it. 'May indorse' merely means that the society may indorse a proper reconveyance upon the mortgage deed. But there is an alternative mode of proceeding. Instead of a reconveyance to the then owner of the equity of redemption the society may indorse a receipt, and then that receipt is to vacate the mortgage and vest the estate in the property 'in the person for the time being entitled to the equity of redemption.' Surely that is the same person as the owner of the equity of redemption in the former part of the section. They are equivalent words; the reconveyance is not to be to one person and the vesting to be in another. They are *alternative modes of getting the legal estate into the same person*, that is, in the owner for the time being of the equity of redemption:" *per* Jessel, M. R., in *Fourth City Mutual Benefit Building Society* v. *Williams*, 14 Ch. D. p. 146.

If, however, a reconveyance were executed by a society *governed by the Act of* 1836, which merely authorizes the giving of a statutory receipt, then such a reconveyance would, it is conceived, be construed and have effect according to the same principles as any other conveyance. In a recent case under the Friendly Societies Act, 1875, which provides (sect. 16, sub-sect. 7) that a receipt endorsed on or annexed to a mortgage to a friendly society shall vacate the same and vest the property therein comprised in the person entitled to the equity of redemption, but says nothing about executing a reconveyance, the trustees of a society instead of giving a receipt executed a reconveyance by deed. It was argued that the same effect must be given to it as if they had given a statutory receipt; but the learned judge (North, J.) declined to adopt this view, holding that the legal estate passed to the grantee under the deed in the ordinary way,

Sect. 42. and that the rights of the parties must be regulated accordingly (*Carlisle Banking Co.* v. *Thompson*, 28 Ch. D. 398; 33 W. R. 119; 53 L. T. 115).

Statutory receipt.

The Courts have frequently been called upon to determine the precise effect to be given to a statutory receipt under the Building Societies Acts. Some of the cases have arisen in connection with societies governed by the Act of 1836, others in connection with societies under the Act of 1874; but the wording of the two statutes on this point is so similar that all the authorities may, it is conceived, be considered as applying with almost equal force to either Act. It appears then to be now settled that when a society, being a legal mortgagee, is paid off and gives a receipt in the prescribed form, the effect is to shift the legal estate out of the society and vest it in the person *who in equity is best entitled to call for it*, although such person may not be the one who paid off the society. Thus if there are successive equitable mortgagees and the society is paid off by the mortgagor, the effect will be to vest the legal estate in the equitable incumbrancer who is first in point of time; but if the society is paid off by a subsequent equitable incumbrancer who has no notice of prior incumbrances, then he as having the best equity will be the person in whom the legal estate will vest. The question in each case is, Who of all the persons interested in the equity of redemption has the best right to call for a conveyance of the legal estate? See *Pease* v. *Jackson*, 3 Ch. 576; 37 L. J. Ch. 725; 17 W. R. 1; 32 J. P. 757; *Lawrence* v. *Clements*, 31 L. T. 670; *Fourth City Mutual Benefit Building Society* v. *Williams* and *Marson* v. *Cox*, 14 Ch. D. 140; 49 L. J. Ch. 245; 28 W. R. 572; 42 L. T. 615, where *Pease* v. *Jackson* is discussed by Jessel, M. R.; *Robinson* v. *Trevor*, 12 Q. B. D. 423; 53 L. J. Q. B. 85; 32 W. R. 374; 50 L. T. 190; *Sangster* v. *Cochrane*, 28 Ch. D. 298; 54 L. J. Ch. 301; 33 W. R. 221; 51 L. T. 889; 49 J. P. 327; *Stamers* v. *Preston*, 9 Ir. C. L. R. 351. *Prosser* v. *Rice*, 28 Beav. 68, cannot now be relied on.

In *Pease* v. *Jackson*, a legal mortgage was made to a building society and a subsequent equitable charge given to the plaintiffs. The defendants on the mortgagor's request paid off the society. A receipt was accordingly endorsed on the mortgage and the deeds handed to the defendants, and the mortgagor executed a fresh mortgage to them, receiving at the same time a further advance. The defendants had no notice of the plaintiffs' charge. Lord Romilly, M. R., held, following his own decision in *Prosser* v. *Rice*, that the plaintiffs were entitled to priority (3 Ch. 578, n.; 16 W. R. 58). On appeal, however, Lord Cairns reversed this decision, holding that the defendants had the better equity and therefore that the rule "*Qui prior est tempore, potior est jure*" did not apply; and he decided, first, that on the satisfaction of the mortgage the legal estate vested either in the mortgagor or in the persons who had the best right to call for it, in either of which cases it had passed to the defendants; but secondly, that the defendants were not entitled to tack their further advance. In the concluding portion of his judgment Lord Cairns stated that he had decided the case on the ground of the better equity, and this no doubt is the correct view; see *Fourth City Mutual Benefit Building Society* v. *Williams*, and the judgment of Baggallay, L. J., in *Robinson* v. *Trevor*, 12 Q. B. D. p. 429. Sect. 42.

Tacking further advance.

The second part of the decision in *Pease* v. *Jackson*, however, viz. that under such circumstances there is no right to tack, did not commend itself to the late Master of the Rolls, Sir George Jessel; see his Lordship's judgment in *Marson* v. *Cox*, 14 Ch. D. p. 150, where he expressed the opinion that if the legal estate passed by the statute at all it passed altogether and for all purposes, and all the usual consequences must follow. Lord Cairns's decision, however, on this point was followed by Hall, V.-C., in *Lawrence* v. *Clements*, by the Court of Appeal in *Robinson* v. *Trevor*, and by Kay, J., in *Sangster* v. *Cochrane*, and must be taken to be the law. It should be observed that *Pease* v. *Jackson* was decided under the Act of 1836, whereas *Marson* v. *Cox* was a case under the Act of 1874. Possibly this distinction may afford some means of reconciling the conflicting opinions of Lord Cairns and Sir George Jessel on the point in question.

Sangster v. Cochrane.

Sangster v. *Cochrane* was a peculiar case. The facts were as follows: In 1872 four houses were mortgaged to a building

Sect. 42. society. In 1881 the plaintiff paid off the society at the mortgagor's request; and a receipt was endorsed in the usual way, the deeds were handed to the plaintiff, and a mortgage executed to him for a larger amount. The mortgagor having become bankrupt the plaintiff desired to take possession, and then discovered that in 1877 the mortgagor had sold and conveyed one of the houses to the defendant. The mortgagor, who was a solicitor, had acted for the defendant on the occasion of the sale and had suppressed the fact of the mortgage to the society. Under these circumstances Mr. Justice Kay held, following the previous decisions, though not agreeing with them, that the effect of the receipt was to vest the legal estate in the plaintiff and give him, to the extent of the money he paid to the society, priority over the defendant.

Effect of the receipt on the covenants in the mortgage.

Another question that has arisen in connection with this subject is, What is the effect of a statutory receipt on the covenants in the mortgage?

In *Farmer* v. *Smith*, 4 H. & N. 196; 28 L. J. Ex. 226; 5 Jur. N. S. 533, n.; 7 W. R. 362; 32 L. T. (O. S.) 371; 23 J. P. 230, the estimated duration of a terminating society was thirteen years. The Court held, first, that on the construction of the rules and the mortgage deed an advanced member was entitled to redeem on payment of his subscriptions to the end of the thirteenth year, but would remain liable to pay subscriptions until 120*l*. a share had been realised for every member; and secondly, that the covenant in the mortgage deed extended to the payment of these subscriptions subsequent to the thirteen years, and that the right to sue on the covenant would not be affected by the endorsement of a receipt. See also *Sparrow* v. *Farmer*, 26 Beav. 511; 28 L. J. Ch. 537; 5 Jur. N. S. 530; 33 L. T. (O. S.) 216.

Harvey v. *Municipal Building Society.*

In the recent case of *Harvey* v. *Municipal Permanent Investment Building Society*, 26 Ch. D. 273; 53 L. J. Ch. 1126; 32 W. R. 557; 51 L. T. 408, however, the Court of Appeal held that where a member has executed a mortgage to secure advances and all payments due from him to the society, the endorsement of a receipt in accordance with sect. 42 is absolutely conclusive as against the society, and precludes them from saying that *anything* remains due from the member, even though the receipt was given under a mistake. Cotton, L. J., in his judgment, says:—" We must give effect to the words of the Act, which say that the receipt 'shall vacate the mortgage or further charge or debt.' It is contended that the alternative form of the clause points to a difference between a mortgage and a debt, and that the latter word only refers to a case where there is no mortgage. But even if it were so it would come to the same thing, for if the mortgage is vacated, the debt due on the covenant in the mortgage is also vacated. The society has therefore precluded itself from saying that there is any debt due, even though the receipt was given under a mistake. The counsel for the respondents raised two points, the first was that if all the monies were not in fact paid, the statutory effect of the receipt did not arise. But that is not so; to say that after the indorsement is made the parties were left free to reopen the question as to the amount due would be to repeal the section. The second argument was that [the] two alternative provisions are really only two alternative modes of re-vesting the property in the mortgagor, but such a contention would strike out part of the second alternative. The receipt has, under the statute, not only the effect of re-vesting the property, but also of vacating the mortgage; therefore, in my opinion, the receipt precludes the society from saying that anything remains due on the mortgage. Then it is said that the debt on the plaintiff's original obligation on the shares still remains, though the mortgage is gone; but, in my opinion, it is clear that the mortgage covenant is to cover *not only the mortgage money and interest but all the payments due on the shares, and even if all such payments have not been made, the debt is gone by reason of the indorsement.* The case of *Sparrow* v. *Farmer* was referred to, but when we look at the facts of that case we find that all that was decided there was, that though the mortgage debt was so far gone that the shareholder was able to redeem his property, yet he still remained liable for payments in respect of shares still subsisting. But here all

Sect. 42.

Sect. 42.

which was payable down to the time when the mortgage was satisfied is covered by the receipt, and there is no claim for payments accrued due since, but for sums due before the mortgage was vacated. Therefore that decision has no bearing on the present case." Lord Justice Fry in his judgment says:—"Then it was said that though the liability on the mortgage was satisfied, the liability on the shares remained; *but all liability on the shares was merged in the mortgage, and as that is vacated the debt is gone also.*" It may seem somewhat difficult to reconcile this decision with *Farmer* v. *Smith*, which does not appear to have been cited. It should be remembered however that the two cases were decided under different Acts of Parliament, and that the earlier Act makes the receipt vacate the mortgage or further charge only, while under the later Act the effect of the receipt is to vacate the mortgage or further charge *or debt.*

Priestly v. *Hopwood.*

In *Priestly* v. *Hopwood*, 4 N. R. 239; 10 L. T. 646; 12 W. R. 1031; 28 J. P. 628, the plaintiff executed a mortgage to the society in the usual way, and then sold the equity of redemption to the defendant, who covenanted to pay "all subscriptions and other payments which should become due thenceforth in respect of the plaintiff's shares by virtue of the rules of the society;" but the shares remained in the plaintiff's name. One of the rules provided that the managers might "determine the amount of money to be paid by any mortgagor in full for the claims of the society upon his property, on payment of which the share or shares in respect of which the security was made should become wholly extinguished." The society having passed a resolution enabling members to redeem their mortgages on payment of 60*l*. 10*s*. per share the defendant paid this sum on each of the plaintiff's shares and the usual receipt was endorsed on the mortgage. The Court held that the effect of the resolution and receipt was to extinguish the plaintiff's shares, and consequently to release the plaintiff from all liability to the society and the defendant from all liability to the plaintiff.

Form of receipt.

For the form of receipt, see *post*, p. 153.

Sect. 43.

Penalties.

43. If any society hereafter formed under this Act, or any persons representing themselves to be a society under this Act, commence business without first obtaining a certificate of incorporation under this Act, or if any society under this Act makes default in forwarding to the registrar any returns or information by this Act required, or in inserting in any deposit book or acknowledgment or security for loan the matters required by section fifteen of this Act to be inserted therein, or makes a return wilfully false in any respect, the person or persons by whom business shall have been so commenced, or by whom such default shall have been made, or who shall have made such wilfully false return, shall be liable for every day business is so carried on, or for every such default or false return, upon summary conviction before justices at the complaint of the registrar, to a penalty not exceeding five pounds. If any society under this Act receives loans or deposits in excess of the limits prescribed by this Act, the directors or committee of management of such society receiving such loans or deposits on its behalf shall be personally liable for the amount so received in excess.

Default in forwarding returns.

The provisions of this section as to default in forwarding returns to the registrar are similar to those of sect. 27 of the Companies Act, 1862, as to which see *Gibson* v. *Barton*, L. R. 10 Q. B. 329; 44 L. J. M. C. 81; 23 W. R. 858; 32 L. T. 396; 39 J. P. 628; *R.* v. *Newton*, 48 L. J. M. C. 77; 43 J. P. 351; *Edmonds* v. *Foster*, 45 L. J. M. C. 41; 24 W. R. 368; 33 L. T. 690; 40 J. P. 151.

Personal liability of directors for loans in excess of borrowing powers.

As to the meaning of the words "in excess of the limits prescribed by this Act," see *Looker* v. *Wrigley*, *Leigh* v. *Wrigley*, cited in note to sect. 15, *ante*, p. 107.

Sect. 44.

Regulations.

44. One of Her Majesty's principal secretaries of state may from time to time make regulations respecting the fees, if any, to be paid for the transmission, registration, and inspection of documents under this Act, and generally for carrying this Act into effect. The registrar shall give his certificates in the forms contained in the schedule to this Act respectively.

Treasury Regulations, 1884.

The Treasury Regulations issued in December, 1884, under the authority of this section, will be found at p. 164, *infra*.

Forms of certificates.

The forms of certificates now in use are those prescribed by the Building Societies Act, 1877; see sect. 6 of that Act, *infra*, p. 159.

SCHEDULE.

FORM OF BOND.

KNOW all men by these presents, that we, A. B., of , one of the officers of the Building Society, established at in the county of , and C. D. of (as surety on behalf of the said A. B.), are jointly and severally held and firmly bound to the said society in the sum of to be paid to the said society, for which payment well and truly to be made we jointly and severally bind ourselves, and each of us by himself, our and each of our heirs, executors, and administrators, firmly by these presents, sealed with our seals. Dated the day of in the year of our Lord .

Whereas the above-bounden A. B. hath been duly appointed to the office of of the Building Society, established as aforesaid, and he, together with the above-bounden C. D. as his surety, have entered into the above-written bond, subject to the condition hereinafter contained: Schedule.

Now, therefore, the condition of the above-written bond is such, that if the said A. B. shall and do render a just and true account of all monies received and paid by him, and shall and do pay over all the monies remaining in his hands, and assign and transfer or deliver all securities and effects, books, papers, and property of or belonging to the said society in his hands or custody, to such person or persons as the said society shall appoint, according to the rules of the said society, together with the proper or legal receipts or vouchers for such payments, then the above-written bond shall be void and of no effect, otherwise shall be and remain in full force and virtue.

Form of Receipt to be endorsed on Mortgage or further Charge.

The Building Society hereby acknowledge to have received all monies intended to be secured by the within [*or* above] written deed.

In witness whereof the seal of the society is hereto affixed this day of by order of the board of directors [*or* committee of management] in presence of secretary [*or* manager]. (L.S.)

[*Other witnesses, if any required by the rules of the society.*]

Forms of Certificate to be given under this Act.

[Other forms are substituted for these by the Building Societies Act, 1877, *infra*, p. 159.]

THE BUILDING SOCIETIES ACT, 1875.

38 VICT. c. 9.

An Act to repeal section eight of the Building Societies Act, 1874, *and make other provision in lieu thereof.* [22nd April, 1875.]

WHEREAS by the Building Societies Act, 1874, the Act of the session of the sixth and seventh years of the reign of His late Majesty King William the Fourth, chapter thirty-two, intituled "An Act for the regulation of benefit building societies," was repealed, subject as in the recited Act mentioned, and by section eight of the said Building Societies Act, 1874, it was enacted as follows:

"Every society, the rules of which have been certified under the said repealed Act, shall be deemed to be a society under this Act, and may obtain a certificate of incorporation under this Act, and thereupon its rules shall, so far as the same are not contrary to any expressed provisions of this Act, continue in force until altered or rescinded as hereinafter mentioned:"

And whereas the words in the said section, whereby existing societies not having a certificate of incorporation are deemed to be societies under the Building Societies Act, 1874, were inserted through inadvertence:

Be it therefore enacted by the Queen's most excellent Majesty, by and with the advice and consent of the lords spiritual and temporal, and commons, in this present Parliament assembled, and by the authority of the same, as follows:

1. Section eight of the Building Societies Act, 1874, is hereby repealed as from the date of the commencement of such last-mentioned Act: Provided that such repeal shall not affect any certificate of incorporation given, or any other thing heretofore done or suffered in pursuance of such section before the date of the passing of this Act.

Repeal of s. 8 of 37 & 38 Vict. c. 42.

This section, as appears by the preamble, was rendered necessary by the error which had crept into sect. 8 of the Act of 1874, the effect of which was to bring societies established under the Act of 1836 within the Act of 1874, *whether they had obtained a certificate of incorporation or not.* It accordingly repeals sect. 8 as from November 2nd, 1874, but with a saving clause in respect of anything done or suffered in pursuance thereof between that date and April 22nd, 1875. The result is, that societies certified under the Act of 1836 were, in the interval between November 2nd, 1874, and April 22nd, 1875, governed by the Act of 1874, although not incorporated under that Act. A loan made to an unincorporated society during that interval, was accordingly held by the Court of Appeal to be valid on this ground; but the Court was of opinion that a loan made before November 2nd, 1874, if otherwise invalid, was not made valid thereby, although continued during the interval. See *Re Guardian Permanent Benefit Building Society*, cited in note to sect. 8 of the Act of 1874, *ante*, p. 99. Sect. 2 of the Act of 1875 now provides that a society established under the Act of 1836 may obtain a certificate of incorporation, *and thereupon* shall be deemed to be a society under the Act of 1874.

2. From and after the passing of this Act every society, the rules of which have been certified under

Substitution of clause for

Sect. 2.

s. 8 of 37 & 38 Vict. c. 42.

the said Act of the session of the sixth and seventh years of the reign of His late Majesty King William the Fourth, chapter thirty-two, intituled "An Act for the regulation of benefit building societies," may obtain a certificate of incorporation under the Building Societies Act, 1874, and thereupon shall be deemed to be a society under that Act; and its rules shall, so far as the same are not contrary to any express provisions of that Act, continue in force until altered or rescinded as in that Act mentioned.

See note to sect. 1, *ante*, p. 155.

Short title.

3. This Act may be cited as the Building Societies Act, 1875.

THE BUILDING SOCIETIES ACT, 1877.

40 & 41 Vict. c. 63.

An Act to amend the Building Societies Act, 1874.
[14th August, 1877.]

Whereas it is expedient to amend the laws relating to building societies:

Be it enacted by the Queen's most excellent Majesty, by and with the advice and consent of the lords spiritual and temporal, and commons, in this present parliament assembled, and by the authority of the same, as follows:

1. This Act shall be construed as one with "The Building Societies Act, 1874" (herein termed, "the principal Act"), and "The Building Societies Act, 1875," and may be cited as "The Building Societies Act, 1877," or, together with the said Acts, as "The Building Societies Acts."

Short title, &c. 37 & 38 Vict. c. 42. 38 & 39 Vict. c. 9.

2. Any society under the principal Act may change its chief office in the manner its rules direct, or, if there be no such direction, then at a general meeting specially called for the purpose, in the manner set forth in the rules of the society; and no alteration of rule shall be necessary upon such change, nor shall the provisions of section eighteen of the principal Act apply to such change. Notice of every such change shall be given by the secretary

Societies may change their chief offices.

Notice of such change to

Sect. 2.

be sent to registrar.

of the society to the registrar within seven days after such change, and shall be registered by him, and he shall give a certificate of such registration.

For sect. 18 of the Act of 1874 see *ante*, p. 112.

The notice of a change of office must be in the form prescribed by the Treasury Regulations, 1884 (Treasury Regulations, 1884, r. 24, *infra*, p. 170).

Amendment of 37 & 38 Vict. c. 42, s. 27.

3. Section twenty-seven of the principal Act shall be read as if the word "now" were omitted therefrom.

For sect. 27 of the Act of 1874 see *ante*, p. 122.

See note to next section.

Rights held in trust to vest in societies.

4. All rights of action and other rights and interests in real and personal estate whatsoever held in trust for any society heretofore incorporated under the principal Act shall, on the passing of this Act, vest in the society without any conveyance or assignment whatsoever, except in the case of stocks and securities in the public funds of Great Britain and Ireland, and estates in copyhold or customary hereditaments the title to which cannot be transferred without admittance.

The effect of sects. 3 and 4 of this Act and of sect. 27 of the Act of 1874 appears to be as follows:—In the case of a society under the old law which obtained a certificate of incorporation in the interval between November 2nd, 1874, and August 14th, 1877, so much only of the property of the society vested in it on its incorporation as belonged to or was held in trust for the society on November 2nd, 1874 (sect. 27); but all property held in trust for such a society on August 14th, 1877, vested in the society on that date (sect. 4).

In the case of any society under the old law obtaining a

certificate of incorporation since August 14th, 1877, the property belonging to or held in trust for it vests in the society immediately on its incorporation (sect. 27; sect. 3).

Registration of union of societies or of transfer of engagements to operate as effectual conveyance of funds and property of uniting societies to the united society and to society to which engagements are transferred.

5. The registration by the registrar of the notice of the union of any societies, or of the transfer of the engagements of any society to another society, in terms of and subject to the provisions of section thirty-three of the principal Act, shall operate as an effectual conveyance, transfer, and assignment, as at the date of the said registration, of the funds, property, and assets of the societies so uniting to the united society, or of the society transferring its engagements to the society to which such engagements may be transferred, as may be set forth in the instrument of union or transfer of engagements, without any conveyance, transfer, or assignment whatsoever, save and except in the case of stocks and securities in the public funds of Great Britain and Ireland, and estates in copyhold or customary hereditaments the title to which cannot be transferred without admittance: provided always, that such union or transfer of engagements shall not affect the rights of any creditor of either or any society uniting or transferring its engagements.

See sect. 33 of the principal Act, and note thereto, *ante*, p. 133.

Forms in schedule to be used.

6. The forms in the schedule to this Act shall henceforth be used under the Building Societies Acts.

This section does away with the forms of certificate contained in the schedule to the Act of 1874; the form of bond, however, and the form of the statutory receipt given in that schedule remain unaffected.

Schedule.

SCHEDULE.

CERTIFICATE OF INCORPORATION.

The Registrar of Building Societies in [England, Scotland, *or* Ireland] hereby certifies that the Building Society, established at , in the county of , is incorporated under "The Building Societies Act, 1874."

This day of , 18 .

[*Seal of Central Office, or signature of Assistant Registrar of Friendly Societies.*]

CERTIFICATE OF REGISTRATION OF ALTERATION OF RULES.

The Registrar of Building Societies in [England, Scotland, *or* Ireland] hereby certifies that the foregoing alterations of [*or* addition to] the rules of the Building Society, established at , in the county of , are registered under "The Building Societies Act, 1874."

This day of , 18 .

[*Seal of Central Office, or signature of Assistant Registrar of Friendly Societies.*]

CERTIFICATE OF REGISTRATION OF CHANGE OF NAME.

The Registrar of Building Societies in [England, Scotland, *or* Ireland] hereby certifies that the registered name of the Building Society, established at , in the county of , is changed from the date hereof to the name following: Schedule.

This day of , 18 .

[*Seal of Central Office, or signature of Assistant Registrar of Friendly Societies.*]

Certificate of Alteration of Chief Office.

The Registrar of Building Societies in [England, Scotland, *or* Ireland] hereby certifies that the registered chief office of the Building Society, established at , in the county of , is changed from the date hereof to the office or place following:

This day of , 18 .

[*Seal of Central Office, or signature of Assistant Registrar of Friendly Societies.*]

THE BUILDING SOCIETIES ACT, 1884.

47 & 48 Vict. c. 41.

An Act to amend the Building Societies Act, 1874.

[7th August, 1884.]

Whereas it is expedient to amend the laws relating to building societies:

Be it enacted by the Queen's most excellent Majesty, by and with the advice and consent of the lords spiritual and temporal, and commons, in this present parliament assembled, and by the authority of the same, as follows:

Construction and short title.

1. This Act shall be construed as one with the Building Societies Act, 1874, and the Building Societies Act, 1875, and the Building Societies Act, 1877, and may be cited as the Building Societies Act, 1884, or, together with the said Acts, as the Building Societies Acts.

Definition of word "disputes."

2. The word "disputes" in the Building Societies Acts, or in the rules of any society thereunder, shall be deemed to refer only to disputes between the society and a member, or any representative of a member in his capacity of a member of the society, unless by the rules for the time being it shall be otherwise expressly provided; and in the absence of such express provision, shall not apply to any dis-

Sect. 2.

pute between any such society and any member thereof, or other person whatever, as to the construction or effect of any mortgage deed, or any contract contained in any document, other than the rules of the society, and shall not prevent any society, or any member thereof, or any person claiming through or under him, from obtaining in the ordinary course of law any remedy in respect of any such mortgage or other contract to which he or the society would otherwise be by law entitled: provided always, that nothing in this Act shall apply to any dispute pending at any time before the passing of this Act between any such society and any member thereof, or other person, which before the passing of this Act shall have been actually referred, or agreed to be referred, to arbitration, or as to which the jurisdiction of any court of law shall have been adjudged to be excluded by a decision of any court of competent jurisdiction in an action or suit between the society and any member thereof or other person.

See note to sect. 34 of the principal Act, *ante*, p. 135.

TREASURY REGULATIONS, 1884.

BUILDING SOCIETIES ACTS.

In pursuance of the powers vested in me by the above-mentioned statutes, I, the Right Honourable Sir William George Granville Vernon Harcourt, one of Her Majesty's Principal Secretaries of State, hereby revoke the Regulations made thereunder, and make the following Regulations in lieu thereof:—

(1.) Every application for a certificate of incorporation to a society in existence on the 2nd November, 1874, shall be made by a person authorized by a general meeting of the society, specially called for the purpose, and shall be in the Form A. annexed hereto, and shall be accompanied by the following documents:—

(a) A copy of the rules of the society as they exist at the date of the application.

(b.) A statutory declaration by the applicant in the Form B. annexed hereto.

If the Registrar at the time the application is received by him has not received from the clerk of the peace for the county in which the society is established a transcript of the certified and enrolled rules of the society, he shall make application to the clerk of the peace for the same, and if the same is not received by him within seven days of such application, shall, as soon as practicable, acquaint the applicant for incorporation therewith, who must furnish evidence that the rules are certified as provided by 37 & 38 Vict. c. 42, s. 11, before the society can be incorporated.

(2.) Every application for a certificate of incorporation to a society about to be established, shall be in the Form C. annexed hereto, and shall be accompanied by two printed copies of the rules marked and signed, as mentioned in the said Form.

(3.) An alteration of the rules of a society may be either—

(a.) A partial alteration, consisting of the addition of a new rule or part of a rule or rules to the existing rules, or of the substitution of a new rule or part of a rule or rules for any of the existing rules, or of a rescission of any of the existing rules or any part thereof without any substitution, or of more than one or all of those modes; or,

(b.) A complete alteration consisting of the substitution of an entire set of rules for the existing set of rules.

(4.) An application for the registration of a partial alteration of rules must be made by three members and the secretary of the society, and must be made in the Form D. annexed hereto, and must be accompanied by a statutory declaration in the Form E. annexed hereto, and by a printed copy of the existing rules, and by the following documents:—

(a.) If the partial alteration consists of the addition or substitution of a new rule or part of a rule or rules, two copies of such rule or part of a rule or rules, each copy being marked Y. and signed by each of the applicants.

(b.) If the partial alteration consists of the rescission of any of the rules without any substitution, two copies of the resolution for such rescission, each copy being marked Y. and signed by each of the applicants.

The Registrar before registering the partial alteration of rules, shall ascertain that it is in conformity with the Building Societies Acts.

(5.) An application for the registration of a complete alteration of rules shall be made by three members and the secretary of the society, and shall be in the Form F. annexed hereto, and must be accompanied by a statutory declaration in Form E. annexed hereto, and by a printed copy of the existing rules and by two printed copies of the new rules, each copy being marked Z. and signed by each of the applicants; and the Registrar before registering the new set of rules, shall ascertain that it provides for all matters which, by 37 & 38 Vict. c. 42, s. 16, are to be provided for by rules, and is in conformity with the Building Societies Acts.

(6.) The certificate of registry of an alteration of rules shall be delivered to the applicants attached to one of the copies of the alteration.

(7.) The last words in the name of any society established and incorporated under the Building Societies Acts, shall be "Building Society;" and no change of name by any society shall be registered unless the new name ends with those words; and the

Registrar may refuse to allow the insertion in the name of any society about to be established and applying for incorporation under the said Acts, or the retention in the name of any society which seeks to change its name, of any words implying that the society is other than a building society.

Change of Name.

(8.) Every society changing its name shall give notice to the Registrar in the Form G. annexed hereto, accompanied by a statutory declaration in the Form H. annexed hereto. The Registrar, before issuing a certificate of registration of change of name, shall ascertain that the new name is not identical with that of any society previously registered, or so nearly resembling the same as to be calculated to deceive; and in the event of such identity or resemblance, may require the society desiring to change its name to satisfy him that such previously registered society is not subsisting, or, if subsisting, that it is in course of being terminated or dissolved, and consents to such registration.

Transfer of Stock.

(9.) Every application to the Registrar to direct a transfer of stock shall follow, as near as may be, the Form I. annexed hereto, and shall be accompanied by a statutory declaration in the Form K. annexed hereto, or as near thereto as the facts admit, and by the certificate of the stock in respect of which the application is made.

(10.) Before making the application, the society shall submit to the Registrar for examination a draft copy, on foolscap paper, written on one side only, of the proposed application and declaration.

(11.) The Registrar before directing the transfer, may require further proof of any statement in the application.

(12.) The Registrar shall give a direction in the Form L. annexed hereto so framed in each case as to suit the particular circumstances, and shall register the same and deliver the same to the applicants, endorsed with the word "Registered," and duly authenticated.

Dissolution.

(13.) The instrument of dissolution shall be on foolscap paper in the Form M. annexed hereto, and shall be signed in duplicate, and accompanied by a statutory declaration in the Form N. annexed hereto.

(14.) The Registrar shall return one of the duplicates to the society, with a certificate in the Form O. annexed hereto.

(15.) Alterations in the instrument of dissolution shall be signed, declared to and certified in like manner.

(16.) When a society is dissolved otherwise than by an instrument of dissolution, notice of the commencement of the dissolution shall be given to the Registrar in duplicate, within fourteen days from such commencement, in the Form P. annexed hereto, and the Registrar shall return one copy to the society, endorsed with the word "Registered," and duly authenticated.

(16a.) When a society is wound up either voluntarily under the supervision of the Court or by the Court, notice of the commencement of the winding up shall be given to the Registrar in duplicate, within fourteen days from the date of the order for winding up subject to the supervision of the Court, or of the order for winding up by the Court, as the case may be, in the Form P a. hereto annexed, and the Registrar shall return one copy to the society, endorsed with the word "Registered," and duly authenticated.

(17.) Notice of the termination of every dissolution shall be given to the Registrar in duplicate, within fourteen days from such termination, in the Form Q. annexed hereto, and the Registrar shall return one copy to the society, endorsed with the word "Registered," and duly authenticated.

(17a.) Notice of the termination of every winding up subject to the supervision of the Court or by the Court shall be given in duplicate to the Registrar within fourteen days from the termination of such winding-up in the Form Q a. hereto annexed, and the Registrar shall return one copy to the society, endorsed with the word "Registered," and duly authenticated.

Union of Societies or Transfer of Engagements.

(18.) Where two or more societies unite, notice shall be given to the Registrar in duplicate in the Form R. annexed hereto, and the Registrar shall return one copy to the united society, endorsed with the word "Registered," and duly authenticated.

(19.) Where a society transfers its engagements to another, notice shall be given to the Registrar in duplicate in the Form S. annexed hereto, and the Registrar shall return one copy to the transferee society, endorsed with the word "Registered," and duly authenticated.

Arbitration.

(20.) The submission of a dispute to the Registrar shall be in duplicate in the Form T. annexed hereto. Where the rules of the society provide that disputes shall be submitted to the Registrar, and either party to the dispute refuses or neglects to fill up and sign the portion of the submission relating to his case, the other party may send the submission to the Registrar. The Registrar may require either party to support any statement in the submission by statutory declaration.

(21.) If the Registrar desires the parties to appear, notice shall be given in the Form V. annexed hereto.

(22.) The award of the Registrar shall be in the Form W. annexed hereto.

(23.) If any order for discovery be necessary, it shall be in the Form X. annexed hereto.

(24.) The notice of change of the chief office of a society shall be in Form Y.

Fees.

(25.) The following fees shall be payable under the Acts :—

	£	s.	d.
For the certificate of incorporation of a society	1	0	0
For the certificate of registry of an alteration of rules	0	10	0

	£	s.	d.
For the certificate of registry of a change of name	0	10	0
For a direction to transfer stock .	1	0	0
For the certificate of registry of an instrument of dissolution, or alteration therein	0	10	0
For registry of notice of the commencement or termination of a dissolution or winding up	0	2	6
For registry of union or transfer . .	0	10	0
For an award by the Registrar on a dispute	1	0	0
And, if more than one hearing or an adjournment becomes necessary, then 1*l.* more for every hearing after the first, and for every adjournment.			
For an order for discovery . . .	0	10	0
For every document required to be authenticated by the Registrar, not chargeable with any other fee .	0	2	6
For every inspection on the same day of documents (whether one or more), in the custody of the Registrar, relating to one and the same society . .	0	1	0
For every copy or extract of any document in the custody of the Registrar, not exceeding 216 words 1*s.*, and if exceeding that number 4*d.* per folio of 72 words, in addition to the fee for authentication.			

Authentication of Documents by Registrar.

(26.) Every document under the Building Societies Acts, bearing the seal of the central office for registry of Friendly Societies, or the signature of the Assistant-Registrar of Friendly Societies for Scotland or Ireland, as the case may require, shall be deemed to be duly authenticated for the purposes of the said Acts and the Regulations made thereunder.

(27.) Where a document is tendered for registry which appears to the Registrar substantially to comply with the provisions of the Building Societies Acts the Registrar may dispense with the use of any of the forms prescribed by the Regulations, but nothing in this Regulation contained shall hinder the Registrar from refusing to register a document not in the prescribed forms when it shall appear to such Registrar to be unnecessarily long, or to contain extraneous matter.

(28.) The Registrar may also modify any such forms to suit particular cases, and may dispense with the obligation to supply a duplicate of any document where such obligation is imposed only by the Regulations.

Whitehall,
December, 1884.

For societies registered in Scotland the address "43, New Register House, Edinburgh," and in Ireland "9, Upper Ormond Quay, Dublin," will be substituted for "28, Abingdon Street, Westminster."

FORM A.

Building Societies Acts.

Application for a Certificate of Incorporation to a Society existing on November 2, 1874.

——— Building Society.

This application for a certificate of incorporation under the above-mentioned Act to the ——— Building Society, which on the 2nd of November, 1874, was a building society existing under the Act 6 & 7 Will. IV. c. 32, is made by the person whose name is subscribed at the foot hereof.

Accompanying this application are sent a copy of the rules of the society, as they exist at the date of the application, and a statutory declaration by the applicant (in the form required by the Regulations of the Secretary of State) to the effect that he was authorized to make this application by a general meeting of the society specially called for the purpose.

Signed ———.

Address ———.
Date ———.

To the Registrar of Building Societies,
28, Abingdon Street, Westminster,
London, S.W.

FORM B.

Building Societies Acts.

Declaration accompanying Application in Form A.

——— Building Society.

——— of ——— do solemnly and sincerely declare that at a general meeting of the ——— Society, specially called for the purpose, authority was duly given to me to make application for the incorporation of the said society under the above-mentioned Acts; and that the rules of the said society have been certified under the 6 & 7 Wm. IV. c. 32.

And I make this solemn declaration conscientiously believing the same to be true, and by virtue of the provisions of the Statutory Declarations Act, 1835.

Taken and received before me, one of
Her Majesty's justices of the peace
for the county of ———, at ———,
in the said county, this ——— day
of ———, 18—,

FORM C.

Building Societies Acts.

Application for a Certificate of Incorporation to a Society about to be established.

——— Building Society.

1. This application for a certificate of incorporation for a society intended to be established under the above-mentioned Acts as a building society, under the name of the ——— Building Society, is made by the four persons whose names are subscribed at the foot hereof.

2. The name of the society and chief office or place of meeting for the business of the society are set forth in rule No. ———.

3. The manner in which the stock or funds of the

society are to be raised, the terms upon which paid up shares (if any) are to be issued and repaid, and whether preferential shares are to be issued, and if so, within what limits, if any; and whether the society intends to avail itself of the borrowing powers contained in the Acts, and, if so, within what limits, which do not exceed the limits prescribed by the Acts, are set forth in rule No. ———.

4. The purposes to which the funds of the society are to be applied and the manner in which they are to be invested, are set forth in rule No. ———.

5. The terms upon which shares may be withdrawn, and upon which mortgages may be redeemed, are set forth in rule No. ———.

6. The manner of altering and rescinding the rules of the society, and of making additional rules, is set forth in rule No. ———.

7. The manner of appointing, remunerating, and removing the board of directors or committee of management, auditors, and other officers, is set forth in rule No. ———.

8. The manner of calling general and special meetings of the members is set forth in rule No. ———.

9. Provision for an annual or more frequent audit of accounts, and inspection by the auditors of the mortgages and other securities belonging to the society is made by rule No. ———.

10. Whether disputes between the society and any of its members, or any person claiming by or through any member, or under the rules, shall be settled by reference to the Court, or to the Registrar, or to arbitration, is determined by rule No. ———.

11. Provision for the device, custody, and use of the seal of the society, and that it shall bear the registered name thereof, is made by rule No. ———.

12. Provision for the custody of the mortgage deeds and other securities belonging to the society is made by rule No. ———.

13. The powers and duties of the board of directors or committee of management and other officers are set forth in rule No. ———.

14. The fines and forfeitures to be imposed on members of the society are set forth in rule No. ———.

15. The manner in which the society shall be terminated or dissolved, and whether it is terminating or permanent, are set forth in rule No. ———.

16. In other respects the rules are in conformity with the above-mentioned Acts.

17. Accompanying this application are sent two printed copies of the rules, each marked P. and signed by each of the applicants.

(Signed) 1. ———, Member.
2. ———, Member.
3. ———, Member.
4. ———, Secretary.

*

*Here insert the address to which the answer to the application is to be sent.

Dated the ——— day of ———, 18—.

To the Registrar of Building Societies,
28, Abingdon Street, Westminster,
London, S.W.

FORM D.

Building Societies Acts.

Application to register a Partial Alteration of Rules.

——— Building Society. Register No. ———.

This application to register a partial alteration of the rules of the ——— Building Society is made by the four persons whose names are subscribed at the foot hereof.

With this application are sent :—

(a.) A printed copy of the registered rules marked to show where and in what way they are altered :

(b.) Two printed [*or* written] copies of the alteration, each marked O., signed by each of the applicants :

(c.) A statutory declaration of an officer of this society, that in making the alteration of rules now submitted for registry, the provisions of sect. 18 of the 37 & 38 Vict. c. 42 have been complied with.

(Signed) 1. ——— Member.
2. ——— Member.
3. ——— Member.
4. ——— Secretary.

Address ———,
Date ——— day of ——— 18—.

To the Registrar of Building Societies,
Abingdon Street, Westminster.

FORM E.

Building Societies Acts.

Declaration accompanying Alteration of Rules.

——— Building Society. Register No. ———.

I, ——— of ———, an officer of the above-named society, do solemnly and sincerely declare that in making the alteration of the rules of the said society, the application for the registration of which is appended to this declaration, the provisions of sect. 18 of the 37 & 38 Vict. c. 42 have been complied with.

And I make this solemn declaration, conscientiously believing the same to be true, and by virtue of the provisions of the Statutory Declarations Act, 1835.

Taken and received before me, one of Her Majesty's justices of the peace for the county of ———, at ———, in the said county, this ——— day of ———, 18—,

---

FORM F.

Building Societies Acts.

Application for Registry of Complete Alteration of Rules.

——— Building Society. Register No. ———.

1. This application for the registration of a complete alteration of the registered rules of the ——— Building Society is made by the four persons whose names are subscribed at the foot hereof.

2. The complete alteration submitted for registration is the substitution of the set of rules, two printed copies of which (each copy marked P. and signed by each of the applicants) accompany this application, for the set of rules already registered.

3. The name of the society, and chief office or place of meeting for the business of the society are set forth in rule No. ———.

4. The manner in which the stock or funds of the society are to be raised, the terms upon which paid-up shares (if any) are to be issued and repaid, and whether preferential shares are to be issued, and if so, within what limits, if any; and whether the society intends to avail itself of the borrowing powers contained in the Acts, and, if so, within what limits, which do not exceed the limits prescribed by the Acts, are set forth in rule No. ———.

5. The purposes to which the funds of the society are to be applied, and the manner in which they are to be invested, are set forth in rule No. ———.

6. The terms upon which the shares may be withdrawn, and upon which mortgages may be redeemed, are set forth in rule No. ———.

7. The manner of altering and rescinding the rules of the society, and of making additional rules, is set forth in rule No. ———.

8. The manner of appointing, remunerating and removing the board of directors or committee of management, auditors and other officers, is set forth in rule No. ———.

9. The manner of calling general and special meetings of the members is set forth in rule No. ———.

10. Provision for an annual or more frequent audit of the accounts, and inspection by the auditors of the mortgages and other securities belonging to the society, is made by rule No. ———.

11. Whether disputes between the society and any of its members, or any person claiming by or through

any member, or under the rules, shall be settled by reference to the Court, or to the Registrar, or to arbitration, is determined by rule No. ———.

12. Provision for the device, custody and use of the seal of the society, and that it shall bear the registered name thereof, is made by rule No. ———.

13. Provision for the custody of the mortgage deeds and other securities belonging to the society is made by rule No. ———.

14. The powers and duties of the board of directors or committee of management and other officers are set forth in rule No. ———.

15. The fines and forfeitures to be imposed on members of the society are set forth in rule No.———.

16. The manner in which the society shall be terminated or dissolved, and whether it is terminating or permanent, are set forth in rule No. ———.

17. This application is also accompanied by a printed copy of the existing rules and by a statutory declaration of ———, an officer of the said society, to the effect that in making the alteration of rules now submitted for registration the provisions of sect. 18 of the 37 & 38 Vict. c. 42 have been complied with.

(Signed) 1. ——— Member.
2. ——— Member.
3. ——— Member.
4. ——— Secretary.

Address ———.
Date ———.

To the Registrar of Building Societies,
28, Abingdon Street, Westminster, S.W.
——— day of ——— 18—.

FORM G.

Building Societies Acts.

Notice to Registrar of Change of Name.

[Name already registered.] —— Building Society. Register No. —.

Notice is hereby given, that at a meeting of the ——— Building Society called for the purpose, held on the ——— day of ———, ———, it was resolved by three-fourths of the members present :—

"That the name of the society be changed to ——— Building Society."

——— Member.
——— Member.
——— Member.
——— Secretary.

Address ———.

Date ——— day of ——— 18—.

To the Registrar of Building Societies,
28, Abingdon Street, Westminster.

FORM H.

Building Societies Acts.

Declaration as to Change of Name.

[Name already registered.] —— Building Society. Register No.—.

I ——— of ——— an officer of the above-named society, do solemnly and sincerely declare that in making the change of name, notice of which is appended to this declaration, the provisions of sect. 22 of the 37 & 38 Vict. c. 42 have been duly complied with.

And I make this solemn declaration, conscientiously believing the same to be true, and by virtue of the provisions of the Statutory Declarations Act, 1835.

Taken and received before me, one of Her Majesty's justices of the peace for the said county of ——, at ——, in the said county, this —— day of —— 18—.

FORM I.

Building Societies Acts.

Application for Direction to transfer Stock.

—— Building Society. Register No.—.

1. This application is made by the four persons whose names are subscribed at the foot hereof, being the secretary [*if not, state which other officer*] and three members of the board of directors [*or* committee of management] of the —— Building Society.

2. For the purpose of making an investment in the public funds, the said society [*or* the board of directors, *or* the committee of management of the said society] did on the —— day of —— appoint —— of —— in the county of —— [*here name and describe all the trustees then appointed*] to be trustees.

3. On the —— day of —— the sum of —— was invested in the purchase of —— stock transferable at the Bank of England [*or* Ireland] in the names of the said trustees, and the same is still

standing in their names, as follows :—[*state exactly in what names the stock stands*].

4. The said ——— is absent from England [*or* Ireland] [*or* became bankrupt on the ——— day of ———, *or* filed a petition (*or* executed a deed) for liquidation of his affairs by assignment or arrangement, or for composition with his creditors on the ——— day of ———, *or* has become a lunatic, *or* died on the ——— day of ———, *or* has not been heard of for ——— years, and it is not known whether he is living or dead].

5. On the ——— of ——— the said society [*or* the board of directors, *or* the committee of management of the said society] removed the said ——— from his appointment as one of the said trustees, and appointed ——— [*give full name and description*] in his place.

6. Since such removal, application has been made in writing to the said [*removed trustee*] to join in the transfer of the said stock into the names of the said [*here give the names of the other trustees, and the new trustee appointed in the place of the one removed*] as trustees for the said society, but he has refused to comply [*or*, has not complied] with such application. [*This paragraph may be omitted or varied as the facts require.*]

7. This application to the Registrar is made pursuant to 37 & 38 Vict. c. 42, sect. 26, that he may direct the said stock to be transferred into the names of the said ——— as trustees for the society, by ——— [*this blank should be filled by the names of the surviving or continuing trustee or trustees, if any, and if they be willing and able to make the transfer; but if*

there be no such trustee, or if he or they refuse or be unable to make the transfer, then by the words the accountant-general or deputy or assistant accountant-general of the said bank; *and a full statement of the facts and of the grounds of such refusal or inability should be made*].

——— Secretary [*or* officer].

The seal must be applied and witnessed in the manner directed by the rules of the society.

(Seal of the Society.)

———
———
——— } Members of the Board or Committee.

Address ———.
Date ——— day of ——— 18—.
To the Registrar of Building Societies,
28, Abingdon Street, Westminster.

FORM K.

Building Societies Acts.

Declaration verifying Statements in an Application for direction to transfer Stock.

——— Building Society. Register No—.

——— of ——— in the county of ——— do solemnly and sincerely declare that I am the secretary [*or other officer, naming the office*] of the ——— Building Society.

That ———, ———, and ———, whose names are subscribed at the foot of the application hereto annexed, are members of the board of directors [*or* committee of management] of the said society.

That on the ——— day of ———, 18—, ———

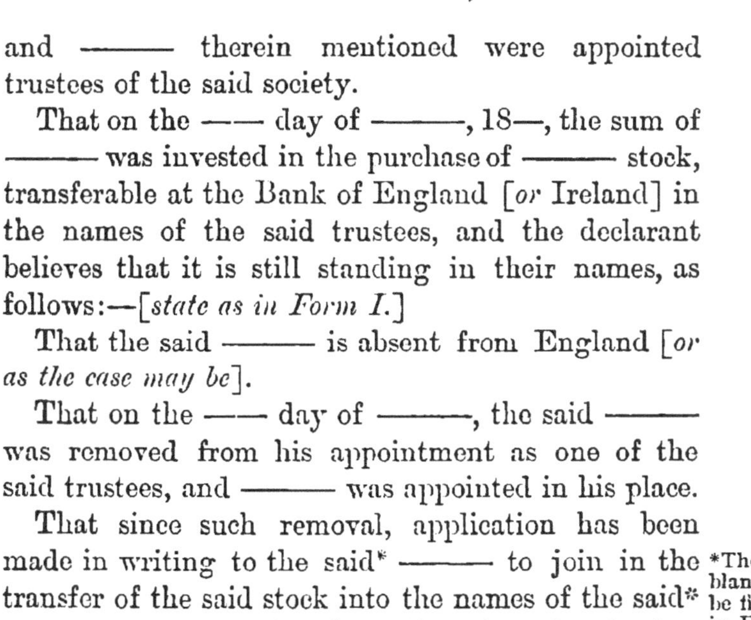

and ——— therein mentioned were appointed trustees of the said society.

That on the —— day of ———, 18—, the sum of ——— was invested in the purchase of ——— stock, transferable at the Bank of England [*or* Ireland] in the names of the said trustees, and the declarant believes that it is still standing in their names, as follows:—[*state as in Form I.*]

That the said ——— is absent from England [*or as the case may be*].

That on the —— day of ———, the said ——— was removed from his appointment as one of the said trustees, and ——— was appointed in his place.

That since such removal, application has been made in writing to the said* ——— to join in the transfer of the said stock into the names of the said* ——— as trustees for the said society, but he has refused to comply [*or*, has not complied] with such application. [*This paragraph may be omitted or varied as the facts require.*]

*These blanks will be filled as in Form I.

And I make this solemn declaration, conscientiously believing the same to be true, and by virtue of the provisions of the Statutory Declarations Act, 1835.

Taken and received before me, one of Her Majesty's justices of the peace for the said county of ———, at ———, in the said county, this ——— day of ———, 18—. }

FORM L.

Building Societies Acts.

Direction by the Registrar to transfer Stock.

Whereas it has been made to appear to the Registrar of Building Societies that —— stock, transferable at the Bank of England [*or* Ireland] is now standing in the names of ——, ——, and ——, who are trustees for the —— Building Society, incorporated under the abovementioned Acts.

And that the said —— is absent from England [*or as the case may be*].

And that —— has been appointed trustee for the said society in place of the said ——.

The Registrar of Building Societies hereby directs, pursuant to sect. 26 of the Building Societies Act, 1874, that the said sum of —— so standing in the books of the Governor and Company of the Bank of England [*or* Ireland] in the names of the said —— be transferred in the said books by the said —— into the names of the said ——, *or*,

And that there is no trustee of the said society, or that the surviving or continuing trustee or trustees refuse or are unable to transfer the said stock.

The Registrar of Building Societies hereby directs, pursuant to sect. 26 of the Building Societies Act, 1874, that the said sum of ——, so standing in the books of the Governor and Company of the Bank of England [*or* Ireland] be transferred in the said books by the accountant-general, or deputy or assistant accountant-general, of the said bank into the names of the said ——.

Address ——. Date ——, 18—.

[*To be authenticated as provided by Regulation* 26.]

FORM M.

Building Societies Acts.

Instrument of Dissolution.

——— Building Society. Register No. —.

Instrument of dissolution of the ——— Building Society made the ——— day of ———, pursuant to the Act 37 & 38 Vict. c. 42, s. 32, and signed by not less than three-fourths of the members holding not less than two-thirds of the number of shares in the said society.

It is agreed and declared as follows :—

1. The liabilities and assets of the society are the following [*here set them forth in detail*].
2. The number of members is ———, the number of shares is ———, the amount standing to the credit of the members in the books of the society is ———.
3. The society owes to depositors the sum of ———, and to other creditors the sum of ———, and such sums shall be paid out of the first moneys which shall be received by the trustees hereby appointed [*or as the case may be*].
4. After payment of the claims of depositors and other creditors, the funds and property of the society shall be appropriated and divided among the members thereof in the proportion of the amount standing to each member's credit in the books of the society [*or as the case may be*].
5. *A.*, *B.*, and *C.* [*giving full names, addresses, and descriptions*], are hereby appointed trustees for the special purpose of the dissolution,

and shall be remunerated by the sum of £——— [*or as the case may be*].

[*Here insert any other provisions the society desires to make as to the dissolution.*]

Number of shares held by members signing.

Signatures of members.

Signatures of trustees.

The seal must be applied and witnessed in the manner directed by the rules of the society.

(Common seal of the society.)

FORM N.

Building Societies Acts.

Declaration to accompany Instrument of Dissolution.

——— Building Society. Register No. —.

I, ———, of ———, an officer of the above-named society, do solemnly and sincerely declare that the instrument of dissolution* appended to this declaration is signed by not less than three-fourths of the members, holding not less than two-thirds of the number of shares in the said society.

* [*or* the alteration of the instrument of dissolution.]

And I make this solemn declaration, conscientiously believing the same to be true, and by virtue of the provisions of the Statutory Declarations Act, 1835.

Taken and received before me, one of Her Majesty's justices of the peace for the said county of ———, in the said county, this ——— day of ———, 18—.

FORM O.

Building Societies Acts.

Certificate of Registration of Instrument of Dissolution.

The Registrar of Building Societies in [England, Scotland, *or* Ireland] hereby certifies that the foregoing instrument of dissolution* of the ——— Building Society, established at ———, in the county of ———, is registered under the Building Societies Acts.

* [*or* alteration of the instrument of dissolution.]

This ——— day of ———, 18—.

[*To be authenticated as provided by Regulation* 26.]

FORM P.

Building Societies Acts.

Notice of Commencement of Dissolution where no Instrument of Dissolution is executed.

To be given within 14 days.

——— Building Society. Register No. —.

To the Registrar of Building Societies,
28, Abingdon Street, Westminster.

Notice is hereby given, that, in pursuance of the rules of the above-mentioned society, *or* of a resolution duly passed in pursuance of the rules of the society on the ——— day of ———,

The dissolution of the society commenced on the ——— day of ———.

(Seal of society.)

The seal must be applied and witnessed in the manner directed by the rules of the society.

Name and address to which registered copy is to be sent. } ———

Date ———, 18—.

FORM P *a*.

Building Societies Acts.

Notice of Commencement of Winding up.

To be given within 14 days of order of Court.

——— Building Society. Register No. —.

To the Registrar of Building Societies,
28, Abingdon Street, Westminster.

Notice is hereby given that the voluntary winding up, subject to the supervision of the Court, *or* the winding up by the Court, of the above-mentioned society commenced on the ——— day of ———.

The seal must be applied and witnessed in the manner directed by the rules of the society.

(Seal of the society.)

Name and address to which registered copy is to be sent. } ———

Date ———, 18—.

FORM Q.

Building Societies Acts.

Notice of Termination of Dissolution.

To be given within 14 days.

——— Building Society. Register No. —.

To the Registrar of Building Societies,
28, Abingdon Street, Westminster.

Notice is hereby given, that, pursuant to the instrument of dissolution [*or* rules, *as the case may be*] of the above-mentioned society, the dissolution thereof terminated on the ——— day of ———.

——— The trustees for the purpose of the dissolution,
——— [*or*, three members and the secretary if the dissolution
——— is not by instrument.]

Name and address to which registered copy is to be sent. ———

Date ———, 18—.

FORM Q *a*.

Building Societies Acts.

Notice of Termination of Winding up.

To be given within 14 days.

——— Building Society. Register No. —.

To the Registrar of Building Societies,
28, Abingdon Street, Westminster.

Notice is hereby given that the voluntary winding up, subject to the supervision of the Court, *or* the winding up by the Court, of the above society terminated on the ——— day of ———.

——— Liquidator *or* liquidators.
——— *or*
——— Official liquidator *or* liquidators.

Name and address to which registered copy is to be sent. ———

Date ———, 18—.

FORM R.

Building Societies Acts.

Notice of Union of Societies.

(*A*)——— Building Society. Register No. —.
(*B*)——— Building Society. Register No. —.

To the Registrar of Building Societies,
28, Abingdon Street, Westminster.

Notice is hereby given, that at a general meeting convened for the purpose and held pursuant to 37 & 38 Vict. c. 42, s. 33, on the ——— day of ———, 18—, the (*A*)——— Building Society above mentioned, passed by three-fourths of the members, holding not less than two-thirds of the whole number of shares, present at such meeting, the following resolution to unite with the (*B*)——— Building Society :—

[*Here give the words of the resolution as passed.*]

And that at a general meeting convened for the purpose and held pursuant to 37 & 38 Vict. c. 42, s. 33, on the ——— day of ———, 18—, the said (*B*)——— Building Society passed, by three-fourths of the members, holding not less than two-thirds of the whole number of shares, present at such meeting, the following resolution to unite with the said (*A*)——— Building Society :—

[*Here give the words of the resolution as passed.*]

And that the following are the terms of the said union :—[*State the terms.*]

And that it is intended that the united societies shall henceforth be called the ——— Building Society.

Accompanying this notice is a copy of the rules intended to be henceforth adopted by the united society [which are the rules of the ——— Building Society.]

(Seal of the (*A*) Building Society.)
(Seal of the (*B*) Building Society.)

The seals must be applied and witnessed in the manner directed by the rules of the societies respectively.

Name and address to which registered copy is to be sent. } ———

Date ———, 18—.

FORM S.

Building Societies Acts.

Notice of Transfer of Engagements.

——— Building Society. Register No. —.

To the Registrar of Building Societies,
28, Abingdon Street, Westminster.

Notice is hereby given, that at a general meeting convened for the purpose and held pursuant to 37 & 38 Vict. c. 42, s. 33, on the ——— day of ———, 18—, the above-mentioned society resolved, by three-fourths of the members, holding not less than two-thirds of the whole number of shares, present at such meeting, to transfer its engagements to the ——— Building Society, Register No. —.

And that at a general meeting convened for the purpose and held pursuant to 37 & 38 Vict. c. 42, s. 33, on the ——— day of ———, 18—, the said [*Transferee*] Building Society resolved, by three-fourths of the members, holding not less than two-thirds of the whole number of shares, present at such meeting, to accept such transfer and to undertake the engagements of the said [*Transferor*] Building Society.

And that the following are the terms of the said transfer: [*State the terms.*]

The seals must be applied and witnessed in the manner directed by the rules of the societies respectively.

(Seal of the Transferor Society.)
(Seal of the Transferee Society.)

Name and address to which registered copy is to be sent. } ———

Date ——— 18—.

FORM T.

Building Societies Acts.

Submission of a Dispute.

The part within brackets is not necessary where the rules direct disputes to be referred to the Registrar.

Dispute between ——— and the ——— Building Society. Register No. —.

[The above-named parties agree to submit the dispute between them to the Registrar.

——— Signature of Claimant. (Seal of Society.)]

The said ——— submits as follows:—

1. That he is a member of the said Society [*or claims by or through a member, or under the rules, as the case may be*].

2. That ——— [*give particulars of the claim or contention*].

3. That his case is proposed to be supported by the evidence of the following witnesses, and by the production of the following documents:— [*give list*].

Signature ———.
Address ———.
Date ——— 18—.

The said society submit as follows:—

1. That they dispute the claim [*or* contention] of the said ——— on the following grounds:— [*state grounds of dispute*].
2. That their case is proposed to be supported by the evidence of the following witnesses, and the production of the following documents:— [*give list*].

(Seal of Society.)

Date ———, 18—.

The seal must be applied and witnessed in the manner directed by the rules of the society.

FORM V.

Building Societies Acts.

Notice of Hearing.

Dispute between ——— and the ——— Building Society.

Take notice, that the Registrar of Building Societies will proceed to hear and determine the matter in dispute, which has been referred to the Registrar pursuant to the said Acts on ——— the ——— day of ——— next, at ——— o'clock, at 28, Abingdon Street, Westminster [*or as the case may be*].

Dated ——— day of ———, 18—.

[*To be authenticated as provided by Regulation* 26.]

FORM W.

Building Societies Acts.

Award of Registrar.

In the matter of a dispute between ——— and the ——— Building Society, Register No. —, referred to the Registrar pursuant to the above-mentioned Acts.

The Registrar of Building Societies in England [Scotland *or* Ireland] awards as follows :—[*here state the terms of the award*].

——— day of ———, 18—.

[*To be authenticated as provided by Regulation* 26.]

FORM X.

Building Societies Acts.

Order for Discovery.

In the matter of a dispute between ——— and the ——— Building Society, Register No. —, referred to me pursuant to the above-mentioned Acts.

The Registrar of Building Societies in England [Scotland *or* Ireland] orders and directs as follows :—

1. That, within fourteen days from the service of this order, the said ——— [*society or name of party*] do deposit at [*state where*] for inspection by the parties the following documents:—[*state the documents*].

2. That on the ——— day of ——— next, at ——— o'clock, ——— [*an officer of the society] do appear at the place above named, and make discovery of all things within his knowledge [*as such officer] relative to the following matters:—[*state the matters as to which discovery is granted*].

*These words will be omitted if the discovery is to be made by the other party to the dispute.

Date ——— day of ———.

[*To be authenticated as provided by Regulation* 26.]

FORM Y.

Building Societies Acts.

Notice of change of Chief Office.

——— Building Society. Register No. —.

To the Registrar of Building Societies in England.

Notice is hereby given that the Registered Chief Office of the ——— Building Society, established at *———, in the county of ———, is changed to the office or place following: ———, ———.

*State present Registered Chief Office.

Date ———, 18—. *Secretary.*

ACT OF SEDERUNT

Regulating the Proceedings in Liquidations in the Sheriff Courts of Scotland, under the Building Societies Act, 1874.

Edinburgh, 17*th March*, 1882.

Whereas by the Building Societies Act, 1874, 37 & 38 Vict. c. 42, s. 32, sub-s. 4, it is enacted that a society under the said Act may terminate or be dissolved "by winding up either voluntarily under the supervision of the Court, or by the Court, if the Court shall so order, on the petition of any member authorised by three-fourths of the members present at a general meeting of the society specially called for the purpose to present the same on behalf of the society, or on the petition of any judgment creditor for not less than fifty pounds, but not otherwise;" and that "general orders for regulating the proceedings of the Court under this section may be from time to time made by the authority for the time being empowered to make general orders for the Court:"

And whereas, by sect. 4 of the said statute, it is enacted that the Court in this Act means:—

"In England the County Court of the district in which the chief office or place of meeting for the business of the society is situate; in Scotland the

Sheriff's Court of the county in which such office or place of meeting is situate:"

The Lords enact and ordain as follows:—

1. All applications presented to the Court for the winding up of a society registered under the said Act, either voluntarily under the supervision of the Sheriff Court, or by the Court, shall be by petition, in form as nearly as may be of petitions under the Act 39 & 40 Vict. c. 70 (Sheriff Court Act, 1876), and the Court shall order service and advertisement thereof in the *Edinburgh Gazette*, and such further advertisement if any as the Court may consider necessary, and shall appoint the said petition to be heard on such early day as may be suitable.

2. The said petition shall be printed, and every shareholder and creditor of the company shall be entitled to receive from the solicitor of the petitioner a copy thereof on demand at his office.

3. The Court on the day appointed may hear the petitioner's proof in support of the petition, and may also hear any parties interested in support thereof or in opposition thereto, and also any application which may follow thereon in the course of the winding up, either in open Court or in chambers, and may order such answers as may be deemed necessary; and may adjourn the hearing; and after such inquiry, by proof or otherwise, as may be deemed necessary, the Court may order the society to be wound up, or may dismiss the petition, or may make such other order as may be just.

4. The Court may, as to all matters relating to the winding up, have regard to the wishes of the creditors or members, as proved by sufficient evidence; and

may direct meetings of the creditors or members to be summoned, held, and conducted in such manner as may be directed, for the purpose of ascertaining their wishes, and may appoint a person to act as chairman of any such meeting, and to report the result of such meeting to the Court. In the case of creditors regard is to be had to the value of the debt due to each creditor; and in the case of members, to the number of votes conferred on each member by the regulations of the society, or, failing such regulations, to the number of shares held by each member.

5. For the purpose of winding up a society, a liquidator shall be appointed. The shareholders may nominate a liquidator at any meeting held by them, and called in terms of the 32nd section of the statute 37 & 38 Vict. cap. 42, for the purpose of resolving to wind up the society under supervision of the Court, and of presenting a petition to the Court to that effect; and the Court shall confirm the nomination so made, unless sufficient cause to the contrary be shown. If the Court do not confirm the nomination, or if no such nomination has been made before the presenting of the petition, the Court shall, at the hearing of the said petition, or at any subsequent time, nominate a liquidator, either provisionally or otherwise. In the case of winding up by the Court, the liquidator shall be nominated by the Court. The Court may also determine whether any and what security shall be given by the liquidator; and every appointment of a liquidator shall be advertised in such manner as the Court may appoint.

6. Any liquidator may resign; or may be removed by the Court on due cause shown; and any vacancy in the office of a liquidator shall be filled up by the Court. There shall be paid to the liquidator such salary or remuneration by way of percentage or otherwise as the Court may direct.

7. When in course of winding up the society, it shall be necessary to carry on the business thereof for a time, or to make up titles to heritable property, or to compromise claims with contributories, these powers shall only be exercised with the sanction of the Court, obtained upon a note presented to the Court setting forth the grounds upon which the powers are asked for. The Court may, on the presentation of such note, order such intimation thereof as shall be deemed suitable and expedient in the circumstances. And further, it shall be competent to the liquidator to apply to the Court for instruction and direction in regard to any matter wherein, in his judgment, such instruction and direction are necessary.

8. The liquidator shall have power to appoint a law agent to assist him in the performance of his duties, and also with sanction of the Court to appoint a factor for taking charge of or managing any of the properties of the society.

9. Where a society is being wound up voluntarily under the supervision of the Court, the liquidator may from time to time during the continuance of such winding up call general meetings of the members of the society; and in the event of the winding up continuing for more than one year the liquidator shall call a general meeting of the members at the

end of the first year, and of each succeeding year from the commencement of the winding up, or as soon thereafter as may be convenient, and shall lay before such meeting an account showing his acts and dealings, and the manner in which the winding up has been conducted during the preceding year.

10. The liquidator shall, as soon as may be after an order is made for winding up a society, make up and lodge in process a state showing—

(1) The liabilities and assets of the society in detail.

(2) The number of members, and the amounts standing to their credit in the books of the society.

(3) The liabilities of members of the society in terms of sects. 13 and 14 of the Building Societies Act and of the rules of the society.

(4) The claims of depositors and other creditors and the provision to be made for their payment.

(5) The sums to be repaid to the members, if any, after payment of the debts due by the society.

And such state may be objected to by any person having interest, and may be amended from time to time. And the Court may, after such notice or advertisement as may be thought proper, and after hearing any party or parties sanction and approve of such state, or disapprove thereof, and if the same be sanctioned and approved of, the Court may authorise the funds to be distributed in terms of such state; and thereafter, on being satisfied that payment has been made to the creditors of the society and depositors so far as possible, and to the members of the society in terms of the said state, or when any sum or sums payable to any member or members of the society have not been claimed, that such consignation thereof has been made by the liquidator as the Court may direct, the Court shall declare the winding up of the said society to be at an end, and the society dissolved, discharge the liquidator of his whole actings and intromissions, and appoint his bond of caution, if any, to be delivered up.

11. The accounts of the liquidator shall be audited annually. The audit shall be made by such person as the Court may select, whether he be an auditor of Court or not, and the auditor shall report to the Court the audit so made. If it shall appear to the auditor that any payment by the liquidator should be disallowed, or that any charge has been incurred, as against the estate, which was unnecessary, or that any sum ought to have been, but is not brought into account, he shall, in his report, bring the same under the notice of the Court, setting forth the grounds of his opinion, and the Court shall pronounce judgment upon the matter so reported upon as may seem just.

12. The Court may, in the event of the assets being insufficient to satisfy the liabilities, make an order as to the payment out of the estate of the society of the costs, charges, and expenses incurred in winding up the society in such order of priority as may be considered just.

13. The liquidator shall lodge all money received by him on account of the society in one of the banks in Scotland established by Act of Parliament or Royal

Charter, in a separate account or on deposit, in his name as such liquidator, within seven days after the receipt thereof, unless the Court has otherwise directed. If the liquidator shall keep in his hands more than 50*l.* of money belonging to the society for more than seven days he shall be charged in his account with a sum at the rate of twenty per cent. per annum on the excess of the said sum of 50*l.* for such time as it shall be in his hands beyond the said seven days, and the Court may, in respect of any such retention, disallow the salary or remuneration of such liquidator, or may remove him from his office.

14. In every case where the Court shall order service, such service may be made by registered letter if the Court authorize it.

And the lords appoint this Act to be inserted in the Books of Sederunt, and to be published in common form.

JOHN INGLIS, *I.P.D.*

RULES

OF THE

—— PERMANENT BUILDING SOCIETY*

(*As altered on Incorporation*, ——, 18—).

INDEX.

---

* The following rules are those of one of the largest and most successful societies in England. The society was founded a good many years ago, and was subsequently incorporated under the Act of 1874, on which occasion various alterations were made in the rules. The most noticeable feature in these rules is that very wide powers are given to the directors—an excellent plan, if, as in the case of this society, the services of first-rate men can be secured. The author is indebted to the kindness of a friend for permission to print these rules.

Name. Office. Object.

1. THIS society, which was founded in 18—, shall be called the ——— Permanent Building Society. The chief office or place of meeting for the business of the society is ———. Its object shall be to raise and maintain, by the subscriptions of the members, and by loan as hereinafter provided, a stock or fund for investment upon the security of freehold, copyhold or leasehold property, by way of mortgage, pursuant to the Building Societies Act, 1874.

Members. Shares. Receipts. Residence. Notices.

2. Every person subscribing for a share shall be a member. Every member on entering the society shall state his name, place of abode and occupation, which shall be entered in a register to be kept at the office, and upon changing his residence shall give notice thereof within one month afterwards, or be fined one shilling.

In respect of any share or deposit registered in the name of one person only, a receipt signed by such person shall be alone a good discharge for any payment by the society on account of such share or deposit.

If any share shall be held by two or more persons jointly, the person whose name shall stand first upon the register of shareholders shall alone be entitled to vote, in respect of such share. If any share or deposit shall be held by two or more persons jointly, the person whose name shall stand first upon the books of the society shall alone be entitled to receive notices and communications in respect of such share or deposit; but the receipt of any one of such joint holders shall be a good discharge to the society for any profit or interest paid in respect of such share or deposit.

For the withdrawal of any principal money the signatures of all the joint owners shall be required.

The board shall have power to decline to register any share or deposit in more than three names, and may decline to issue any share to any person whose membership they may consider detrimental to the society.

Notices to members or depositors.

3. Every notice or communication to a member or depositor may be served by being left at his place of abode, as described on the register, or addressed to him there, and sent prepaid by post. Notices or communications for members or depositors paying through an agent may be served by being sent to such agent in either of such ways.

Entrance fees. Subscriptions. Holidays. Fines.

4. Every member, on entering the society or taking an additional share, shall pay an entrance fee of one shilling per share. The nominal value of every share shall be 30*l.*; and shares may be issued from time to time in the discretion of the board, and upon such terms as they may think fit, but no preferential shares shall be issued.

The subscriptions on every share on which no advance shall have been made (except completed or paid-up shares) shall be due on the first Monday in each month, and be four shillings per month, and shall be paid in advance, and payments becoming due on Christmas Day, or any Bank Holiday, may be made on the next day. Members making default in paying their subscriptions on unadvanced shares shall pay, for any share in arrear, a fine of one penny per month, or part of a month, and such fines shall be enforced if the payments be not received at the office by the Monday after the day on which they become due, and may be deducted at the time of making the next or any subsequent payment.

If in any case the amount due for fines on unadvanced shares shall equal the amount which would be payable on withdrawal, the board shall have power to cancel such shares.

Interest or profit.

5. The board may allow interest on the amount paid upon completed and subscribing shares respectively, at such rates as they shall think fit.

Remittances.

6. All payments shall be made at the office, and no amount, however transmitted, shall be placed to the credit of the member or depositor sending it, until the money is actually received at the office.

Agents.

7. Any number of members may (subject to the approbation of the board) appoint any member of the society as their agent for the transmission of their money, and the board will make to such agent such allowance as they may think fit, but the society shall not be responsible for any act or default on the part of any such agent.

Pass-Book.

8. Every member shall be furnished with a pass-book, and a copy of the rules of the society, for which he shall pay one shilling, in which his payments shall be entered, and his account with the society from time to time made up. In the month of December, in every year, such pass-books must be left at or sent to the office to be made up and audited.

Loss of pass-book.

9. Any member losing his pass-book shall give the secretary immediate notice of the loss, and on paying two shillings and sixpence shall be furnished with a duplicate.

10. If any person other than the member to whom

it shall belong shall produce any pass-book (either duplicate or original), and represent himself to be the member therein named, and shall thereupon withdraw or receive any money in respect of the account therein contained, neither the society nor any of its officers shall be responsible for the same, unless notice of the loss of such pass-book shall have been previously given, and the money so obtained shall be deemed to have been paid to the member whose book shall have been so produced.

11. The funds of the society are to be employed by the board in making advances to members in such order and to such amount as shall be determined by the board, and all money not so employed shall be from time to time invested upon mortgage of freehold, leasehold, or copyhold property, or other security, as provided by the Building Societies Act, 1874, in such manner as the board shall direct. **Employment of funds.**

The board may also from time to time place any money temporarily on deposit, in any joint stock bank.

12. Every member receiving an advance shall give security by mortgage to the satisfaction of the board. The member receiving the advance shall repay the amount with such premium and interest by such monthly or other instalments as shall be agreed upon. Every member entitled to or having received an advance, and being in arrear with any of his payments in respect of such advance, shall be fined after the rate of threepence for every share or part of a share for each monthly or other payment in arrear; such fines shall be enforced if the payments be not received at the office by the Monday after the day on **Security. Repayments. Premium. Interest. Fines. Deeds.**

which they become due, and may be deducted at the time of making the next or any subsequent payment. The mortgage deeds and all other securities belonging to the society shall be kept in the fire-proof strong rooms at the office of the society, except when in the custody of and required by the solicitor for the purposes of the society.

Bye-laws. 13. The directors shall have power from time to time to make bye-laws for the regulation of the society according to the rules.

Titles to property. 14. It shall be the duty of the solicitor carefully to investigate and present to the board a written report and opinion upon the title to every property offered as security for an advance. In the case of leaseholds such report shall state whether the solicitor has had the opportunity of investigating the title of the lessor or sub-lessor in addition to that of the borrower; together with any information in his possession which may assist the board in judging whether it will be safe to dispense with the investigation of such superior title. No advance shall be made upon any property which shall be mortgaged to any other persons than the society, nor until it has been surveyed on behalf of the society.

Mortgage deeds. 15. Every member may have, at his own expense, an official copy of his mortgage security delivered to him, certified by the signature of the solicitor.

Releases. 16. Whenever the money secured by any mortgage or further charge shall have been paid, all documents of title in the possession of the society relating to the mortgage or further charge which shall have been so redeemed, shall be given up; and the society shall, at the request and costs of the member, execute a release of the mortgage or further charge by a receipt in the form set forth in the schedule to the Building Societies Act, 1874, or may reconvey or assure the premises in question as the member may direct. Provided, that if there shall be any principal money owing by such member, in respect of any other mortgage or further charge, he shall not be entitled to the delivery of such documents without the consent of the board.

17. All expenses incurred by the society, or any officer or agent, in respect of any property mortgaged, or offered in security by any member, may, if the board think fit, be paid out of the society's funds in the first instance, and in that case shall be recoverable from the member, with interest at five per cent., as rent in arrear, or charged in the same way as if it were principal money, and in the meantime shall be a charge upon all property mortgaged by the member to the society, and all funds of the member in their hands. **Expenses.**

18. If any member, having received an advance and secured the payment thereof upon any property, shall sell such property, it shall be lawful for the purchaser, subject to the approval of the board, upon becoming a member in his stead, to take the said property, chargeable with the mortgage debt, and all payments in respect thereof due to the society, and with the expense of the transfer, if not paid at the time, and the purchaser, or new member, shall thenceforth become answerable to the society for the said debt and payment, and the board may, if they see no objection, release such member so selling from all future liability in respect thereof, provided that **Sales, &c., of property.** **Redemptions.** **Mortgages by non-members.** **Releases.** **Letting, &c.**

such transfer be prepared by the solicitor to the society, at the expense of the member.

Mortgages by members of the society, executed prior to ———, 18—, may be redeemed at any time on payment of the balance of the principal and premium secured by the mortgage, together with all other charges due by the member, and interest to the 30th June, or the 31st of December, which shall first accrue next after the payment is made, after being credited with a proportion of the premium to be regulated by the bye-laws. Mortgages by members of the society, executed on or after ———, 18—, may be redeemed at any time on payment of the principal secured by the mortgage, together with all other charges due by the member, and interest at five per cent. upon the balance due on the 31st of December preceding to the date of the redemption, together with an amount equal to three months' interest upon the principal due at the date of redemption.

Mortgages by persons other than members shall be subject to the ordinary equitable rules of redemption, subject to any special arrangement between the board and the mortgagor.

The board may, from time to time, at the request of any mortgagor, accept any other security by mortgage in manner hereinbefore specified, or by way of further charge on any other property already mortgaged to the society, in the place of any existing security, and such last-mentioned security may be thereupon duly released. The board may also release any portion of any mortgaged property if they shall be satisfied with the security of the property left on mortgage, and make any arrangement with regard to the sale or letting by lease or agreement, and the general management or disposal of any mortgaged property which they may deem desirable or beneficial to the society, but only with the consent of the mortgagor so long as he shall not be in arrear with his repayments in respect of such property.

19. Any member may (subject to the approval of the board) transfer his share to any other person, on payment of all arrears and fines, together with a transfer fee of one shilling per share, or part of a share; but no transfer shall be valid unless made and recorded in the manner to be from time to time directed by the board. **Transfers.**

20. Any member may withdraw the subscriptions standing to his credit, and such proportion of the profit as shall be from time to time determined by the board, at any time after the expiration of one month from the time when he shall have given notice in writing of his intention to do so, and left his pass-book at the office; any depositor may withdraw the deposits standing to his credit, at any time after the expiration of the term of notice agreed upon, but if the money in hand shall be at any time insufficient to pay all the depositors and members having given notice to withdraw, the depositors shall, in all cases, have precedence; and subject thereto, depositors and members shall be paid in rotation, according to the priority of their notices. **Withdrawal of money.**

21. If it shall appear to the board that any member or depositor has become lunatic, and that there is no committee of his effects (although the **Lunacy of members or depositors.**

contrary may, in either case, be the fact), any person appearing to have care of such member or depositor may, with the consent of the board, withdraw the amount standing to his credit, or any portion thereof, in manner aforesaid; and such withdrawal, with such consent as aforesaid, shall be considered as the valid act of such member or depositor, and be binding on him and his representatives.

Death of members or depositors.

22. In case any member or depositor to whose credit any sum of money not exceeding fifty pounds shall be standing in the books of the society shall die, and the board shall be satisfied that no will was made and left by such deceased member or depositor, and that no letters of administration have been or will be taken out (although the contrary may, in either case, be the fact), it shall be lawful for the board to pay such money to the person whom they shall think entitled to the effects of the deceased member or depositor, and every such payment shall, so far as respects any claim against the society, or any of its officers or members, be binding and valid upon and against the next of kin of such deceased member or depositor and his lawful representatives, if any such there should then or thereafter be.

Profits.

23. At the end of every year such portion of the profits as the board shall think equitable shall be carried to a reserve fund, and the remainder shall be placed to the credit of the investing shareholders who have subscribed for one year and upwards by way of bonus or interest, in such proportions as the board may direct, but no portion of such profit shall be paid to any member until his share is completed or with-

drawn, when such portion may be payable, as the board may from time to time direct.

24. The board may, whenever they think it conducive to the interest of the society, receive deposits of the members or any other persons, or borrow money to be applied in aid of the funds of the society, upon such terms as they may think fit, and such money may be repaid out of the funds of the society, with interest and all expenses incidental to the transaction, provided that the total amount so received on deposit or loan shall not at any time exceed two-thirds of the amount for the time being secured to the society by mortgage from its members. Specific notice shall be given by the board to every depositor by endorsement on the deposit certificate, that all deposits are received subject to the provisions of Rules 2, 3, 6, 20, 21, 22, and 24, regarding deposits, a copy of which rules shall be given to the depositor, or endorsed on the deposit certificate. Deposits and loans.

25. The business of the society shall be conducted by a board of directors, of such a number of members, not exceeding twenty-four, as shall be determined by the annual meeting. Each director elected after ———, 18—, must hold investing shares on which not less than 150*l.* shall be permanently at his credit. The remuneration of the board shall be such sum as from time to time shall be voted by the members at a general meeting, and in the event of no alteration being made the amount last voted shall be payable. Directors.

26. The board of directors shall have power to appoint an executive committee and other committees, with such powers and such remuneration as they may Directors. Committees. Documents.

deem expedient; and to conduct and manage the affairs of the society in all things according to their discretion, subject only to the rules for the time being; and from time to time to authorize all instruments or documents to be given, issued, signed, made, or produced, which they shall deem necessary or proper in conducting the affairs of the society in accordance with the Building Societies Act, 1874.

Directors. General meeting. Auditors. Elections.

27. One-third in number (or the number nearest to one-third) of the directors shall retire annually, the order of retirement being determined by rotation, and the vacancies shall be supplied by the members at the annual general meeting, and the retiring directors shall be eligible without notice of nomination for re-election. Twenty-eight days' previous notice in writing shall be given to the board by any member intending to propose himself, or any other member not being a retiring director or auditor for election as a director or auditor of the society; such notice shall contain the name, address, and occupation of the member to be proposed, and shall be exhibited in the offices of the society for at least seven days previous to such meeting. If, on the occasion of any election of directors, there shall be more candidates than vacancies, the election shall be conducted by the existing board for the time being in such a manner, and at such time and place, as they may think fit.

Payments.

28. No payment shall be made out of the funds of the society except by order of the board; and all payments shall be made by cheques upon the bankers, signed by two members of the board, and countersigned by the secretary.

Trustees. Seal.

29. The board shall have power from time to time

to elect and appoint one or more fit and proper person or persons to be a trustee or trustees of the society, as occasion may require.

The seal of the society shall be kept at the chief office in the custody of the board, and shall be applied to such documents as shall from time to time be directed by them. The device thereof is prefixed to these rules.

30. The board of directors shall appoint the secretary of the society. He shall not, without the consent of the board of directors, accept any other official engagement, and his salary shall be determined by the board of directors. The secretary shall give all notices, and convene and attend all meetings, and record all minutes of the proceedings thereat; he shall prepare the annual general statement of the affairs of the society hereafter named, and shall submit it to the auditors at least fourteen days before every annual meeting. He shall also conduct the general business of the society, under the direction of the board, and he shall make all returns required to be sent to the registrar. Secretary

31. The board of directors shall appoint a solicitor to the society. The solicitor shall conduct all legal business of the society, and attend, when required, all meetings of the board, for which he shall be allowed the usual professional charges. Solicitor.

32. At every annual meeting the members shall elect and appoint two members, who, with one to be appointed by the board, shall audit the accounts of the ensuing year, and at the same time inspect the mortgages and other securities belonging to the society. Auditors.

Balance sheets. 33. The board shall, at the end of each year, prepare, or cause to be prepared, a general statement of the funds and effects of or belonging to the society, specifying in whose custody or possession the said funds or effects shall be then remaining, together with an account of all sums of money received and expended since the publication of the previous periodical statement, and the same shall be certified by two of the said auditors, and countersigned by the secretary, and a copy of such statement shall be sent to the members at least three days before the annual meeting.

Members' accounts. 34. Any member or his agent shall be allowed to inspect his account in the society's books at all reasonable times.

Indemnity. 35. No director, trustee, or other officer of this society, shall be responsible for, or liable to make good, any deficiency which may arise in the funds of the society otherwise than by reason of his wilful default; but every such officer shall be answerable for the money and property actually received by him on account of the society, until he shall have disposed of the same in accordance with these rules.

Vacancies. 36. If any director, trustee, or auditor, shall become bankrupt, compound or compromise with, or make an assignment for the benefit of his creditors, or become insane, or shall signify his wish to retire from his office, or shall refuse, neglect, or become incapable to act therein, or if any director shall cease to be qualified as provided by Rule 25, the board shall remove him therefrom.

Vacancies. 37. If any vacancy shall occur in the office of trustee, director, auditor, or other office, other than such as is provided for by these rules, such vacancy may in each case be supplied by the board. Any director so appointed shall hold office only so long as the vacating director would have done.

38. Any rule may be altered or rescinded, and any additional rule may be made by the vote of three-fourths of the members present, and entitled to vote at a special meeting called for the purpose, of which meeting notice shall have been given to the members in the manner provided by Rule 42—provided that any alterations voted, which in the opinion of the board would be injurious to the society, may be suspended for two months by the board for the purpose of being submitted to a poll of the whole of the members by means of voting papers, and shall be decided upon by a majority of votes so given.

Alteration of rules.

39. A general meeting of the members shall be held annually in the month of February or March to receive the report of the directors for the past year, and for general purposes; and a special meeting shall be held whenever directed by the board; and they shall give such directions at any time upon the written request of any twenty members of the society, who shall give to the secretary written notice of the proposals to be made to such special meeting; and deposit with the secretary such sum of money as the board shall deem sufficient to pay all the expenses of convening and holding such meeting; and every special meeting convened at the request of the members, shall decide whether such expenses shall be paid by the society, or out of the money so deposited.

Annual and special meetings.

All meetings of the members shall be held at such time and place as the board shall appoint. No resolution shall be brought forward at any general or special meeting, except such as arise upon the report of the directors, unless twenty-eight days' previous notice, in writing, of such resolutions shall have been given to the board.

Voting. 40. In every case not otherwise provided for, all questions submitted to meetings shall be decided by votes of the majority of the members present and entitled to vote; and such votes shall be first taken by show of hands, or by voting papers, upon which the decision of the chairman shall be final, unless a scrutiny shall be demanded, in which case it shall be taken, at such time and place as the board may determine; and then such members of six months' standing, whose subscriptions are not in arrear, including the chairman, shall have one vote; and if there shall be an equality of votes, the chairman shall give the casting vote.

Adjournments. 41. Any meeting of members, or of any committee, may be adjourned or removed from one place to another, any number of times, by resolution of such meeting; and every meeting by adjournment or removal, as aforesaid, shall be deemed a continuation of the original meeting.

Notices of meetings. 42. Notices of all meetings of the members shall be conspicuously posted in the offices of the society, at least three weeks before the day of meeting, and shall, unless called by circular, be advertised in two daily and two weekly London newspapers, and such other papers as the board may think proper, at least two weeks before the day of meeting; and such notices shall be deemed sufficient to convene any meeting of members.

43. Every dispute between the board and any member or person claiming by or through any member or under the rules on which the decision of the board shall not be deemed satisfactory, shall be settled by reference to the registrar, under the Building Societies Act, 1874. Arbitration.

44. Each member, requiring a reference to arbitration, shall deposit with the secretary 1*l.* on account of costs. The costs and expenses of the arbitration, including such deposit, shall be in the discretion of the registrar. Arbitration.

45. In the construction of these rules a month shall be held to be a calendar month. The word "year" shall mean the society's year, and the society's first year shall be taken to expire with the ——— day of ———, 18—; and by the word "board" shall be understood "board of directors;" and whenever any word importing the singular number or the masculine gender only is used, it shall be held to include and apply to the plural number or feminine gender, as the case may be, and *vice versâ*, unless there shall be something in the subject or context repugnant to such construction. Interpretation.

46. The society may be dissolved in the manner prescribed by the Building Societies Act, 1874, s. 32. Dissolution.

MORTGAGE OF LEASEHOLDS TO A PERMANENT BUILDING SOCIETY.

THIS INDENTURE made the ——— day of ——— 18— Between A. B. of &c. (hereinafter called the mortgagor) of the one part and the ——— Building Society incorporated under the Building Societies Act 1874 (hereinafter called the society) of the other part WHEREAS by an indenture of lease dated the ——— day of ——— and made between C. D. of the one part and E. F. of the other part All that &c. [*parcels from the lease*] with the appurtenances were demised to the said E. F. his executors administrators and assigns for the term of ——— years from the ——— day of ——— at the yearly rent of £——— and subject to covenants by the lessee and conditions therein contained AND WHEREAS the said premises are now vested in the mortgagor for the residue of the said term of ——— years AND WHEREAS the mortgagor is a member of the society and has agreed to borrow the sum of £——— in respect of his ——— advanced shares therein for the term of ——— years and to assure the premises to the society to secure the repayment of such sum with interest and premium as hereinafter mentioned NOW THIS INDENTURE WITNESSETH that in consideration of the premises and of the sum of £——— paid out of the funds of the society on the execution hereof to the mortgagor (of which sum he doth hereby acknowledge the receipt) The mortgagor as beneficial owner hereby demises unto the society all the said hereditaments and premises by the said indenture of the ——— day of ——— expressed to be demised To HOLD the said premises unto the society for the residue of the said term of ——— years (except the last three days thereof) by way of mortgage for securing the discharge by the mortgagor in accordance with the rules and bye-laws of the society of the sum of £——— (being the aggregate amount of the said cash advance and an agreed premium therefor) and of all subscriptions fines interest and other sums if any which before such discharge may be owing by the mortgagor to the society upon the above-mentioned shares or upon any other share or shares therein or in any other way AND IT IS AGREED that if three of the monthly subscriptions herein provided for shall be in arrear and unpaid or if default be made by the mortgagor in observance or performance of some agreement covenant rule or bye-law herein contained or incorporated by reference or otherwise or if the mortgagor shall be bankrupt or in insolvent circumstances or make any general arrangement with his creditors whether by deed or otherwise then and in any and each of such events the society may at any time thereafter and from time to time in their absolute discretion without any further consent of the mortgagor do all any or either of the following acts that is to say—Require immediate payment from the mortgagor of the full amount that at the date of such request would be necessary for the redemption of this mortgage in accordance with the rules and bye-laws of the society or distrain for the amount of any monthly subscriptions and fines which shall be in arrear and unpaid and of any payments made by the society under the powers hereby conferred upon them as for rent in arrear upon a common demise or enter into possession of the premises or receipt of the rents and profits thereof or appoint a collector of such rents and profits at a reasonable remuneration or demise the premises or any part thereof for any terms and upon any conditions or complete any unfinished buildings thereon or repair the premises when and as the society shall deem any repair needful or expedient and for such purposes enter into such contracts as they may think proper or expedient or insure any buildings on the said premises from fire in such sums as the society shall deem expedient or pay [the ground rent or] any rates or taxes and all costs charges expenses and outgoings incurred or payable in respect of the premises And may either before or after doing any such act as aforesaid and subject or not to any such demise sell the premises or any part thereof by public auction or private contract subject or not to any special or other conditions as to title or otherwise and buy in or rescind contracts and resell without responsibility for loss and do all things necessary for effectuating demises and sales And shall out of the said rents and profits and moneys arising from sales or any or either of them so far as the same will extend firstly pay [the ground rent and] the rates and taxes in respect of the premises and all such costs charges expenses and outgoings as aforesaid together with interest thereon respectively at the rate of five pounds per centum per annum from the respective times of any such payments and next retain all subscriptions fines interest premium and other moneys due or owing by the mortgagor to the society in respect of the above-mentioned shares or any other share or shares therein in accordance with the rules and bye-laws of the society and after discharge of all moneys intended to be hereby secured pay the surplus (if any) to the mortgagor AND IT IS AGREED that the receipts of the society or of any authorized officer or agent of the society shall discharge lessees tenants occupiers purchasers and other persons paying rents profits purchase and other moneys to the society from the same and from seeing to the application thereof. And that no lessee tenant occupier purchaser or other person shall be bound to inquire whether any monthly subscriptions are in arrear or whether default has been made as aforesaid or whether any money remains on the security of these presents or whether the conditions of sale were proper or otherwise as to the propriety or regularity of any exercise of any power hereby conferred or be affected by notice actual or constructive to the contrary AND IT IS FURTHER AGREED that in case the mortgagor shall commit any breach of any covenant or agreement included herein the society shall be entitled to exercise any of the rights or powers thereupon arising at any time thereafter notwithstanding any time given by the society to the mortgagor or receipt of any moneys or other act done by the society and which but for this clause might have been construed to be a waiver of such breach AND the mortgagor hereby covenants with the society that he the mortgagor will during the continuance of this security duly and punctually pay to the proper officer and at the office for the time being of the society the monthly subscription of——— on the [first Monday] in every calendar month commencing with the month of——— next until the whole of the said sum of £——— and interest at the rate of five pounds per centum per annum from the ——— day of ——— shall have been duly paid to the society or discharged as aforesaid such interest to be calculated for the present year on the said sum of £——— and for each succeeding year on the amount remaining due to the society on the thirty-first day of December in the year last preceding and to be then debited to the account of the mortgagor in the books of the society AND THAT the mortgagor will upon demand pay to the society all and every sums or sum of money which they shall expend under or in execution of the powers hereby conferred on them with interest for the same after the rate of five pounds per centum per annum from the respective times of the payment thereof AND WILL keep the buildings now or hereafter standing on the premises in good repair and also insured against loss or damage by fire to the amount of three-fourths of the value at least in such names office and manner as shall from time to time be required by the society and deposit every policy for such insurance with the society and produce the receipts for the payment of such insurance [and of the ground-rent payable in respect of the premises] within seven days after the first day on which the same respectively shall become payable or sooner on request to the proper officer and at the office for the time being of the society

AND THAT if the premises shall be sold as aforesaid and if the rents and profits (if any) received by the society and the moneys produced by the sale shall be deficient to answer the trusts hereinbefore declared thereof the mortgagor will immediately pay to the society the sum necessary to make up such deficiency AND THAT after any sale or sales shall have been made by the society the mortgagor will stand possessed of the premises sold for the last three days of the term granted by the said indenture of lease upon trust for the purchaser or purchasers of the said premises and will assign the same as such purchaser or purchasers shall direct AND IT IS HEREBY AGREED that the position and powers of the mortgagor with regard to demising or letting the premises hereby assured or any part thereof shall be the same in all respects as they would have been prior to the passing of the Conveyancing and Law of Property Act 1881 AND FURTHER that the rules and bye-laws for the time being of the society shall apply to this mortgage and be taken by reference as incorporated herein except so far as the same have been waived by these presents AND LASTLY that where the context allows the expressions the "mortgagor" and "society" used herein include besides the mortgagor and society herein named all persons deriving title under them respectively IN WITNESS &c.

MORTGAGE OF FREEHOLDS AND COPYHOLDS TO A TERMINATING BUILDING SOCIETY.

THIS INDENTURE made the —— day of —— 18— Between A. B. of &c. a member of the —— Building Society incorporated under the Building Societies Act 1874 (hereinafter called the mortgagor) of the one part and the said —— Building Society (hereinafter called the society) of the other part WITNESSETH that in consideration of the sum of £—— on the execution of these presents paid by the society to the mortgagor being the amount to which he is entitled in respect of —— shares held by him in the society (the receipt whereof he hereby acknowledges) the mortgagor doth hereby covenant with the society that he will duly and punctually pay to the society all subscriptions and other moneys which according to the rules for the time being of the society shall from time to time become payable in respect of the said —— shares and also will duly observe all the rules of the society AND THIS INDENTURE ALSO WITNESSETH that for the consideration aforesaid the mortgagor as beneficial owner doth hereby grant unto the society and their assigns All that &c [*parcels*] To HOLD the said premises unto and to the use of the society and their assigns in fee simple PROVIDED ALWAYS that if the mortgagor shall pay to the society all the subscriptions and other moneys which according to the rules for the time being of the society shall from time to time become payable in respect of the said ——— shares and shall observe and perform all the same rules and the covenants herein contained then the society shall at any time thereafter upon the request and at the cost of the mortgagor endorse upon these presents a proper statutory receipt under their common seal for all moneys intended to be hereby secured and thereupon these presents shall be vacated AND THIS INDENTURE ALSO WITNESSETH that for the consideration aforesaid the mortgagor as beneficial owner doth hereby covenant with the society that he and all other necessary parties (if any) will forthwith surrender into the hands of the lord of the manor of ——— in the county of ——— according to the custom thereof All that &c. [*parcels*] To the use of the society and their assigns or of any persons or person nominated by the society for that purpose their heirs and assigns according to the custom of the said manor and by and under the rents fines suits and services therefor due and of right accustomed but subject to a condition for making void the said surrender corresponding with the proviso hereinbefore contained for vacating these presents AND ALSO that until such surrender shall be made he and his heirs will stand seised of the same premises in trust for the society and their assigns and subject to the same equity of redemption to which the same would have been subject if so surrendered as aforesaid AND IT IS HEREBY AGREED AND DECLARED that the society may at any time hereafter without any further consent on the part of the mortgagor take possession of the said mortgaged premises or any part thereof and may appoint any person or persons to receive the rents thereof on behalf of the society at such remuneration as the society shall think fit and may lease the said premises or any part thereof for such term or terms of years and upon such conditions and in such manner in all respects as the society shall think fit and may sell the said premises or any part thereof at such time in such manner and upon and subject to such conditions in all respects as the society may deem expedient and may buy in or rescind or vary any contract for sale and re-sell without being responsible for any loss occasioned thereby PROVIDED ALWAYS that the society shall not exercise the aforesaid powers of taking possession appointing a receiver leasing and sale unless and until default shall have been made for ——— monthly meetings of the society in the payment of some subscription or other moneys which shall have become payable in respect of the said ——— shares according to the rules of the society or in the observance or performance of the said rules or of the covenants herein contained or unless and until the mortgagor shall have become bankrupt or made some composition or arrangement with his creditors PROVIDED ALSO that no such taking of possession appointment of a receiver lease or sale by the society as aforesaid shall be impeachable by reason of the proviso lastly hereinbefore contained and no purchaser lessee or other person dealing with the society shall be bound to inquire if any money is owing on the security of these presents or into the right of the society to exercise any of the said powers AND IT IS HEREBY AGREED AND DECLARED that a receipt under the seal of the society or under the hand of any authorized officer or agent of the society for any money payable to the society by virtue of these presents shall be a good discharge to the person or persons paying the same AND IT IS HEREBY FURTHER AGREED AND DECLARED that the society shall out of the moneys which shall arise from any exercise of the aforesaid powers in the first place discharge all the expenses incurred in or about the collection or receipt of such moneys or otherwise in respect of the premises and in the next place apply such moneys in or towards satisfaction of the moneys owing according to the aforesaid rules in respect of the said shares or otherwise owing on this security (and for this purpose in case of a sale under the power hereinbefore contained all moneys which would at any time afterwards become due in respect of the said shares according to the rules of the society shall be considered as due and owing at the time of such sale) and shall pay the surplus if any to the mortgagor AND IT IS HEREBY AGREED AND DECLARED that Nos. ——— and ——— of the present registered rules of the society or any rules hereafter to be substituted for the same rules respectively having reference to the completion of unfinished buildings and to insurance from loss by fire or such of the same rules respectively as having regard to the nature and intent thereof are capable of applying to this transaction shall apply thereto as if here inserted *mutatis mutandis* and also that the other rules for the time being of the society so far as capable of applying to this transaction and except so far as hereby expressly varied or as inconsistent with any of the provisions of these presents shall also (though not expressly herein referred to) apply to this transaction AND the mortgagor hereby covenants with the society that he will during the continuance of this security observe and perform all the rules for the time being of the society relating to or affecting the premises herein comprised AND LASTLY IT IS HEREBY AGREED AND DECLARED that the expression "the mortgagor" shall unless such interpretation be inconsistent with the context be construed to include his heirs executors administrators and assigns IN WITNESS &c.

CONVEYANCE OF AN EQUITY OF REDEMPTION BY AN ADVANCED MEMBER, THE SOCIETY CONCURRING.

THIS INDENTURE made the —— day of —— 18— Between A. B. of &c. of the first part the —— Building Society (hereinafter called the society) of the second part and C. D. of &c. of the third part WHEREAS by an indenture of lease dated &c. and made between E. F. of the one part and the said A. B. of the other part All that &c. [*parcels from the lease*] were demised unto the said A. B. from the —— day of —— for the term of —— years at the yearly rent of £—— and subject to the covenants by the lessee and conditions therein contained AND WHEREAS by an indenture of mortgage dated the —— day of —— and made between the said A. B. of the one part and the society of the other part the hereditaments and premises comprised in and demised by the said indenture of lease were demised unto the society for all the residue then unexpired of the said term granted by the said indenture of lease (except the last three days thereof) by way of mortgage for securing the discharge by the said A. B. in accordance with the rules and bye-laws of the society of the sum of £——— being the full amount of his ——— advanced shares and one-third of another of such shares therein with agreed premium thereon and of all subscriptions fines interest and other sums if any which before such discharge might become payable by the said A. B. to the society upon any shares whether under those presents or in any other way AND in the indenture now in recital are contained certain powers of distress and entry upon the said premises and of perception of the rents and profits thereof and of demising and selling the same and certain other powers to take effect in the events therein mentioned AND WHEREAS the amount now required to redeem the said recited mortgage security in accordance with the rules and bye-laws of the society is the sum of £——— and no more AND WHEREAS the said A. B. has agreed with the said C. D. for the sale to him of the said premises subject to the said mortgage debt and for the transfer to him of his said advanced shares in the society for the sum of £——— and with his approval has applied to the directors of the society to permit such transfer and to release him from future liability under the said recited indenture of mortgage and to accept that of the said C. D. in lieu thereof which the said directors have agreed to do and that the society should join herein AND WHEREAS the said A. B. has transferred his said advanced shares in the society to the said C. D. before the execution hereof NOW THIS INDENTURE WITNESSETH that in pursuance of the said agreement and in consideration of the sum of £——— to the said A. B. paid by the said C. D. upon the execution hereof (the receipt whereof the said A. B. doth hereby acknowledge) and also in consideration of the said C. D. taking upon himself the said mortgage debt so due to the society as aforesaid He the said A. B. as beneficial owner doth hereby assign unto the said C. D. his executors administrators and assigns All the said hereditaments and premises by the said indenture of lease expressed to be demised To hold the said premises unto the said C. D. his executors administrators and assigns for the residue of the said term of ——— years At the rent and subject to the covenants by the lessee and conditions in the said indenture of lease reserved and contained and henceforth to be paid performed and observed And also subject to the said indenture of mortgage and to the term thereby created and to the payment of all moneys intended to be thereby secured AND the said C. D. doth hereby covenant with the said A. B. that he the said C. D. his executors administrators or assigns will henceforth pay the rent reserved by and perform all the covenants by the lessee and conditions contained in the said indenture of lease and keep the said A. B. his heirs executors and administrators indemnified against all proceedings costs damages claims demands and liability for non-payment of the said rent or breach of the said covenants or any of them AND the said C. D. doth hereby covenant with the society their successors and assigns that he the said C. D. his executors administrators or assigns shall and will from time to time and at all times hereafter during the continuance of the said mortgage security duly and punctually pay or cause to be paid to the person at the times and in manner therein mentioned the several monthly subscriptions and payments therein mentioned and provided for until the whole of the moneys intended to be thereby secured shall be fully paid to the society or discharged in accordance with the rules and bye-laws of the society in that behalf And shall and will in all other respects well and truly observe and perform fulfil and keep all and every the covenants and agreements in the said hereinbefore recited indenture of mortgage contained on the part of the said A. B. his heirs executors administrators or assigns so far as the same now remain to be observed and performed fulfilled and kept And moreover that nothing herein contained shall in any way preclude or prejudice the exercise of the powers of sale or any other of the powers contained in the said recited indenture of mortgage or the trusts and provisoes ancillary thereto but that the same shall be exercisable in all respects as if the society had not joined in these presents And the society in consideration thereof do hereby release unto the said A. B. his heirs executors and administrators all claims suits and causes of suit whatsoever in respect of the said recited indenture of mortgage without prejudice nevertheless to any existing liability on his or their part for anything done or omitted to be done by him contrary to the covenants contained in the said recited indenture of mortgage up to the day of the execution of these presents IN WITNESS &c.

INDEX.

PRINTED BY C. F. ROWORTH, GREAT NEW STREET, FETTER LANE, E.C.

October, 1885.

A CATALOGUE
OF
LAW WORKS,
PUBLISHED BY
STEVENS AND SONS,
119, CHANCERY LANE, LONDON, W.C.
(And at 14, Bell Yard, Lincoln's Inn).

NOTE.—*All letters to be addressed to Chancery Lane,* NOT *to Bell Yard.*

A Catalogue of Modern Law Works *(including the leading American, Indian, Irish and Scotch); together with a complete Chronological List of all the English, Irish and Scotch Reports, Abbreviations used in reference to Law Reports and Text Books, and an Index of Subjects, 8vo, cloth, corrected to January 1885. (Post free for two stamps.)*

Acts of Parliament.—*Public and Local Acts from an early date, may be had of the Publishers of this Catalogue, who have also on sale the largest collection of Private Acts, relating to Estates, Enclosures Railways, Roads. &c., &c.*

ACTION AT LAW.—Foulkes' Elementary View of the Proceedings in an Action in the Supreme Court, with a Chapter on Matters and Arbitrations.—(Founded on "SMITH'S ACTION AT LAW.") By W. D. I. FOULKES, Esq., Barrister-at-Law. Third Edition. Demy 12mo. 1884. 7*s.* 6*d.*

"The entire work will be invaluable to students, and it will often prove a handy book of reference to busy practitioners."—*Law Times.*

ADMIRALTY.—Roscoe's Admiralty Practice.—A Treatise on the Jurisdiction and Practice of the Admiralty Division of the High Court of Justice, and on Appeals therefrom, with a chapter on the Admiralty Jurisdiction of the Inferior and the Vice-Admiralty Courts. With an Appendix containing Statutes, Rules as to Fees and Costs, Forms, Precedents of Pleadings and Bills of Costs. By E. S. ROSCOE, Esq., Barrister-at-Law. Second Edition. Revised and Enlarged. Demy 8vo. 1882. 1*l.* 4*s.*

"A clear digest of the law and practice of the Admiralty Courts."
"A comprehensive and useful manual of practice."—*Solicitors' Journal.*

ADVOCACY.—Harris' Hints on Advocacy. Conduct of Cases Civil and Criminal. Classes of Witnesses and suggestions for Cross-Examining them, &c., &c. By RICHARD HARRIS, Barrister-at-Law. Seventh Edition. (Further Revised.) Royal 12mo. 1884. 7*s.* 6*d.*

"Full of good sense and just observation. A very complete Manual of the Advocate's art in Trial by Jury."—*Solicitors' Journal.*
"A book at once entertaining and really instructive. . . . Deserves to be carefully read by the young barrister whose career is yet before him."—*Law Magazine.*

AGRICULTURAL LAW.—Beaumont's Treatise on Agricultural Holdings and the Law of Distress as regulated by the Agricultural Holdings (England) Act, 1883, with Appendix containing Full Text of the Act, and Precedents of Notices and Awards. By JOSEPH BEAUMONT, Esq., Solicitor. Royal 12mo. 1883. 10*s.* 6*d.*

Cooke's Treatise on the Law and Practice of Agricultural Tenancies.—New edition, in great part rewritten with especial reference to Unexhausted Improvements, with Modern Forms and Precedents. By G. PRIOR GOLDNEY, of the Western Circuit, and W. RUSSELL GRIFFITHS, LL.B., of the Midland Circuit, Barristers-at-Law. Demy 8vo. 1882. 1*l.* 1*s.*

Griffith's Agricultural Holdings (England) Act, 1883, containing an Introduction; a Summary of the Act, with Notes; the complete Text of the Act, with Forms, and a specimen of an Award under the Act. By W. RUSSELL GRIFFITHS, LL.B., of the Midland Circuit. Uniform with "Cooke's Agricultural Tenancies." Demy 8vo. 1883. 5*s.*

Spencer's Agricultural Holdings (England) Act, 1883, with Explanatory Notes and Forms; together with the Ground Game Act, 1880. Forming a Supplement to "Dixon's Law of the Farm." By AUBREY J. SPENCER, B.A., Esq. Barrister-at-Law, and late Holder of Inns of Court Studentship. Demy 8vo. 1883. 6*s.*

"The general effect of the Act of 1883 is clearly and concisely stated in the Introduction, and the annotation of both Acts is very well done. Thirty-nine forms are given, and a good index."—*Law Times.*

ANNUAL DIGEST.—Mews'.—*Vide* "Digest."

ARBITRATION.—Russell's Treatise on the Power and Duty of an Arbitrator, and the Law of Submissions and Awards; with an Appendix of Forms, and of the Statutes relating to Arbitration. By FRANCIS RUSSELL, Esq., M.A., Barrister-at-Law. Sixth Edition. By the Author and HERBERT RUSSELL, Esq., Barrister-at-Law. Royal 8vo. 1882. 36*s.*

"The cases are carefully collected, and their effect is clearly and shortly given. . . . . . This edition may be commended to the profession as comprehensive, accurate and practical.'—*Solicitors Journal.*

ARTICLED CLERKS.—Rubinstein and Ward's Articled Clerks' Handbook.—Being a Concise and Practical Guide to all the Steps Necessary for Entering into Articles of Clerkship, passing the Preliminary, Intermediate, Final, and Honours Examinations, obtaining Admission and Certificate to Practise, with Notes of Cases, Suggestions as to Mode of Reading and Books to be read during Articles, and an Appendix. Third Edition. By J. S. RUBINSTEIN and S. WARD, Solicitors. 12mo. 1881. 4*s.*

"No articled clerk should be without it."—*Law Times.*

Shearwood.—*Vide* "Examination Guides."

ARTICLES OF ASSOCIATION.—Palmer.—*Vide* "Conveyancing."

ASSETS, ADMINISTRATION OF.—Eddis' Principles of the Administration of Assets in Payment of Debts. By ARTHUR SHELLY EDDIS, one of Her Majesty's Counsel. Demy 8vo. 1880. 6*s.*

AUSTRALASIAN COLONIES.—Wood's Laws of the Australasian Colonies as to the Administration and Distribution of the Estate of Deceased Persons; with a Preliminary Part on the Foundation and Boundaries of those Colonies, and the Law in force in them. By JOHN DENNISTOUN WOOD, Esq., Barrister-at-Law. Royal 12mo. 1884. 6*s.*

*** *All standard Law Works are kept in Stock, in law calf and other bindings.*

AVERAGE.—**Hopkins' Hand-Book of Average**, to which is added a chapter on Arbitration.—Fourth Edition. By MANLEY HOPKINS, Esq., Author of "A Manual of Marine Insurance," &c. Demy 8vo. 1884. 1*l.* 1*s.*

"The work is eminently practical, and exhibits the results of practical experience in every branch of the subject with which it deals, and the book may properly find its place in the library of every lawyer who occupies himself with ships and shipping."—*Law Journal:*

Lowndes' Law of General Average.—English and Foreign. Fourth Edition. By RICHARD LOWNDES. Author of "The Law of Marine Insurance," &c. (*In preparation.*)

BALLOT.—**FitzGerald's Ballot Act.**—With an INTRODUCTION. Forming a Guide to the Procedure at Parliamentary and Municipal Elections. Second Edition. By GERALD A. R. FITZGERALD, M.A., Esq., Barrister-at-Law. Fcap. 8vo. 1876. 5*s.* 6*d.*

BANKING.—**Walker's Treatise on Banking Law.** Second Edition. By J. D. WALKER, Esq., Barrister-at-Law. Demy 8vo. 1885. 15*s.*

"An able and concise treatise. . . . The chapter on Principal and Surety is one of much general interest. . . . The style is clear and precise."—*Law Times.*

BANKRUPTCY.—**Chitty's Index, Vol. I.**—*Vide* "Digests."

Gray's Bankruptcy Manual.—The Bankruptcy Act, 1883, and the Rules, Orders, Forms and Scales thereunder, with short Notes, giving cross-references, references for comparisons with the corresponding provisions of the old Statutes and Rules, and Cases incorporated, and References for all the Reported Decisions, an **Introduction**, showing the Changes effected by the Act, an **Analysis** of the Act, an Appendix on the Debtors' Acts, &c., Tables of Statutes, Rules and Cases, and a **Full Index**. Second Edition. By GEO. G. GRAY, LL.D., Esq., Barrister-at-Law. 8vo. 1884. 12*s.* 6*d.*

Haynes' Lectures on Bankruptcy; originally delivered before the members of the Liverpool Law Students' Association. By JOHN F. HAYNES, LL.D., Author of the "Student's Statutes," the "Student's Leading Cases," &c. Royal 12mo. 1884. 5*s.*

"Well worthy of the student's perusal."—*Solicitors' Journal.*

Joel's Manual of Bankruptcy and Bills of Sale Law, with analytical Notes to the Bankruptcy Act, 1883, and references to the leading Cases in Bankruptcy, under the 1849, 1861 and 1869 Acts, and the Bills of Sale Acts, 1854, 1866, 1878, and 1882, and Debtors Acts, 1869 and 1878, together with Rules, Orders, and Forms, Forms of Deeds of Composition, Bills of Sale, and Rules of Interpleader, &c. By J. EDMONDSON JOEL, Esq., Barrister-at-Law. Demy 8vo. 1884. 1*l.* 5*s.*

Lawrance's Precedents of Deeds of Arrangement between Debtors and their Creditors; including Forms of Resolutions for Compositions and Schemes of Arrangement under the Bankruptcy Act, 1883. By GEORGE WOODFORD LAWRANCE, M.A., of Lincoln's Inn, Esq., Barrister-at-Law. 8vo. 1884. 5*s.*

"A small but useful collection of precedents by a draftsman very familiar with the subject."—*Law Journal*, August 9th, 1884.

Rigg's Bankruptcy Act, 1883, and the Debtors Act, 1869, with the Rules and Forms belonging thereto, and the Bills of Sale Acts, 1878 and 1882. Edited with a Commentary. By JAMES McMULLEN RIGG, Esq., Barrister-at-Law. Royal 12mo. 1884. 10*s.* 6*d.*

***** *All standard Law Works are kept in Stock, in law calf and other bindings.***

BANKRUPTCY.—*Continued.*

Salaman's Analytical Index to the Bankruptcy Act, 1883.—By JOSEPH SEYMOUR SALAMAN, Esq., Solicitor. Uniform with the Act, 1883. *Net*, 3*s*.

Williams' Law and Practice in Bankruptcy: comprising the Bankruptcy Act, 1883, the Debtors Acts, 1869, 1878, and the Bills of Sale Acts, 1878 and 1882. Third Edition. By R. VAUGHAN WILLIAMS and W. VAUGHAN WILLIAMS, assisted by EDWARD WM. HANSELL, Esqrs., Barristers-at-Law. Demy 8vo. 1884. 1*l*. 8*s*.

"We miss nothing in the book which is necessary material for understanding the new system."—*Law Journal.*

Willis' Law and Practice in Bankruptcy under the Bankruptcy Act of 1883, and the Rules and Forms, with Notes. By E. COOPER WILLIS Esq., one of Her Majesty's Counsel, assisted by A. R. WHITEWAY, Esq., Barrister-at-Law. Demy 8vo. 1884. 1*l*. 10*s*.

"The book before us has a special merit in the practical tone in which it is written. The notes upon sect. 44 are an excellent example of this virtue. . . . The index is up to the standard of the rest of the book."—*Law Times.*

"The index appears full and well arranged, and the notes give a good account of the cases bearing on the sections of the Act."—*Law Journal.*

"The book is extremely well printed, and the index—the work of Mr. Whiteway—is all that cou'd be desired."—*Solicitors' Journal.*

BILLS OF LADING.—A Treatise on the Law of Bills of Lading. By EUGENE LEGGETT, Solicitor and Notary Public. Demy 8vo. 1880. 1*l*. 1*s*.

BILLS OF SALE.—Fithian's Bills of Sale Acts, 1878 and 1882. With an Introduction and Explanatory Notes showing the changes made in the Law with Respect to Bills of Sale, together with an Appendix of Precedents, Rules of Court, Forms, and Statutes. Second Edition. By EDWARD WILLIAM FITHIAN, Esq., Barrister-at-Law. Royal 12mo. 1884. 6*s*.

"The notes appear thoroughly reliable."—*Law Times*, March 22, 1884.

"Mr. Fithian's book will maintain a high place among the most practically useful editions of the Bills of Sale Acts."—*Law Magazine.*

Joel.—*Vide* "Bankruptcy."

BOOK-KEEPING.—Matthew Hale's System of Book-keeping for Solicitors, containing a list of all books necessary, with a comprehensive description of their objects and uses for the purpose of Drawing Bills of Costs and the rendering of Cash Accounts to clients; also showing how to ascertain profits derived from the business; with an Appendix. Demy 8vo. 1884. 5*s*. 6*d*.

"We think this is by far the most sensible, useful, practical little work on Solicitors' book-keeping that we have seen."—*Law Students' Journal.*

CANALS.—Webster's Law Relating to Canals: Comprising a Treatise on Navigable Rivers and Canals; and including all Legislation to the close of the last Session of Parliament, together with the Procedure and Practice in Private Bill Legislation; with a coloured Map of the existing Canals and Navigations in England and Wales. By ROBERT G. WEBSTER, LL.B., of the Inner Temple, Barrister-at-Law; author of "The Trade of the World," etc. Demy 8vo. 1885. 1*l*. 1*s*.

CARRIERS.—Browne on Carriers.—A Treatise on the Law of Carriers of Goods and Passengers by Land and Water. By J. H. B. BROWNE, Esq., Barrister-at-Law. 8vo. 1873. 18*s*.

CHANCERY, *and Vide* "**EQUITY.**"

**** All standard Law Works are kept in Stock, in law calf and other bindings.*

CHANCERY.—*Continued.*

Daniell's Chancery Practice.—The Practice of the Chancery Division of the High Court of Justice and on appeal therefrom, being the Sixth Edition of Daniell's Chancery Practice, with alterations and additions, and references to a companion Volume of Forms. By L. FIELD, E. C. DUNN, and T. RIBTON, assisted by W. H. UPJOHN, Barristers-at-Law. 2 vols. in 3 parts. Demy 8vo. 1882-84. 6*l.* 6*s.*

"There is to be found, in every part of the book we have examined, evidence of great care. . . . It is exactly what it professes to be—a concise and careful digest of the practice."—*Solicitors' Journal.*

"A complete, trustworthy, and indispensable guide to the practice of the Chancery Division."—*Law Times.*

"A mine of information for ready reference whenever the practitioner may have occasion to seek for guidance."—*Law Magazine.*

Daniell's Forms and Precedents of Proceedings in the Chancery Division of the High Court of Justice and on Appeal therefrom. Fourth Edition. With Summaries of the Rules of the Supreme Court, Practical Notes and References to the Sixth Edition of "Daniell's Chancery Practice." By CHARLES BURNEY, B.A. (Oxon.), a Chief Clerk of the Hon. Mr. Justice Chitty. Royal 8vo. 1885. 2*l.* 10*s.*

"Many of the chapters have been revised by persons specially qualified to deal with their contents."—*Law Quarterly Review*, July, 1885.

Morgan's Chancery Acts and Orders.—The Statutes, Rules of Court and General Orders relating to the Practice and Jurisdiction of the Chancery Division of the High Court of Justice and the Court of Appeal. With Copious Notes. Sixth Edition. By the Right Hon. GEORGE OSBORNE MORGAN, one of Her Majesty's Counsel, and E. A. WURTZBURG, Barrister-at-Law. Royal 8vo. 1885. 1*l.* 10*s.*

"This work we have had in constant use for the last few weeks, and we have no hesitation in saying that the present state of the Harmonious Whole, so far as relates to the Chancery Division, is made to appear as intelligible as under the circumstances can reasonably be expected."—*Law Quarterly Review*, July, 1885.

"The present edition of this valuable work is marked by a care and completeness which leave comparatively little to be desired."—*Solicitors' Journal*, May 9, 1885.

Morgan and Wurtzburg's Chancery Costs.—*Vide* "Costs."

Peel's Chancery Actions.—A Concise Treatise on the Practice and Procedure in Chancery Actions under the Rules of the Supreme Court, 1883.—Third Edition. By SYDNEY PEEL, of the Middle Temple, Esq., Barrister-at-Law. Demy 8vo. 1883. 8*s.* 6*d.*

"A valuable little treatise."—*Law Times.*

"Enriched with a very full list of cases bearing upon the practice of the Chancery Division, giving references to all the Reports."—*Law Journal.*

"The book will give to the student a good general view of the effect on chancery practice of the Judicature Acts and Orders."—*Solicitors' Journal.*

CHANCERY PALATINE OF LANCASTER.—Snow and Winstanley's Chancery Practice.—The Statutes, Consolidated and General Orders and Rules of Court relating to the Practice, Pleading and Jurisdiction of the Court of Chancery, of the County Palatine of Lancaster. With Copious Notes. By THOMAS SNOW and HERBERT WINSTANLEY, Esqrs., Barristers-at-Law. Royal 8vo. 1880. 1*l.* 10*s.*

*** *All standard Law Works are kept in Stock, in law calf and other bindings.*

COLLISIONS.—Lowndes' Admiralty Law of Collisions at Sea.—8vo. 1867. *7s. 6d.*

Marsden's Treatise on the Law of Collisions at Sea. With an Appendix containing Extracts from the Merchant Shipping Acts, the International Regulations for preventing Collisions at Sea; and local Rules for the same purpose in force in the Thames, the Mersey, and elsewhere. Second Edition. By REGINALD G. MARSDEN, Esq., Barrister-at-Law. Demy 8vo. 1885. 1*l.* 1*s.*

COMMERCIAL LAW.—The French Code of Commerce and most usual Commercial Laws. With a Theoretical and Practical Commentary, and a Compendium of the judicial organization and of the course of procedure before the Tribunals of Commerce; together with the text of the law; the most recent decisions, and a glossary of French judicial terms. By L. GOIRAND, Licencié en droit. Demy 8vo. 1880. 2*l.* 2*s.*

COMMON LAW.—Allen.—*Vide* "Pleading."

Ball's Short Digest of the Common Law; being the Principles of Torts and Contracts. Chiefly founded upon the works of Addison, **with Illustrative Cases**, for the use of Students. By W. EDMUND BALL, LL.B., late "Holt Scholar" of Gray's Inn, Barrister-at-Law and Midland Circuit. Demy 8vo. 1880. 16*s.*

"The principles of the law are very clearly and concisely stated."—*Law Journal.*

Ball.—*Vide* "Leading Cases" and "Torts."

Bullen and Leake.—*Vide* "Pleading."

Chitty's Archbold's Practice of the Queen's Bench Division of the High Court of Justice and on Appeal therefrom to the Court of Appeal and House of Lords in Civil Proceedings. Fourteenth Edition. By THOS. WILLES CHITTY, assisted by J. ST. L. LESLIE, Esqrs., Barristers-at-Law. 2 Vols. Demy 8vo. 1885. 3*l.* 13*s.* 6*d.*

Chitty's Forms.—*Vide* "Forms."

Fisher's Digest of Reported Decisions in all the Courts, with a Selection from the Irish; and references to the Statutes, Rules and Orders of Courts from 1756 to 1883. Compiled and arranged by JOHN MEWS, assisted by C. M. CHAPMAN, HARRY H. W. SPARHAM and A. H. TODD, Barristers-at-Law. In 7 vols. Royal 8vo. 1884. 12*l.* 12*s.*

*** *Annual Supplement for* 1884. *Royal* 8*vo.* 12*s.* 6*d.*

Foulkes.—*Vide* "Action."

Napier's Concise Practice of the Queen's Bench and Chancery Divisions and of the Court of Appeal, with an Appendix of Questions on the Practice, and intended for the use of Students. By T. BATEMAN NAPIER, Barrister-at-Law. Demy 8vo. 1884. 10*s.*

Shirley.—*Vide* "Leading Cases."

Smith's Manual of Common Law.—For Practitioners and Students. Comprising the fundamental principles and the points most usually occurring in daily life and practice. By JOSIAH W. SMITH, B.C.L., Q.C. Ninth Edition. 12mo. 1880. 14*s.*

COMMONS AND INCLOSURES.—Chambers' Digest of the Law relating to Commons and Open Spaces, including Public Parks and Recreation Grounds. By GEORGE F. CHAMBERS, Esq., Barrister-at-Law. Imperial 8vo. 1877. 6*s.* 6*d.*

COMPANY LAW.—**Palmer's Private Companies,** their Formation and Advantages; or, How to Convert your Business into a Private Company, and the benefit of so doing. With Notes on "Single Ship Companies." Fifth Edition. By F. B. PALMER, Esq., Barrister-at-Law. 12mo. 1884. *Net*, 2*s*.

Palmer.—*Vide* "Conveyancing" and "Winding up."

Palmer's Shareholders' and Directors' Legal Companion.—A Manual of every-day Law and Practice for Promoters, Shareholders, Directors, Secretaries, Creditors and Solicitors of Companies, under the Companies' Acts, 1862 to 1883. Fifth Edition. With an Appendix on the Conversion of Business Concerns into Private Companies. By F. B. PALMER, Esq., Barrister-at-Law. 12mo. 1885. *Net*, 2*s*. 6*d*.

Thring.—*Vide* "Joint Stocks."

COMPENSATION.—**Cripps' Treatise on the Principles of the Law of Compensation.** Second Edition. By C. A. CRIPPS, Esq., Barrister-at-Law. Demy 8vo. 1884. 16*s*.

"A complete treatise on the subject in which it professes to deal."—*Law Times.*

"A remarkably well-written treatise."—*Solicitors' Journal.*

CONTINGENT REMAINDERS.—**An Epitome of Fearne on Contingent Remainders and Executory Devises.** Intended for the Use of Students. By W. M. C. Post 8vo. 1878. 6*s*. 6*d*.

"The student will find a perusal of this epitome of great value to him."—*Law Journal.*

CONTRACTS.—**Addison on Contracts.**—Being a Treatise on the Law of Contracts. Eighth Edition. By HORACE SMITH, Esq., Barrister-at-Law, Recorder of Lincoln, Author of "A Treatise on the Law of Negligence," &c. Royal 8vo. 1883. 2*l*. 10*s*.

"To the present editor must be given all praise which untiring industry and intelligent research can command. He has presented the profession with the law brought down to the present date clearly and fully stated."—*Law Times.*

"This edition of Addison will maintain the reputation of the work as a satisfactory guide to the vast storehouse of decisions on contract law."—*Solicitors' Journal.*

Fry.—*Vide* "Specific Performance."

Leake on Contracts.—An Elementary Digest of the Law of Contracts. By STEPHEN MARTIN LEAKE, Barrister-at-Law. Demy 8vo. 1878. 1*l*. 18*s*.

Pollock's Principles of Contract.—Being a Treatise on the General Principles relating to the Validity of Agreements in the Law of England. **Fourth Edition.** By FREDERICK POLLOCK, Esq., Barrister-at-Law. Demy 8vo. 1885. 1*l*. 8*s*.

Smith's Law of Contracts.—Eighth Edition. By V. T. THOMPSON, Esq., Barrister-at-Law. Demy 8vo. 1885. 1*l*. 1*s*.

"The best introduction to the law of contracts which can be put before the student."—*Law Journal*, Jan. 31, 1885.

CONVEYANCING.—**Dart.**—*Vide* "Vendors and Purchasers."

Greenwood's Manual of Conveyancing.—A Manual of the Practice of Conveyancing, showing the present Practice relating to the daily routine of Conveyancing in Solicitors' Offices. To which are added Concise Common Forms and Precedents in Conveyancing. Seventh Edition. Edited by HARRY GREENWOOD, M.A., Esq., Barrister-at-Law. Demy 8vo. 1882. 16*s*.

"We should like to see it placed by his principal in the hands of every articled clerk. One of the most useful practical works we have ever seen."—*Indermaur's Law Students' Journal.*

*** *All standard Law Works are kept in Stock, in law calf and other bindings.*

CONVEYANCING.—*Continued.*

Humphry's Common Precedents in Conveyancing. Adapted to the Conveyancing Acts, 1881-82, and the Settled Land Act, 1882, &c., together with the Acts, an Introduction, and Practical Notes. Second Edition. By HUGH M. HUMPHRY, M.A., Esq., Barrister-at-Law. Demy 8vo. 1882. 12*s.* 6*d.*

"The collection of Precedents is sufficiently comprehensive for ordinary use, and is supplemented by concise foot notes mainly composed of extracts from statutes necessary to be borne in mind by the draftsman."—*Law Magazine.*

"A work that we think the profession will appreciate."—*Law Times.*

Palmer's Company Precedents.—For use in relation to Companies subject to the Companies' Acts, 1862 to 1883. Arranged as follows :—Agreements, Memoranda and Articles of Association, Resolutions, Notices, Certificates, Prospectus, Debentures, Policies, Private Companies, Writs, Petitions, Judgments and Orders, Winding-up, Reconstruction, Amalgamation, Arrangements, Special Acts. With Copious Notes. Third Edition. By FRANCIS BEAUFORT PALMER, of the Inner Temple, Esq., Barrister-at-Law. Royal 8vo. 1884. 1*l.* 12*s.*

"To those concerned in getting up companies, the assistance given by Mr. Palmer must be very valuable, because he does not confine himself to bare precedents, but by intelligent and learned commentary lights up, as it were, each step that he takes. . . There is an elaborate index."—*Law Times.*

Prideaux's Precedents in Conveyancing.—With Dissertations on its Law and Practice. Thirteenth Edition. By FREDERICK PRIDEAUX, late Professor of the Law of Real and Personal Property to the Inns of Court, and JOHN WHITCOMBE, Esqrs., Barristers-at-Law. 2 vols. Royal 8vo. 1885. 3*l.* 10*s.*

"The most useful work out on Conveyancing."—*Law Journal.*

"This work is accurate, concise, clear, and comprehensive in scope, and we know of no treatise upon conveyancing which is so generally useful to the practitioner."—*Law Times.*

"The conciseness and scientific precision of these Precedents of the Future are at once pleasing and startling."—*Law Magazine.*

"The student who, in good time before his examination, can peruse these most valuable dissertations and refer to some of the precedents will have an immense advantage over those who have not done so."—*Law Students' Journal.*

Turner's Duties of Solicitor to Client as to Partnership Agreements, Leases, Settlements and Wills.— By EDWARD F. TURNER, Solicitor, Lecturer on Real Property and Conveyancing, and one of the Assistant Examiners for Honours to the Incorporated Law Society, Author of "The Duties of Solicitor to Client as to Sales, Purchases, and Mortgages of Land." (Published by permission of the Council of the Incorporated Law Society.) Demy 8vo. 1884. 10*s.* 6*d.*

"The work has our full approval, and will, we think, be found a valuable addition to the student's library."—*Law Students' Journal.*

CONVICTIONS.—**Paley's Law and Practice of Summary Convictions under the Summary Jurisdiction Acts, 1848 and 1879**; including Proceedings preliminary and subsequent to Convictions, and the responsibility of convicting Magistrates and their Officers, with Forms. Sixth Edition. By W. H. MACNAMARA, Esq., Barrister-at-Law. Demy 8vo. 1879. 1*l.* 4*s.*

**** ***All standard Law Works are kept in Stock, in law calf and other bindings.***

COPYRIGHT.—Slater's Law relating to Copyright and Trade Marks, treated more particularly with Reference to Infringement; Forming a Digest of the more important English and American decisions, together with the Practice of the English Courts and Forms of Informations, Notices, Pleadings, and Injunctions. By JOHN HERBERT SLATER, of the Middle Temple, Esq., Barrister-at-Law. Demy 8vo. 1884. 18s.

CORONERS.—Jervis on the Office and Duties of Coroners.—With Forms and Precedents. Fourth Edition. By R. E. MELSHEIMER, Esq., Barrister-at-Law. Post 8vo. 1880. 12s.

COSTS.—Morgan and Wurtzburg's Treatise on the Law of Costs in the Chancery Division of the High Court of Justice.—Being the Second Edition of Morgan and Davey's Costs in Chancery. With an Appendix, containing Forms and Precedents of Bills of Costs. By the Right Hon. GEORGE OSBORNE MORGAN, one of Her Majesty's Counsel, and E. A. WURTZBURG, Esq., Barrister-at-Law. Demy 8vo. 1882. 1*l.* 10*s.*

"Cannot fail to be of use to solicitors and their Chancery managing clerks."—*Law Times.*

Scott's Costs in the High Court of Justice and other Courts. Fourth Edition. By JOHN SCOTT, of het Inner Temple, Esq., Barrister-at-Law. Demy 8vo. 1880. 1*l.* 6*s.*

Summerhays and Toogood's Precedents of Bills of Costs in the Chancery, Queen's Bench, Probate, Divorce and Admiralty Divisions of the High Court of Justice; in Conveyancing; the Crown Office; Lunacy; Arbitration under the Lands Clauses Consolidation Act; the Mayor's Court, London; the County Courts; the Privy Council; and on Passing Residuary and Succession Accounts; with Scales of Allowances; Rules of Court relating to Costs; Forms of Affidavits of Increase, and of Objections to Taxation. Fourth Edition. By WM. FRANK SUMMERHAYS, and THORNTON TOOGOOD, Solicitors. Royal 8vo. 1883. 1*l.* 8*s.*

"On looking through this book we are struck with the minuteness with which the costs are enumerated under each heading; and the 'Table of Contents' shows that no subject matter has been omitted. . . . . We have no doubt the work will meet with the same approval, and be as useful in the Solicitor's office, as heretofore."—*Law Journal.*

Webster's Parliamentary Costs.—Private Bills, Election Petitions, Appeals, House of Lords. Fourth Edition. By C. CAVANAGH, Esq., Barrister-at-Law. Post 8vo. 1881. 20s.

COUNTY COURTS.—Pitt-Lewis' County Court Practice.—**A Complete Practice of the County Courts,** including Admiralty and Bankruptcy, embodying the Acts, Rules, Forms and Costs, with Additional Forms and a Full Index. Second Edition. By G. PITT-LEWIS, of the Middle Temple and Western Circuit, Esq., Barrister-at-Law, sometime Holder of the Studentship of the Four Inns of Court, assisted by H. A. DE COLYAR, Esq., Barrister-at-Law. In 2 parts. Demy 8vo. 1883-84. 2*l.* 10*s.*

"It is very clearly written, and is always practical. The Index is very elaborate, and there is an excellent tabular Index to the County Court Acts and Rules."—*Solicitors' Journal.*

"One of the best books of practice which is to be found in our legal literature."—*Law Times.*

"Mr. Pitt-Lewis has, in fact, aimed—and we are glad to say successfully—at providing for the County Courts' practitioner what 'Chitty's Archbold' and 'Daniell's Chancery Practice' have long been to practitioners in the High Court."—*Law Magazine.*

*** *All standard Law Works are kept in Stock, in law calf and other bindings.*

CRIMINAL LAW.—Archbold's Pleading and Evidence in Criminal Cases.—With the Statutes, Precedents of Indictments, &c., and the Evidence necessary to support them. Nineteenth Edition. By WILLIAM BRUCE, Esq., Stipendiary Magistrate for the Borough of Leeds. Demy 8vo. 1878. 1*l.* 11*s.* 6*d.*

Mews' Digest of Cases relating to Criminal Law from 1756 to 1883, inclusive.—By JOHN MEWS, assisted by C. M. CHAPMAN, HARRY H. W. SPARHAM, and A. H. TODD, Barristers-at-Law. Royal 8vo. 1884. 1*l.* 1*s.*

Roscoe's Digest of the Law of Evidence in Criminal Cases.—Tenth Edition. By HORACE SMITH, Esq., Barrister-at-Law, Recorder of Lincoln, Editor of "Addison on Contracts," &c. Royal 12mo. 1884. 1*l.* 11*s.* 6*d.*

"We have looked for a considerable number of the recent cases, and have found them all correctly stated."—*Solicitors' Journal*, August 16, 1884.

Russell's Treatise on Crimes and Misdemeanors.—Fifth Edition. By SAMUEL PRENTICE, Esq., one of Her Majesty's Counsel. 3 vols. Royal 8vo. 1877. 5*l.* 15*s.* 6*d.*

"What better Digest of Criminal Law could we possibly hope for than 'Russell on Crimes?'"—*Sir James Fitzjames Stephen's Speech on Codification.*

Shirley's Sketch of the Criminal Law.—By W. SHIRLEY SHIRLEY, Author of "Leading Cases made Easy," assisted by C. M. ATKINSON, Esqrs., Barristers-at-Law. Demy 8vo. 1880. 7*s.* 6*d.*

"As a primary introduction to Criminal Law, it will be found very acceptable to Students."—*Law Students' Journal.*

DIARY.—Lawyer's Companion (The), Diary, and Law Directory for 1886.—For the use of the Legal Profession, Public Companies, Justices, Merchants, Estate Agents, Auctioneers, &c., &c. Edited by J. TRUSTRAM, of Lincoln's Inn, Esq., Barrister-at-Law; and contains Tables of Costs in Conveyancing, &c.; Monthly Diary of County, Local Government, and Parish Business; Oaths in Supreme Court; Summary of Legislation of 1885; Alphabetical Index to the Practical Statutes; a Copious Table of Stamp Duties; Legal Time, Interest, Discount, Income, Wages and other Tables; Probate, Legacy and Succession Duties; and a variety of matters of practical utility. PUBLISHED ANNUALLY. Fortieth Issue. 1886. (*Nearly ready.*)

Contains the most complete List published of the English Bar, and London and Country Solicitors, with date of admission and appointments, and is issued in the following forms, octavo size, strongly bound in cloth:—

		s.	*d.*
1.	Two days on a page, plain	5	0
2.	The above, INTERLEAVED for ATTENDANCES	7	0
3.	Two days on a page, ruled, with or without money columns	5	6
4.	The above, with money columns, INTERLEAVED for ATTENDANCES	8	0
5.	Whole page for each day, plain	7	6
6.	The above, INTERLEAVED for ATTENDANCES	9	6
7.	Whole page for each day, ruled, with or without money cols.	8	6
8.	The above, INTERLEAVED for ATTENDANCES	10	6
9.	Three days on a page, ruled blue lines, without money cols.	5	0

The Diary contains memoranda of Legal Business throughout the Year.

"An excellent work."—*The Times.*

"Contains all the information which could be looked for in such a work, and gives it in a most convenient form and very completely."—*Solicitors' Journal.*

"The 'Lawyer's Companion and Diary' is a book that ought to be in the possession of every lawyer, and of every man of business."

"The 'Lawyer's Companion' is, indeed, what it is called, for it combines everything required for reference in the lawyer's office."—*Law Times.*

"It is a book without which no lawyer's library or office can be complete."—*Irish Law Times.*

*** *All standard Law Works are kept in Stock, in law calf and other bindings.*

DECISIONS OF SIR GEORGE JESSEL.—Peter's Analysis and Digest of the Decisions of Sir George Jessel, late Master of the Rolls; with Full Notes, References and Comments, and copious Index. By APSLEY PETRE PETER, Solicitor, Law Society Prizeman. Demy 8vo. 1883. 16s.

"A perusal of the book in its present entire state further demonstrates with what neatness and conciseness the author has summarised and digested the judgments of the great judge who delivered them, with what care he has collated his references, and how happily his comments are expressed. There is every reason to think that his 'hope that the work may be useful to both the practitioner and student' will be amply realised, not only in this country but the United States."—*Law Journal.*

DICTIONARY.—The Pocket Law Lexicon.—Explaining Technical Words, Phrases and Maxims of the English, Scotch and Roman Law, to which is added a complete List of Law Reports, with their Abbreviations. Second Edition, Enlarged. By HENRY G. RAWSON, Esq., Barrister-at-Law. Fcap. 8vo. 1884. 6s. 6d.

"A wonderful little legal Dictionary."—*Indermaur's Law Students' Journal.*

"A very handy, complete, and useful little work."—*Saturday Review.*

Wharton's Law Lexicon.—Forming an Epitome of the Law of England, and containing full explanations of the Technical Terms and Phrases thereof, both Ancient and Modern; including the various Legal Terms used in Commercial Business. Together with a Translation of the Latin Law Maxims and selected Titles from the Civil, Scotch and Indian Law. Seventh Edition. By J. M. LELY, Esq., Barrister-at-Law, Editor of "Chitty's Statutes," &c. Super-royal 8vo. 1883. 1l. 18s.

"On almost every point both student and practitioner can gather information from this invaluable book, which ought to be in every lawyer's office."—*Gibson's Law Notes.*

"As it now stands the Lexicon contains all it need contain, and to those who value such a work it is made more valuable still."—*Law Times.*

DIGESTS.—Bedford.

Chitty's Index to all the Reported Cases decided in the several Courts of Equity in England, the Privy Council, and the House of Lords, with a selection of Irish Cases, on or relating to the Principles, Pleading, and Practice of Equity and Bankruptcy; from the earliest period. Fourth Edition. By WILLIAM FRANK JONES and HENRY EDWARD HIRST, Esqrs., Barristers-at-Law. Volumes I. and II. contain the Titles "Abandonment" to "Education." Royal 8vo. 1883-85. *Each*, 1l. 11s. 6d.

Volumes III. and IV. are in the press, and will be issued shortly.

"To both counsel and solicitor the book will be invaluable."—*Law Magazine.*

Fisher's Digest of the Reported Decisions of the Courts of Common Law, Bankruptcy, Probate, Admiralty, and Divorce, together with a Selection from those of the Court of Chancery and Irish Courts from 1756 to 1883 inclusive. Founded on Fisher's Digest. By JOHN MEWS, assisted by C. M. CHAPMAN, HARRY H. W. SPARHAM, and A. H. TODD, Barristers-at-Law. 7 vols. Royal 8vo. 1884. 12l. 12s.

*** Annual Supplement for 1884, 12s. 6d.

"To the common lawyer it is, in our opinion, the most useful work he can possess."—*Law Times.*

Mews' Digest of the Reported Decisions for the year 1883. By JOHN MEWS, Esq., Barrister-at-Law Royal 8vo. 16s.

Ditto, ditto for 1884. Royal 8vo. 12s. 6d.

"Compiled with the completeness and accuracy which distinguish the series."—*Law Journal*, Feb. 21, 1885.

****All standard Law Works are kept in Stock, in law calf and other bindings.*

DIGESTS.—*Continued.*

Notanda Digest in Law, Equity, Bankruptcy, Admiralty, Divorce, and Probate Cases.—By H. TUDOR BODDAM and HARRY GREENWOOD and E. W. D. MANSON, Esqrs., Barristers-at-Law.

Third Series, 1873 to 1876 inclusive, half-bound. *Net*, 1*l.* 11*s.* 6*d.*

Ditto, Fourth and Fifth Series, for the years 1877, 1878, 1879, 1880, 1881, 1882, 1883, and 1884, with Index. *Each, net*, 1*l.* 1*s.*

Ditto, Sixth Series, for 1885. By E. W. D. MANSON and PROCKTER T. PULMAN, Esqrs., Barristers at-Law. Plain Copy and Two Indexes, or Adhesive Copy for insertion in Text-Books (without Index). Annual Subscription, payable in advance. *Net*, 21*s.*

*** The numbers are issued every alternate month. Each number contains a concise analysis of every case reported in the *Law Reports, Law Journal, Weekly Reporter, Law Times*, and the *Irish Law Reports*, up to and including the cases contained in the parts for the current month, with references to Text-books, Statutes, and the Law Reports Consolidated Digest, and an ALPHABETICAL INDEX of the subjects contained IN EACH NUMBER.

DISCOVERY.—Hare's Treatise on the Discovery of Evidence.—Second Edition. By SHERLOCK HARE, Barrister-at-Law. Post 8vo. 1877. 12*s.*

Sichel and Chance's Discovery.—The Law relating to Interrogatories, Production, Inspection of Documents, and Discovery, as well in the Superior as in the Inferior Courts, together with an Appendix of the Acts, Forms and Orders. By WALTER S. SICHEL, M.A., and WILLIAM CHANCE, M.A., Esqrs., Barristers-at-Law. Demy 8vo. 1883. 12*s.*

"Of material assistance to those who are much engaged in judges' chambers or in the county courts."—*Law Magazine.*

DIVORCE.—Browne's Treatise on the Principles and Practice of the Court for Divorce and Matrimonial Causes:—With the Statutes, Rules. Fees and Forms relating thereto. Fourth Edition. By GEORGE BROWNE, Esq., Barrister-at-Law. Demy 8vo. 1880. 1*l.* 4*s.*

"The book is a clear, practical, and, so far as we have been able to test it, accurate exposition of divorce law and procedure."—*Solicitors' Journal.*

*** Supplement to above. By L. D. POWLES, Esq., Barrister-at-Law. Demy 8vo. 1884. 6*s.*

EASEMENTS.—Goddard's Treatise on the Law of Easements.—By JOHN LEYBOURN GODDARD, Esq., Barrister-at-Law. Third Edition. Demy 8vo. 1884. 1*l.* 1*s.*

"We are able, as the result of a careful perusal of the new portions of this edition of Mr. Goddard's book, to congratulate the author on the important advance towards completeness made since the last edition, with which we have been familiar for some years. . . . . An indispensable part of the lawyer's library."—*Solicitors' Journal.*

"The book is invaluable: where the cases are silent the author has taken pains to ascertain what the law would be if brought into question."—*Law Journal.*

"Nowhere has the subject been treated so exhaustively, and, we may add, so scientifically, as by Mr. Goddard. We recommend it to the most careful study of the law student, as well as to the library of the practitioner."—*Law Times.*

Innes' Digest of the English Law of Easements.—Third Edition. By Mr. JUSTICE INNES, lately one of the Judges of Her Majesty's High Court of Judicature, Madras. Royal 12mo. 1884. 6*s.*

LUNACY.—Elmer's Practice in Lunacy.—Seventh Edition. (*In preparation.*)

MAGISTERIAL LAW.—Shirley's Elementary Treatise on Magisterial Law, and on the Practice of Magistrates' Courts.—By W. SHIRLEY SHIRLEY, M.A., B.C.L., Esq., Barrister-at-Law. Royal 12mo. 1881. 6*s.* 6*d.*

Wigram.—*Vide* "Justice of the Peace."

MARRIAGE.—Kelly's French Law of Marriage, and the Conflict of Laws that arises therefrom. By EDMOND KELLY, M.A., of the New York Bar, Licencié en Droit de la Faculté de Paris. Royal 8vo. 1885. 6*s.*

Lush.—*Vide* "Husband and Wife."

MARRIAGE SETTLEMENTS.—Banning's Concise Treatise on the Law of Marriage Settlements; with an Appendix of Statutes. By HENRY THOMAS BANNING, M.A., Barrister-at-Law. Demy 8vo. 1884. 15*s.*

"A welcome addition to the library of all those specially interested in its subject. It is tersely and neatly written, and is eminently readable."—*Law Journal.*

MARRIED WOMEN'S PROPERTY.—Smith's Married Women's Property Acts, 1882 and 1884, with an Introduction and Critical and Explanatory Notes, together with the Married Women's Property Acts, 1870 and 1874, &c. Second Edition Revised. By H. ARTHUR SMITH, Esq., Barrister-at-Law. Royal 12mo. 1884. 6*s.*

"There are some excellent critical and explanatory notes, together with a good index, and reference to something like two hundred decided cases."—*Law Times.*

MASTER AND SERVANT.—Macdonell's Law of Master and Servant. Part I, Common Law. Part II, Statute Law. By JOHN MACDONELL, M.A., Esq., Barrister-at-Law. Demy 8vo. 1883. 1*l.* 5*s.*

"Mr. Macdonell has done his work thoroughly and well. He has evidently bestowed great care and labour on his task, and has, therefore, produced a work which will be of real value to the practitioner. The information, too, is presented in a most accessible form."—*Law Times.*

MAYOR'S COURT PRACTICE.—Candy's Mayor's Court Practice.—The Jurisdiction, Process, Practice, and Mode of Pleading in Ordinary Actions in the Mayor's Court, London (commonly called the "Lord Mayor's Court"). **Founded on Brandon.** By GEORGE CANDY, Esq., Barrister-at-Law. Demy 8vo. 1879. 14*s.*

MERCANTILE LAW.—Russell's Treatise on Mercantile Agency. Second Edition. 8vo. 1873. 14*s.*

Smith's Compendium of Mercantile Law.—Tenth Edition. By JOHN MACDONELL, Esq., Barrister-at-Law, Author of "The Law of Master and Servant." (*In preparation*).

Tudor's Selection of Leading Cases on Mercantile and Maritime Law.—With Notes. By O. D. TUDOR, Esq., Barrister-at-Law. Third Edition. Royal 8vo. 1884. 2*l.* 2*s.*

Wilson's Mercantile Handbook of the Liabilities of Merchant, Shipowner, and Underwriter on Shipments by General Vessels. By ALEXANDER WILSON, Solicitor and Notary. Royal 12mo. 1883. 6*s.*

METROPOLIS BUILDING ACTS.—Woolrych's Metropolitan Building Acts, together with such clauses of the Metropolis Management Acts as more particularly relate to the Building Acts, with Notes and Forms. Third Edition. By W. H. MACNAMARA, Esq., Barrister-at-Law. 12mo. 1882. 10*s.*

MINES.—Rogers' Law relating to Mines, Minerals and Quarries in Great Britain and Ireland, with a Summary of the Laws of Foreign States, &c. Second Edition Enlarged. By ARUNDEL ROGERS, Esq., Judge of County Courts. 8vo. 1876. 1*l.* 11*s.* 6*d.*

MORTGAGE.—Coote's Treatise on the Law of Mortgage.—Fifth Edition. Thoroughly revised. By WILLIAM WYLLYS MACKESON, Esq., one of Her Majesty's Counsel. and H. ARTHUR SMITH, Esq , Barrister-at-Law. 2 vols. Royal 8vo. 1884. 3*l.*

"An exhaustive, compendious and reliable treatise on the law of Mortgage."—*Law Times.*

"A complete, terse, and practical treatise for the modern lawyer."—*Solicitors' Journal.*

MUNICIPAL CORPORATIONS.—Bazalgette and Humphreys.—*Vide* "Local and Municipal Government."

Lely's Law of Municipal Corporations.—Containing the Municipal Corporation Act, 1882, and the Enactments incorporated therewith, with a Selection of Supplementary Enactments, including therein the Electric Lighting Act, 1882, with Notes. By J. M. LELY, Esq., Barrister-at-Law. Editor of "Chitty's Statutes," &c. Demy 8vo. 1882. 15*s.*

"An admirable edition of one of the most important consolidating statutes of the year."—*Law Journal.*

MUSIC HALLS.—Geary.—*Vide* "Theatres."

NAVY.—Thring's Criminal Law of the Navy, with an Introductory Chapter on the Early State and Discipline of the Navy, the Rules of Evidence, and an Appendix comprising the Naval Discipline Act and Practical Forms. Second Edition. By THEODORE THRING, Barrister-at-Law, and C. E. GIFFORD, Assistant-Paymaster, Royal Navy. 12mo. 1877. 12*s.* 6*d.*

NEGLIGENCE.—Smith's Treatise on the Law of Negligence. Second Edition. By HORACE SMITH, B.A., Esq., Barrister-at-Law, Recorder of Lincoln, Editor of "Addison on Contracts," &c. Demy 8vo. 1884. 12*s.* 6*d.*

"The work, in its present form, appears to us to be one of great value both to the practitioner and student of law. It is not merely a book of reference, though it is likely to be very valuable in that capacity. It is not merely a digest of decisions arranged under appropriate heads; but it really answers to its title, and is a treatise on the law of negligence."—*Solicitors' Journal*, June 7, 1884.

NISI PRIUS.—Roscoe's Digest of the Law of Evidence on the Trial of Actions at Nisi Prius.—Fifteenth Edition. By MAURICE POWELL, Esq., Barrister-at-Law. 2 vols. Demy 8vo. 1884. 2*l.* 10*s.*

"Continues to be a vast and closely packed storehouse of information on practice at Nisi Prius, and the necessary ingredients of the plaintiffs' and defendants' cases in all the classes of actions commonly tried there."—*Law Journal*, Nov. 8, 1884.

"We do not observe any diminution in the care or accuracy with which the cases have been noted."—*Solicitors' Journal.*

NOTARY.—Brooke's Treatise on the Office and Practice of a Notary of England.—With a full collection of Precedents. Fourth Edition. By LEONE LEVI, Esq., F.S.A., of Lincoln's Inn, Barrister-at-Law. 8vo. 1876. 1*l.* 4*s.*

OATHS.—Braithwaite's Oaths in the Supreme Courts of Judicature.—A Manual for the use of Commissioners to Administer Oaths in the Supreme Courts of Judicature in England and Ireland, &c. Fourth Edition. Re-issue. By T. W. BRAITHWAITE, of the Central Office. Fcap. 8vo. 1884. *Net*, 2*s*. 6*d*.

"The recognised guide of commissioners to administer oaths."—*Solicitors' Journal.*

PARISH LAW.—Steer's Parish Law; being a Digest of the Law relating to the Civil and Ecclesiastical Government of Parishes and the Relief of the Poor. Fourth Edition. By W. H. MACNAMARA, Esq., Barrister-at-Law. Demy 8vo. 1881. 16*s*.

"An exceedingly useful compendium of Parish Law. —*Law Times.*

PARTNERSHIP.—Pollock's Digest of the Law of Partnership.—Third Edition. By FREDERICK POLLOCK, Esq., Barrister-at-Law. Author of "Principles of Contract at Law and in Equity." Demy 8vo. 1884. 8*s*. 6*d*.

"Of the execution of the work, we can speak in terms of the highest praise. The language is simple, concise, and clear."—*Law Magazine.*

"Mr. Pollock's work appears eminently satisfactory . . . the book is praiseworthy in design, scholarly and complete in execution."—*Saturday Review.*

Turner.—*Vide* "Conveyancing."

PATENTS.—Aston's (T.) Patents, Designs and Trade Marks Act, 1883, with Notes and Index to the Act, Rules and Forms. By THEODORE ASTON, Q.C. Royal 12mo. 1884. 6*s*.

Johnson's Patentees' Manual.—Being a Treatise on the Law and Practice of Letters Patent. Especially intended for the use of Patentees and Inventors. Fifth Edition. By JAMES JOHNSON, Barrister-at-Law; and J. HENRY JOHNSON, Solicitor and Patent Agent. Demy 8vo. 1884. 10*s*. 6*d*.

Munro's Patents, Designs and Trade Marks Act, 1883, with the Rules and Instructions, together with Pleadings, Orders and Precedents. By J. E. CRAWFORD MUNRO, Esq., Barrister-at-Law. Royal 12mo. 1884. 10*s*. 6*d*.

"The completeness of the statements as to the new practice should render it acceptable to solicitors as a handy guide on practical points."—*Law Times.*

Thompson's Handbook of Patent Law of all Countries.—By WM. P. THOMPSON, Head of the International Patent Office, Liverpool. Sixth Edition. 12mo. 1884. *Net*, 2*s*. 6*d*.

PAWN.—Turner's Contract of Pawn, as it exists at Common Law, and as modified by the Factors' Acts, the Pawnbrokers' Acts, and other Statutes. By FRANCIS TURNER, Esq., Barrister-at-Law. Second Edition. 8vo. 1883. 12*s*.

Turner's Pawnbrokers' Act, 1872.—With Explanatory Notes. By FRANCIS TURNER, Esq., Barrister-at-Law. Third Edition. 1883. *Net*, 2*s*. 6*d*.

PERPETUITIES.—Marsden's Rule against Perpetuities.—A Treatise on Remoteness in Limitation; with a chapter on Accumulation and the Thelluson Act. By REGINALD G MARSDEN, Esq., Barrister-at-Law. Demy 8vo. 1883. 16*s*.

"Mr. Marsden's work is entitled to be called a new one both in treatment and in design. He has handled a difficult subject with intelligence and clearness."—*Law Times*

PERSONAL PROPERTY.—Shearwood's Concise Abridgment of the Law of Personal Property; showing analytically its Branches and the Titles by which it is held. By J. A. SHEARWOOD, Esq., Barrister-at-Law. 1882. 5*s*. 6*d*.

"Will be acceptable to many students, as giving them, in fact, a ready-made note book."—*Indermaur's Law Students' Journal.*

Smith.—*Vide* "Real Property."

*** *All standard Law Works are kept in Stock, in law calf and other bindings.*

PLEADING.—**Allen's Forms of Indorsements of Writs of Summons, Pleadings, and other Proceedings in the Queen's Bench Division prior to Trial, pursuant to the Rules of the Supreme Court, 1883**; with Introduction, showing the principal changes introduced by these Rules, and a Supplement of Rules and Forms of Pleadings applicable to the other Divisions. By GEORGE BAUGH ALLEN, Esq., Special Pleader, and WILFRED B. ALLEN, Esq., Barrister-at-Law. Royal 12mo. 1883. 18*s.*

"A most excellent handbook and guide to those who are called upon to frame indorsements and pleadings under the new system. . . . A work which will be very useful to most legal practitioners."—*Solicitors' Journal.*

"The learned authors have done their work well and supply a large number of precedents, besides providing useful hints and suggestions."—*Law Magazine.*

Bullen and Leake's Precedents of Pleadings, with Notes and Rules relating to Pleading. Fourth Edition. By THOMAS J. BULLEN, Esq., Special Pleader, and CYRIL DODD, Esq., Barrister-at-Law. Part I. Royal 12mo. 1882. (*Part II. in the press.*) 1*l.* 4*s.*

POISONS.—**Reports of Trials for Murder by Poisoning; by Prussic Acid, Strychnia, Antimony, Arsenic and Aconitine;** including the trials of Tawell, W. Palmer, Dove, Madeline Smith, Dr. Pritchard, Smethurst, and Dr. Lamson. With Chemical Introductions and Notes on the Poisons used. By G. LATHAM BROWNE, Esq., Barrister-at-Law, and C. G. STEWART, Senior Assistant in the Laboratory of St. Thomas's Hospital, &c. Demy 8vo. 1883. 12*s.* 6*d.*

POWERS.—**Farwell on Powers.**—A Concise Treatise on Powers. By GEORGE FARWELL, B.A., of Lincoln's Inn, Esq., Barrister-at-Law. 8vo. 1874. 1*l.* 1*s.*

PROBATE.—**Browne's Probate Practice**: a Treatise on the Principles and Practice of the Court of Probate, in Contentious and Non-Contentious Business. Revised, enlarged, and adapted to the Practice of the High Court of Justice in Probate business. By L. D. POWLES, Barrister-at-Law. Including Practical Directions to Solicitors for Proceedings in the Registry. By T. W. H. OAKLEY, of the Principal Registry, Somerset House. 8vo. 1881. 1*l.* 10*s.*
*** Supplement to above. By L. D. POWLES, Esq., Barrister-at-Law. Demy 8vo. 1884. 6*s.*

PUBLIC HEALTH.—**Bazalgette and Humphreys.**—*Vide* "Local and Municipal Government."

Chambers' Digest of the Law relating to Public Health and Local Government.—With Notes of 1260 leading Cases. The Statutes in full. A Table of Offences and Punishments, and a Copious Index. Eighth Edition (with Supplement corrected to March 9, 1885). Imperial 8vo. 1881. 16*s.*
Or, the above with the Law relating to Highways and Bridges. 1*l.*

PUBLIC MEETINGS.—**Chambers' Handbook for Public Meetings,** including Hints as to the Summoning and Management of them. By GEORGE F. CHAMBERS, Esq., Barrister-at-Law. 12mo. 1878. *Net,* 2*s.* 6*d.*

QUARTER SESSIONS.—Leeming & Cross's General and Quarter Sessions of the Peace.—Their Jurisdiction and Practice in other than Criminal matters. Second Edition. By HORATIO LLOYD, Esq., Judge of County Courts, and H. F. THURLOW, Esq., Barrister-at-Law. 8vo. 1876. 1*l.* 1*s.*

Pritchard's Quarter Sessions.—The Jurisdiction, Practice and Procedure of the Quarter Sessions in Criminal, Civil, and Appellate Matters. By THOS. SIRRELL PRITCHARD, of the Inner Temple, Esq., Barrister-at-Law, Recorder of Wenlock. 8vo. 1875. 2*l.* 2*s.*

RAILWAYS.—Browne and Theobald's Law of Railway Companies.—Being a Collection of the Acts and Orders relating to Railway Companies, with Notes of all the Cases decided thereon, and Appendix of Bye-Laws and Standing Orders of the House of Commons. By J. H. BALFOUR BROWNE, Esq., Registrar to the Railway Commissioners, and H. S. THEOBALD, Esq., Barristers-at-Law. Demy 8vo. 1881. 1*l.* 12*s.*

"Contains in a very concise form the whole law of railways."—*The Times.*

"As far as we have examined the volume the learned authors seem to have presented the profession and the public with the most ample information to be found whether they want to know how to start a railway, how to frame its bye-laws, how to work it, how to attack it for injury to person or property, or how to wind it up." —*Law Times.*

RATES AND RATING.—Castle's Practical Treatise on the Law of Rating. Second Edition. By EDWARD JAMES CASTLE, Esq., Barrister-at-Law. (*In the press.*)

Chambers' Law relating to Rates and Rating; with especial reference to the Powers and Duties of Rate-levying Local Authorities, and their Officers. Being the Statutes in full and brief Notes of 550 Cases. By G. F. CHAMBERS, Esq., Barrister-at-Law. Imp. 8vo. 1878. *Reduced to* 10*s.*

REAL ESTATE.—Foster's Law of Joint Ownership and Partition of Real Estate. By EDWARD JOHN FOSTER, M.A., late of Lincoln's Inn, Barrister-at-Law. 8vo. 1878. 10*s.* 6*d.*

REAL PROPERTY.—Greenwood's Real Property Statutes; comprising those passed during the years 1874—1884, inclusive, consolidated with the earlier statutes thereby amended. With copious notes. Second Edition. By HARRY GREENWOOD, M.A., LL.M., assisted by LEES KNOWLES, M.A., LL.M., Esqrs., Barristers-at-Law. Demy 8vo. 1884. 1*l.* 5*s.*

"The second edition of this useful collection of statutes relating to real property will be heartily welcomed by conveyancers and real property lawyers. In referring to it as a collection of statutes, however, we do not fully describe it, because the method adopted by the author of grouping together the provisions of the various Acts, which are in *pari materiâ*, combined with the fulness and accuracy of the notes, entitles the book to rank high amongst treatises on the law of real property. The plan of the book is to bring together all the statutory provisions relating to a particular subject in one place, so that the reader may have them all before him and be better able to judge of their effect. This is carried out by means of interpolating the sections of one statute in the body of another, and in order to avoid any inconvenience or confusion arising from the system, the interpolated sections are plainly distinguished by being inserted between square brackets; and where it has been thought necessary to notice sections which have been repealed they are always printed in italics. . . . . The notes are full, and well supported by the citation of authorities."—*Law Journal*, Feb. 21, 1885.

Leake's Elementary Digest of the Law of Property in Land.—Containing: Introduction. Part I. The Sources of the Law.—Part II. Estates in Land. By STEPHEN MARTIN LEAKE, Barrister-at-Law. 8vo. 1874. 1*l.* 2*s.*

*** *All standard Law Works are kept in Stock, in law calf and other bindings.*

REAL PROPERTY.—*Continued.*

Shearwood's Real Property.—A Concise Abridgment of the Law of Real Property and an Introduction to Conveyancing. Designed to facilitate the subject for Students preparing for Examination. By JOSEPH A. SHEARWOOD, of Lincoln's Inn, Esq., Barrister-at-Law. Third Edition. Demy 8vo. 1885. 8*s.* 6*d.*

"We heartily recommend the work to students for any examination on real property and conveyancing, advising them to read it after a perusal of other works and shortly before going in for the examination."—*Law Student's Journal.*

"A very useful little work, particularly to students just before their examination." —*Gibson's Law Notes.*

"A very excellent specimen of a student's manual."—*Law Journal.*

"One of the most obvious merits of the book is its good arrangement. The author evidently understands 'the art of putting things.' All important points are so printed as readily to catch the eye."—*Law Times*, April 4, 1885.

Shelford's Real Property Statutes.—Ninth Edition. By T. H. CARSON, Esq., Barrister-at-Law. (*In the press.*)

Smith's Real and Personal Property.—A Compendium of the Law of Real and Personal Property, primarily connected with Conveyancing. Designed as a second book for Students, and as a digest of the most useful learning for Practitioners. By JOSIAH W. SMITH, B.C.L., Q.C. Sixth Edition. (Enlarged, and embodying the alterations made by the recent Statutes.) By the AUTHOR and J. TRUSTRAM, LL.M., of Lincoln's Inn, Barrister-at-Law. 2 vols. Demy 8vo. 1884. 2*l.* 2*s.*

"He (the Author) has given to the student a book which he may read over and over again with profit and pleasure."—*Law Times.*

"Will be found of very great service to the practitioner."—*Solicitors' Journal.*

"The book will be found very handy for reference purposes to practitioners, and very useful to the industrious student as covering a great deal of ground."—*Gibson's Law Notes.*

"A really useful and valuable work on our system of Conveyancing. We think this edition excellently done."—*Law Students' Journal.*

REGISTRATION.—**Rogers.**—*Vide* "Elections."

Coltman's Registration Cases.—Vol. I. Part I. (1879—80.) *Net,* 10*s.* Part II. (1880). *Net,* 3*s.* 6*d.* Part III. (1881). *Net,* 2*s.* Part IV. (1882). *Net,* 4*s.* Part V. (1883). *Net,* 3*s.* 6*d.* Part VI. (1884). *Net,* 2*s.* 6*d.*

RENTS.—**Harrison's Law relating to Chief Rents and other Rentcharges and Lands as affected thereby,** with a chapter on Restrictive Covenants and a selection of Precedents. By WILLIAM HARRISON, Solicitor. Demy 12mo. 1884. 6*s.*

"The plan of the book is excellent, and well carried out, the chapter on 'Restrictive Covenants' and the appendix of precedents will give it additional value."—*Law Magazine.*

ROMAN LAW.—**Greene's Outlines of Roman Law.** Consisting chiefly of an Analysis and Summary of the Institutes. For the use of Students. By T. WHITCOMBE GREENE, Barrister-at-Law. Fourth Edition. Foolscap 8vo. 1884. 7*s.* 6*d.*

Mears' Student's Gaius and Justinian.—The Text of the Institutes of Gaius and Justinian, The Twelve Tables, and the CXVIII. and CXXVII. Novels, with Introduction and Translation by T. LAMBERT MEARS, M.A., LL.D. Lond., of the Inner Temple, Barrister-at-Law. Post 8vo. 1882. 18*s.*

Mears' Student's Ortolan.—An Analysis of M. Ortolan's **Institutes of Justinian,** including the History and Generalization of ROMAN LAW. By T. LAMBERT MEARS, M.A., LL.D. Lond. Second Edition. (*In the press.*)

**** All standard Law Works are kept in Stock, in law calf and other bindings.*

ROMAN LAW.—*Continued.*

Ruegg's Student's "Auxilium" to the Institutes of Justinian.—Being a complete synopsis thereof in the form of Question and Answer. By ALFRED HENRY RUEGG, of the Middle Temple, Barrister-at-Law. Post 8vo. 1879. 5*s.*

"The student will be greatly assisted in clearing and arranging his knowledge by a work of this kind."—*Law Journal.*

Ryan's Questions on Roman Law.—By Lieut.-Colonel E. H. RYAN (late Royal Artillery), Student-at-Law, of Lincoln's Inn. Post 8vo. 1884. 3*s.* 6*d.*

RULES OF THE SUPREME COURT: The Supreme Court Funds Rules. With Introduction, Notes, Forms of Orders in use in the Chancery Registrar's Office, other Practical Forms, and an Index. By M. MUIR MACKENZIE and C. ARNOLD WHITE, Esqrs., Barristers-at-Law. Demy 8vo. 1884. 8*s.* 6*d.*

SALES.—Blackburn on Sales. A Treatise on the Effect of the Contract of Sale on the Legal Rights of Property and Possession in Goods, Wares, and Merchandise. By LORD BLACKBURN. Second Edition. By J. C. GRAHAM, of the Middle Temple, Esq., Barrister-at-Law. Royal 8vo. 1885. 21*s.*

SALES OF LAND.—Clerke and Humphry's Concise Treatise on the Law relating to Sales of Land.—By AUBREY ST. JOHN CLERKE, of the Middle Temple, and HUGH M. HUMPHRY, of Lincoln's Inn, Barristers-at-Law. Royal 8vo. 1885. 1*l.* 5*s.*

"The book is written in the condensed style of the notes to 'Seton on Decrees,' and succeeds admirably in reducing the effect of several cases to a proposition, which is briefly formulated and followed by the authorities on which it is based."—*Law Journal,* June 13, 1885.

"The arrangement is extremely good, and the mode of treatment particularly clear; but the substance is as good as the form . . . . . The work will be very useful to all who are concerned in sales of land, and will be invaluable to young practitioners."—*Law Times,* June 20, 1885.

SETTLED ESTATES STATUTES.—Middleton's Settled Estates Statutes, including the Settled Estates Act, 1877, Settled Land Act, 1882, Improvement of Land Act, 1864, and the Settled Estates Act Orders, 1878, with Introduction, Notes and Forms. Third Edition. With Appendix of Rules and Forms under the Settled Land Act, 1882. By JAMES W. MIDDLETON, B.A., Barrister-at-Law. Royal 12mo. 1882. 7*s.* 6*d.*

"In form the book is very simple and practical, and having a good index it is sure to afford material assistance to every practitioner who seeks its aid."—*Law Journal.*

"The book is intended for the legal adviser and equity draftsman, and to these it will give considerable assistance."—*Law Times.*

"The best manual on the subject of settled estates which has yet appeared."

SHERIFF LAW.—Churchill's Law of the Office and Duties of the Sheriff, with the Writs and Forms relating to the Office. Second Edition. By CAMERON CHURCHILL, B.A., of the Inner Temple, Barrister-at-Law. Demy 8vo. 1882. 1*l.* 4*s.*

"A very complete treatise."—*Solicitors' Journal.*

"Under-sheriffs, and lawyers generally, will find this a useful book."—*Law Mag.*

SHIPPING.—Boyd's Merchant Shipping Laws; being a Consolidation of all the Merchant Shipping and Passenger Acts from 1854 to 1876, inclusive; with Notes of all the leading English and American Cases, and an Appendix. By A. C. BOYD, LL.B., Esq., Barrister-at-Law. 8vo. 1876. 1*l.* 5*s.*

Foard's Treatise on the Law of Merchant Shipping and Freight.—By JAMES T. FOARD, Barrister-at-Law. Royal 8vo. 1880. *Half calf,* 1*l.* 1*s.*

SLANDER.—Odgers.—*Vide* "Libel and Slander."

SOLICITORS.—Cordery's Law relating to Solicitors of the Supreme Court of Judicature.—With an Appendix of Statutes and Rules. By A. CORDERY, of the Inner Temple, Esq., Barrister-at-Law. Demy 8vo. 1878. 14*s.*

"Mr. Cordery writes tersley and clearly, and displays in general great industry and care in the collection of cases."—*Solicitors' Journal.*

Turner.—*Vide* "Conveyancing" and "Vendors and Purchasers."

Whiteway's Hints to Solicitors.—Being a Treatise on the Law relating to their Duties as Officers of the High Court of Justice; with Notes on the Recent Changes affecting the Profession. By A. R. WHITEWAY, M.A., of the Equity Bar and Midland Circuit. Royal 12mo. 1883. 6*s.*

"He writes tersely and practically, and the cases he gives, if not exhaustive of the subject, are numerous and pithily explained. The book will altogether be found of great practical value."—*Law Journal.*

SPECIFIC PERFORMANCE.—Fry's Treatise on the Specific Performance of Contracts.—By the Hon. Sir EDWARD FRY, a Lord Justice of Appeal. Second Edition. By the Author and W. DONALDSON RAWLINS, of Lincoln's Inn, Esq., Barrister-at-Law. Royal 8vo. 1881. 1*l.* 16*s.*

STATUTE LAW.—Wilberforce on Statute Law.—The Principles which govern the Construction and Operation of Statutes. By E. WILBERFORCE, Esq., Barrister-at-Law. 1881. 18*s.*

STATUTES, and *vide* "Acts of Parliament."

Chitty's Collection of Statutes from Magna Charta to 1880.—**A Collection of Statutes of Practical Utility** arranged in Alphabetical and Chronological order, with Notes thereon. The Fourth Edition. By J. M. LELY, Esq., Barrister-at-Law. In 6 very thick vols. Royal 8vo. 1880. 12*l.* 12*s.*

Supplements to above, 44 & 45 *Vict.* (1881). 8*s.* 45 & 46 *Vict.* (1882). 16*s.* 46 & 47 *Vict.* (1883). 14*s.* 47 & 48 *Vict.* (1884). 10*s.* 6*d.* 48 & 49 *Vict.* (1885).

***** This Edition is printed in larger type than former Editions, and with increased facilities for Reference.**

"A very satisfactory edition of a time-honoured and most valuable work, the trusty guide of present, as of former judges, jurists, and of all others connected with the administration or practice of the law."—*Justice of the Peace.*

"The practitioner has only to take down one of the compact volumes of Chitty, and he has at once before him all the legislation on the subject in hand."—*Solicitors' Journal.*

"'Chitty' is pre-eminently a friend in need. Those who wish to know what Acts are in force with reference to a particular subject turn to that head in 'Chitty,' and at once find all the material of which they are in quest. Moreover, they are, at the same time, referred to the most important cases which throw light on the subject."—*Law Journal.*

Public General Statutes, royal 8vo, issued in parts and in complete volumes, and supplied immediately on publication.

SUMMARY CONVICTIONS.—Paley's Law and Practice of Summary Convictions under the Summary Jurisdiction Acts, 1848 and 1879; including Proceedings preliminary and subsequent to Convictions, and the responsibility of convicting Magistrates and their Officers, with Forms. Sixth Edition. By W. H. MACNAMARA, Esq., Barrister-at-Law. Demy 8vo. 1879. 1*l.* 4*s.*

Wigram.—*Vide* "Justice of the Peace."

TAXES ON SUCCESSION.—Trevor's Taxes on Succession.—A Digest of the Statutes and Cases (including those in Scotland and Ireland) relating to the Probate, Legacy and Succession Duties, with Practical Observations and Official Forms. Fourth Edition. By EVELYN FREETH and ROBERT J. WALLACE, of the Legacy and Succession Duty Office. Royal 12mo. 1881. 12*s*. 6*d*.

"Contains a great deal of practical information, which is likely to make it very useful to solicitors."—*Law Journal*.

THEATRES AND MUSIC HALLS.—Geary's Law of Theatres and Music Halls, including Contracts and Precedents of Contracts. By W. N. M. GEARY, J.P. for the county of Kent. With Historical Introduction. By JAMES WILLIAMS, Esqrs., Barristers-at-Law. 8vo. 1885. 5*s*.

TORTS.—Addison on Wrongs and their Remedies.—Being a Treatise on the Law of Torts. By C. G. ADDISON, Esq., Author of "The Law of Contracts." Fifth Edition. Re-written. By L. W. CAVE, Esq., M.A., one of Her Majesty's Counsel (now a Justice of the High Court). Royal 8vo. 1879. 1*l*. 18*s*.

"As now presented, this valuable treatise must prove highly acceptable to judges and the profession."—*Law Times*.

"Cave's 'Addison on Torts' will be recognized as an indispensable addition to every lawyer's library."—*Law Magazine*.

Ball's Leading Cases on the Law of Torts, with Notes. Edited by W. E. BALL, LL.D., Esq., Barrister-at-Law, Author of "Principles of Torts and Contracts." Royal 8vo. 1884. 1*l*. 1*s*.

"We are glad to find that the notes are extremely, and as far as we have been able to discover uniformly, good. Subsequent cases to the 'leading ones' are copiously cited. Distinctions are carefully pointed out, the exact state of the authorities on disputed questions is accurately given, and there is much intelligent and independent criticism."—*Solicitors' Journal*.

"All the cases given are interesting, and most of them are important, and the comments in the Notes are intelligent and useful."—*Law Journal*.

TRADE MARKS.—Hardingham's Trade Marks: Notes on the British, Foreign, and Colonial Laws relating thereto. By GEO. GATTON MELHUISH HARDINGHAM, Consulting Engineer and Patent Agent. Royal 12mo. 1881. *Net*, 2*s*. 6*d*.

Sebastian on the Law of Trade Marks.—The Law of Trade Marks and their Registration, and matters connected therewith, including a chapter on Goodwill. Together with The Patents, Designs and Trade Marks Act, 1883, and the Trade Marks Rules and Instructions thereunder; Forms and Precedents; The Merchandise Marks Act, 1862, and other Statutory enactments; The United States Statutes, 1870—81, and the Rules and Forms thereunder; the Treaty with the United States, 1877. Second Edition. By LEWIS BOYD SEBASTIAN, B.C.L., M.A., Esq., Barrister-at-Law. Demy 8vo. 1884. 1*l*. 1*s*.

"A complete and exhaustive treatise on its subject, and is indispensable to practitioners who have to deal with this branch of law."—*Solicitors' Journal*.

"The late Master of the Rolls in his judgment in *Re* Palmer's Trade Marks, said 'He was glad to see that the well-known writer on trade marks, Mr. Sebastian, had taken the same view of the Act.'"—*The Times*.

"Mr. Sebastian has written the fullest and most methodical book on trade marks which has appeared in England since the passing of the Trade Marks Registration Acts."—*Trade Marks*.

*** *All standard Law Works are kept in Stock, in law calf and other bindings.*

TRADE MARKS.—*Continued.*

Sebastian's Digest of Cases of Trade Mark, Trade Name, Trade Secret, Goodwill, &c., decided in the Courts of the United Kingdom, India, the Colonies, and the United States of America. By LEWIS BOYD SEBASTIAN, B.C.L., M.A., Esq., Barrister-at-Law. 8vo. 1879. 1*l.* 1*s.*

"A digest which will be of very great value to all practitioners who have to advise on matters connected with trade marks."—*Solicitors' Journal.*

TRAMWAYS.—Bazalgette and Humphreys.—*Vide* "Local and Municipal Government."

Sutton's Tramway Acts of the United Kingdom; with Notes on the Law and Practice, an Introduction, including the Proceedings before the Committees, Decisions of the Referees with respect to Locus Standi, and a Summary of the Principles of Tramway Rating, and an Appendix containing the Standing Orders of Parliament, Rules of the Board of Trade relating to Tramways, &c. Second Edition. By HENRY SUTTON, B.A., assisted by ROBERT A. BENNETT, B.A., Barristers-at-Law. Demy 8vo. 1883. 15*s.*

"The book is exceedingly well done, and cannot fail not only to be the standard work on its own subject, but to take a high place among legal text-books."—*Law Journal.*

TRIALS FOR MURDER BY POISONING.—Browne and Stewart.—*Vide* "Poisons."

TRUSTS AND TRUSTEES.—Godefroi's Digest of the Principles of the Law of Trusts and Trustees.—By HENRY GODEFROI, of Lincoln's Inn, Esq., Barrister-at-Law. Demy 8vo. 1879. 1*l.* 1*s.*

VENDORS AND PURCHASERS.—Clerke and Humphry.—*Vide* "Sales of Land."

Dart's Vendors and Purchasers.—By J. HENRY DART, Esq., one of the Six Conveyancing Counsel of the High Court of Justice, Chancery Division. Sixth Edition. By the AUTHOR and WILLIAM BARBER, Esq., Barrister-at-Law. 2 vols. Royal 8vo. (*In preparation.*)

Turner's Duties of Solicitor to Client as to Sales, Purchases, and Mortgages of Land. By EDWARD F. TURNER, Solicitor, Lecturer on Real Property and Conveyancing, and one of the Assistant Examiners for Honours to the Incorporated Law Society for 1882–3. Demy 8vo. 1883. 10*s.* 6*d.*

See also Conveyancing.—"Turner."

"His lectures are full of thought and accuracy, they are lucid in exposition, and what is more, though unfortunately rare in law works, attractive in their style and composition."—*Law Magazine.*

"A careful perusal of these lectures cannot fail to be of great advantage to students, and more particularly, we think, to young practising solicitors."—*Law Times.*

VOLUNTEER LAW.—A Manual of the Law regulating the Volunteer Forces.—By W. A. BURN and W. T. RAYMOND, Esqrs., Barristers-at-Law, and Captains in H.M. Volunteer Forces. Royal 12mo. 1882. *Net*, 2*s.*

WILLS.—Theobald's Concise Treatise on the Law of Wills.—Second Edition. By H. S. THEOBALD, Esq., Barrister-at-Law. Demy 8vo. 1881. 1*l.* 4*s.*

"Mr. Theobald has certainly given evidence of extensive investigation, conscientious labour, and clear exposition."—*Law Magazine.*

"A book of great ability and value. It bears on every page traces of care and sound judgment. It is certain to prove of great practical usefulness."—*Solicitors' Journal.*

"His arrangement being good, and his statement of the effect of the decisions being clear, his work cannot fail to be of practical utility."—*Law Times.*

*** *All standard Law Works are kept in Stock, in law calf and other bindings.*

WILLS.—*Continued.*

Weaver's Precedents of Wills.—A collection of concise Precedents of Wills, with Introduction, Notes, and an Appendix of Statutes. By *Charles Weaver*, B.A. Post 8vo. 1882. 5*s.*

WINDING UP.—Palmer's Winding-up Forms. A collection of 580 Forms of Summonses, Affidavits, Orders, Notices and other Forms relating to the Winding-up of Companies. With Notes on the Law and Practice, and an Appendix containing the Acts and Rules. By FRANCIS BEAUFORT PALMER, Esq., Barrister-at-Law, author of "Company Precedents," &c. 8vo. 1885. 12*s.*

WRECK INQUIRIES.—Murton's Law and Practice relating to Formal Investigations in the United Kingdom, British Possessions and before Naval Courts into Shipping Casualties and the Incompetency and Misconduct of Ships' Officers. With an Introduction. By WALTER MURTON, Solicitor to the Board of Trade. Demy 8vo. 1884. 1*l.* 4*s.*

WRONGS.—Addison.—*Vide* "Torts."
Ball.—"Leading Cases," *vide* "Torts."

STEVENS & SONS' ANNOUNCEMENTS OF

NEW WORKS AND NEW EDITIONS

Carver's Law of Carriage by Sea.—By *T. G. Carver*, of Lincoln's Inn, Esq., Barrister-at-Law. (*In the press.*)

Chitty's Index to all the Reported Cases decided in the several Courts of Equity in England, the Privy Council, and the House of Lords. With a selection of Irish Cases, from the earliest period. The Fourth Edition, wholly revised, reclassified and brought down to the date of publication by *William Frank Jones*, B.C.L., M.A., and *Henry Edward Hirst*, B.C.L., M.A., both of Lincoln's Inn, Esqrs., Barristers-at-Law. In 5 or 6 vols. (*Vols. III. and IV. nearly ready.*)

A Digest of Cases Over-ruled, Dissented from, Questioned Disapproved, Distinguished, and Specially Considered by the English Courts, from 1756 to 1884. Arranged in alphabetical order of their subjects, together with Extracts from the Judgments delivered thereon, and a Complete Index of the Cases. By *C. W. Mitcalfe Dale* and *Rudolf C. Lehmann*, of the Inner Temple, Esqrs., Barristers-at-Law. *Forming a Supplement to Chitty's Index and Fisher's Digest.* (*In preparation.*)

Dart's Vendors and Purchasers.—A Treatise on the Law and Practice relating to Vendors and Purchasers of Real Estate. By *J. Henry Dart*, Esq., one of the Six Conveyancing Counsel of the High Court of Justice, Chancery Division. Sixth Edition. By the *Author* and *William Barber*, Esq., Barrister-at-Law. (*In preparation.*)

Hindmarch on the Law of Patents for Inventions. Second Edition. By *E. Macrory*, and *J. C. Graham*, Esqrs., Barristers-at-Law. (*In preparation.*)

Lowndes' Law of General Average.—English and Foreign. Fourth Edition. By *Richard Lowndes*, Author of "The Law of Marine Insurance," &c. (*In preparation.*)

McArthur's Contract of Marine Insurance.—By *Charles McArthur*, Average Adjuster. (*In the press.*)

Shirley's Selection of Leading Cases in Criminal Law.—By *W. Shirley Shirley*, Esq., Barrister-at-Law, Author of "Leading Cases in the Common Law," &c. (*In preparation.*)

Smith's Compendium of Mercantile Law.—Tenth Edition. By *John Macdonell*, of the Middle Temple, Esq., Barrister-at-Law. (*In preparation.*)

Theobald's Concise Treatise on the Law of Wills. Third Edition. By *H. S. Theobald*, Esq., Barrister-at-Law. (*Nearly ready.*)

Woodfall's Law of Landlord and Tenant.—With a Full collection of Precedents and Forms of Procedure. Thirteenth Edition. By *J. M. Lely*, Esq., Barrister-at-Law. (*In preparation.*)

www.ingramcontent.com/pod-product-compliance
Lightning Source LLC
Chambersburg PA
CBHW031404270326
41929CB00010BA/1316
9783337159160